KINGPIN

ALSO BY RICHARD STRATTON:

Smack Goddess
Slam: The Book (editor, with Kim Wozencraft)
Altered States of America: Outlaws and Icons, Hitmakers and Hitmen
Smuggler's Blues: A True Story of the Hippie Mafia

KINGPIN

PRISONER OF THE WAR ON DRUGS

RICHARD STRATTON

Arcade Publishing • New York

First Edition

Arcade Publishing books may be purchased in bulk at special discounts for sales promotion, corporate gifts, fund-raising, or educational purposes. Special editions can also be created to specifications. For details, contact the Special Sales Department, Arcade Publishing, 307 West 36th Street, 11th Floor, New York, NY 10018 or arcade@skyhorsepublishing.com.

Arcade Publishing® is a registered trademark of Skyhorse Publishing, Inc.®, a Delaware corporation.

Visit our website at www.arcadepub.com.

10 9 8 7 6 5 4 3 2 1

Library of Congress Cataloging-in-Publication Data

Names: Stratton, Richard (Richard H.), author.
Title: Kingpin : prisoner of the war on drugs / Richard Stratton.
Description: New York : Arcade Publishing, [2017] | Includes bibliographical
   references and index.
Identifiers: LCCN 2016053991 (print) | LCCN 2017006981 (ebook) | ISBN
   9781628727265 (alk. paper) | ISBN 9781628727289 (ebook)
Subjects: LCSH: Stratton, Richard (Richard H.) | Prisoners—United
   States—Biography. | Drug traffic—United States—Biography.
Classification: LCC HV9468 .S77 2017 (print) | LCC HV9468 (ebook) | DDC
   365/.6092 [B]—dc23
LC record available at https://lccn.loc.gov/2016053991

Cover design by Erin Seward-Hiatt
Front cover prison photo: iStockphoto

Printed in the United States of America

As you are going with your adversary to the magistrate,
try hard to be reconciled on the way,
or your adversary may drag you off to the judge,
and the judge turn you over to the officer,
and the officer throw you into prison.
I tell you, you will not get out
until you have paid the last penny.

Luke 12:58-59

You want to know what this was really all about? The Nixon campaign in 1968, and the Nixon White House after that, had two enemies: the anti-war left and black people. You understand what I'm saying? We knew we couldn't make it illegal to be either against the war or black, but by getting the public to associate the hippies with marijuana and blacks with heroin, and then criminalizing both heavily, we could disrupt those communities. We could arrest their leaders, raid their homes, break up their meetings, and vilify them night after night on the evening news. Did we know we were lying about the drugs? Of course we did.

John Ehrlichman, Nixon's domestic policy chief

CONTENTS

Author's Note: Prisoner of the War on Plants · ix

Prologue: A Grand Unified Theory of Loneliness · 1

1 · The Glass House · 7

2 · Diesel Therapy · 18

3 · Good Jail · 41

4 · The Best Defense · 64

5 · The Criminal Hilton · 82

6 · Kingpin: A Continuing Criminal Enterprise · 120

7 · A Skyline Turkey · 148

8 · The Great Escape · 159

9 · Cop Killer · 168

10 · Jailhouse Lawyer · 192

11 · Confessions of a Reluctant Onanist—
or, Sex in Jail · 205

12 · The Old Don · 220

13 · Banished · 251

14 · The Tao of Punishment · 265

15 · Uncertainty Principle · 274

16 · Of Time and Space · 285

AUTHOR'S NOTE

PRISONER OF THE WAR ON PLANTS

THIS BOOK IS based on my eight-year stretch as a prisoner of the US government's war on plants—specifically, in my case, the ancient and mysterious cannabis plant. At the end of June 1982, I was arrested by DEA agents, agents with the US marshals' fugitive task force, and LA city cops in the lobby of the Sheraton Senator Hotel at Los Angeles International Airport. I had jumped bail on a federal indictment in the District of Maine, where I was charged with conspiracy to possess with intent to distribute marijuana. The Feds were also after me for any number of other successful hashish and pot smuggling escapades that our group had pulled off over a fifteen-year run as one of the major dope smuggling families of the so-called hippie mafia.

That story, the story of my years as an international marijuana and hashish smuggler, is recounted in my previous book, *Smuggler's Blues*. This book picks up where that one left off—with me in custody in the Los Angeles City Jail, also known as the Glass House, possibly the worst jail in America. It quickly became apparent to me and to lawyers involved in my various federal prosecutions that the government had a hidden agenda. Yes, they were anxious to punish me for my long, illicit love affair with the green, splayed, and spiky-leafed cannabis plant. But their ultimate aim was to get me to roll over and inform on friends and enemies they believed were involved in the marijuana underground.

Chief among those targets the government wished to prosecute was my friend and mentor, the world-renowned author Norman Mailer.

Mailer, who once dubbed himself General Marijuana, was one of the first American writers of any stature to write about his personal use of pot. He had been on the government's enemies list since back in the fifties, when the Civil Service Commission accused him of being a "concealed communist" for his left-leaning politics. Always an outspoken critic of the government, with his efforts to end the war in Vietnam, he became a high priority on the Feds' hit list. Making a drug conspiracy case against Norman Mailer would diminish his voice as a leading author and undercut his credibility by branding him as a dope-smoking pinko outlaw while also enhancing the careers of government agents and prosecutors.

This book tells the story of my journey through the courts and Federal Bureau of Prisons, which I have renamed the Bureau of Punishment (BOP) for reasons that should become apparent as I relate how the government sought to turn me into one of their unhappy stool pigeons. Some names have been changed to protect those outlaws who have yet to be captured and to disguise the identities of the snitches who testified against me. They did what they felt they had to do; I did what I felt I could live with and chose not to cooperate with the government.

Looking back on it all, with those wild and perilous years smuggling weed behind me, I am gratified to see that cannabis is now grown abundantly in all fifty states. It is legal in an ever-increasing number for medicinal use and was recently made legal for recreational enjoyment in six states. The war on plants seems to be winding down. When I walk free in the world and into a marijuana dispensary and see the various cannabis strains displayed in all their legal glory, it appears that the alleged bad guys have actually won, albeit at great cost in money, broken families, prison time, and even untimely death. And yet it seems incomprehensible to me the lengths to which our federal government was and still is willing to go to punish me and others for trafficking in this God-given plant. As I write, the troglodytes of the Drug Enforcement Administration, more concerned with job security than with the truth and justice, refuse to accept that marijuana has proven medicinal value and must be rescheduled to reflect the scientific proof.

All considered, even given the years I had to spend in prison, I am glad that I decided to take the heat and do the time. The government is simply wrong when it comes to criminalizing this plant. As Americans, we have a right to alter our consciousness as we see fit so long as we are not hurting anyone else. And as citizens living in a participatory democracy, we have a right to be heard and listened to by our civil servants. End the war on plants.

Here then is the story of those long eight years spent in the American prison system, where still to this day too many prisoners of this absurd and destructive war are locked up, serving criminal sentences for possessing or dealing in vegetable matter that long ago should have been made legal.

KINGPIN

Prologue

A GRAND UNIFIED THEORY
OF LONELINESS

Segregation Unit, Federal Correctional Institution (FCI)
Ashland, Kentucky, June 1990

SO THIS IS the Hole. Solitary confinement, a prison within a prison. There is a low steel shelf welded to the wall with a thin mattress, no pillow or sheets, and a single coarse wool blanket. A stainless-steel combination sink and seatless shitter squats in the corner. Nothing else. No mirror—I can't see my face. It's Spartan. Clean. No roaches or rats. Not bad as jail cells go. I've seen worse in the eight years I've been down.

This is actually a step up in accommodations from the unit where I was housed before the fight. I'm on the second floor of the old cell house, above the tumult. It's quiet. There is fresh air and sunlight during the day. At night I can see stars in the black sky and feel the soft evening breeze wash in through the high windows and across the tier. The unit I was in is like a big damp barn with bunk beds stacked side-by-side in two-man cubicles the size of animal stalls. Even at night it's noisy. Convicts snoring, farting, crying out, or moaning in their sleep. In the morning: a cacophony of toilets flushing, men snorting and hacking and spitting. Yelling. Cursing. Representing.

Getting locked up in the Hole is like going on vacation from the racket and tension of general population: I am gifted with another irony of prison life.

This joint is old, built back in the twenties to house moonshiners and bootleggers, violators of that other failed Prohibition enforced under the Volstead Act. Now it's filled with prisoners of the war on drugs—pot smugglers and growers, coke dealers, junk merchants, addicts—with a smattering of bank robbers and a few white-collar crooks, many of whom robbed or defrauded to support drug habits. The ghost of Dashiell Hammett whispers that he did a skid bid here back in the fifties for refusing to testify before a government committee investigating suspected communist activity during the Red Scare. No rat Hammett. And screenwriter Dalton Trumbo, another man of conscience, did eleven months in this joint for refusing to testify before the House Un-American Activities Committee. In the unseen world, I keep good company.

I need these spirits to comfort me. Prison is the loneliest place in the world. Surrounded by other men, one is never alone, yet one is always lonely. It's like being forced to live in the men's room at New York's Pennsylvania Station. Thick, fetid air smelling of sweat and piss and shit, crowded with men you might otherwise avoid—still, the loneliness is palpable. You feel empty, like a hole has been gouged in the center of your chest where your heart once was.

Here, in the Hole, separated from the rest of the prisoner population, I am alone with my loneliness.

I'M A SHORT-TIMER, with weeks, possibly only days to go before I am to be released. So what do I do? I succumb to the short-timer syndrome and fuck it all up. I was in the TV room, a place I normally avoid. The Berlin Wall fell a few months ago, and the Soviet Union is in its death throes. Child of the Cold War, I was glued to the TV watching the Evil Empire implode on CNN. But the etiquette of prison TV rooms is as strict as a straitjacket. You don't mess with the schedule, hand-printed and stuck to the wall with a dab of toothpaste. Episodes of *All My Children* or *Days of Our Lives* take precedence over life-changing world events.

So there I am in the TV room watching the news with a few other white convicts. This black guy, Rector, comes in and abruptly changes the channel. There are three things I can do is this situation: one, get up and walk out, go about my business—the smart thing to do; two, stay and watch the soap and pretend I don't object—the weak thing to do; three, get up and confront this guy for changing the channel without showing proper respect—the convict thing to do. I don't really know Rector. We've spoken no more than five words to each other in the five months I've been here since being transferred from the federal joint in America's Siberia, FCI Ray Brook, New York, up near the Canadian border. He's a quiet guy, Rector, keeps to himself, normally respectful. He is muscular, my height, maybe a little taller, ten years younger, and very strong—I've watched him on the weight pile bench-press over three hundred pounds. He works in the prison factory, UNICOR, making whatever it is they make there as he winds down a ten-year bid for armed bank robbery. I, however, am in this crazy intense time limbo with no set release date, waiting day-to-day for a decision from the Regional Office of the Bureau of Punishment to determine exactly when I will walk through the gates and back into the free world.

Reason would dictate that I let this lack of respect on Rector's part pass and get on with my life, such as it is. But prison is an unreasonable place, for we live in a world of damaged men where all that matters is how one carries oneself. Respect is currency here. How broken you are is a determination that lives in the crux of each moment, each encounter. To fail to rise to even the slightest challenge or offense could be the fissure in one's character that allows the stony facade to fall, like the Berlin Wall, exposing the scared weakling within. In that moment, I can't admit even to the possibility that I am driven by a self-destructive urge to blow my release date for fear of going free. No, no, fuck no, that's not me.

"We were watching that," I say and stand. Rector turns and sizes me up.

I don't believe I'm doing this. Everything in me tells me: *Stratton, don't be an asshole. Just let it go.* And yet I can't stop myself, I keep moving toward Rector, to the front of the TV room. It's like watching a guy I don't really know but secretly admire. I see myself reach for the knob and switch the channel back to the news.

Rector swats my hand aside. "Schedule calls for—"

Now he's touched me; a line has been crossed.

"Man," I say, "the fucking Soviet Union is collapsing, and you want to watch soaps? What the fuck's the matter with you?"

Now I'm insulting his intelligence.

"Don't matter what I want," he says, back in my face. "Or you. The schedule—"

"Fuck that schedule. I didn't come to prison for following no schedule." I represent in full convict mode now, surprised at how much of this dog-eat-dog world has settled into my character.

One of the men sitting with me says, "Let it go. You're too short, man."

Rector changes the channel back to the soap. I reach for the knob; he shoves his chest up against me. I push him back and he cocks his arm. The man behind me wraps his arms around me in a bear hug. Rector hauls off and socks me in the side of my head. I might have fallen to the floor if I wasn't being propped up. It's like my friend is restraining me so Rector can beat me down. I struggle free and lunge for Rector. One of the other men in the room runs out to get the guard. I know everything they are doing is to protect me, but it feels like the opposite.

The unit guard races in and hits the panic button on his body alarm. What seems like moments later, as Rector and I roll around on the floor struggling to get a clean shot at one another, the goon squad invades the unit. They descend on us with body shields and truncheons. Rector and I are wrestled onto our bellies and restrained.

Marched out in handcuffs. Delivered here to disciplinary segregation. *The Hole.* He's locked in a cell along the tier. I can hear him cough and pace and do his push-ups. Pace some more.

I hold no beef with Rector. It had nothing to do with him, or with the news or the TV. It was all about me. I know this now in the solitary anguish of this thwarted existence. Some deviant strain in my character wants me to fail. But not right away, not until I am just about to snatch the gold ring. The closer I get to realizing my dreams, my hopes, my desires, the more that stunted nasty twin rears his ugly face and goads me: *You don't deserve this, Stratton. You're a bad seed. Nothing but trouble. All your life you have been wrong. You deserve to suffer. Go ahead and fuck it up, shithead, that's what everyone expects of you anyway. This is exactly where you belong—in a prison.*

Just weeks, maybe even days to go before I am to be released after eight straight years in the custody of the attorney general's designated keeper—the Federal Bureau of Prisons—and I fuck it up. Now, while Bureau of Punishment number crunchers come up with a new release date, I must appear before a disciplinary committee to determine my fate. In a worst-case scenario, I could be charged with assault and pick up a new case and ultimately more time. At a minimum, I expect to get a shot (an internal prison disciplinary charge) for fighting and be stripped of any good-time I have accumulated. Since the negotiation with my Punishment Bureau masters is over good-time, years are in the balance. I could be looking at as much as a two-year hit. This senseless fight with Rector could mean I don't get released for years instead of weeks or days. What a stupid asshole . . .

So, I do my push-ups. I pace. I think. I chastise myself and I wait. And I try to dispel the scariest thought of all: *Who gives a fuck?* Not me. I could spend the rest of my life behind these bars, and it wouldn't mean shit. Because it doesn't matter. In this equation, one plus nothing still equals nothing. My life has no meaning or merit. My alter ego is gratified when I live up to everyone's worst expectations—including my own—because my higher self enjoys engaging the dark side. I will not run from it. When I have no one else to fuck with, I fuck with myself. The worse it gets, the stronger I get—or so I like to think . . . and think . . . and obsess. So much of prison life is lived in the mind.

One thing I have come to appreciate during the eight years I've been locked up is that I alone am to blame for my mistakes. I alone must answer for the mess I made of my life. I have no excuses, no apologies, and no regrets—only repentance. I had all the advantages: white skin and blue eyes; a WASP kid from an old New England Yankee family; a star athlete, high school state wrestling champion. College boy who on a lark started to smuggle pot. And a fatal flaw: hubris, and an addiction to danger. Only in peril did I feel truly alive. So I became an international drug kingpin bringing in multiton loads of the finest cannabis from around the world, because I was addicted to the adrenaline rush I got from risking my life getting over on the Man. And because I saw how stupid and unrealistic their laws were in the first place.

Then, when I was arrested and faced with the choice—*To rat or not to rat, that is the question*—I committed perhaps the one noble act of my life. I took the weight. I bit the bullet. I refused to "cooperate" with the government in their asinine war on plants. I said, "Fuck it. This is my adventure, my delusion of outlaw fame and fortune. Let me now pay the price." And that is liberating. Ultimately, I can hope to get free because it still all comes down to me—and God. I believe in the Creator who made me to endure this test. I don't have to depend on anyone to make things right, and there is no one else to fault when things go wrong.

Locked up alone in a stripped cell, stripped of all external accouterments and distractions—the money; the women; the real estate and boats and planes and trucks and cars; and the readily available inebriants, the best dope and booze—I can finally make peace with my self-destructive evil twin.

Chapter One

THE GLASS HOUSE

Los Angeles City Jail, June 1982

It's ALREADY LATE Friday evening by the time my old nemesis, DEA Special Agent Bernard Wolfshein, and my new captor, Deputy US Marshal James Sullivan, deliver me to the custody of the keepers at the LA City Jail. This is a hard come-down after a spectacular arrest in the lobby of the Sheraton Senator Hotel—or perhaps not. Maybe it is the beginning of a new adventure.

"You'll be okay, right, Rich?" Agent Wolfshein says as he completes the paperwork and I am processed in to the jail. "It's just for a couple of days."

The Wolfman has this way of provoking me with statements framed as questions, questions he must know I cannot answer truthfully. What am I to say? *No! Please, Wolf, don't leave me here! Take me to a hotel. I'll be good, I promise.*

I have no idea what to expect in this place, except that it's . . . jail. Whatever it is, I had it coming. "Yeah," I say and actually manage a small smile for them both. "I'll be fine. You guys take it easy."

Sullivan nods. "You, too. Have a great weekend," he says with the hint of a twinkle in his bright blues eyes and a smirk on his mouth.

"Thanks," I say.

"See you in court Monday," Wolfshein tells me, and they leave.

Two guards march me from booking to one of the housing units. We stop outside the gate and they order me to strip.

"Here?"

We're in the hallway. There are civilians walking around. The walls are made of glass.

"Now," one of the guards instructs me while the second guard stands at parade rest with a truncheon held close at his side. These guys are all business, not a glimmer of compassion. I sense that if I fail to follow their orders, the guy with the baton will club me into submission. So I start to undress. I take off my western-cut, three-piece suit and Lucchese boots and drop them on the floor, stand there in my underpants, thinking how ridiculous my wardrobe is given where I have ended up.

"Everything," he says. "Strip."

I take off my shorts and drop them on the pile of clothes, hoping there are no brown skid marks in the crotch, and am reminded once again of the old-school wisdom imparted to me by my grandmother Ethel Lowell Burnham, dear Ba Ba as we children called her. She would tell me always to make certain I put on clean underpants before going out. If something should happen to me at school or at play, she explained, and I was taken to the nurse's office or, worse yet, to the hospital, and had to undress, best to be sure my underpants were stain-free.

"Lift your nut sack," the hack says and peers at my scrotum as if trying to appraise the family jewels. Then he pulls on a rubber glove and examines my asshole like a proctologist. He inspects the bottoms of my feet, looks between my toes. He checks behind my ears and tells me to ruffle my hair and beard. He leaves me standing naked while they both inspect every inch of every article of my clothing, looking in the pockets, carefully feeling along the seams of my pants, checking the cuffs, and inspecting the heels of my boots for hidden compartments. My dick and nuts shrivel up in their own embarrassment. From the neck up, I'm in that state where nothing affects me. *I don't give a fuck.* It doesn't matter what they do to me, the worst has already happened—I have been arrested yet again. I know the drill. Nothing to do now but submit to the experience while maintaining my perspective: *This too shall pass.*

"Get dressed," the guard says at last.

THE HOUSING UNITS are rectangular rooms the size of a tennis court with thick Plexiglas outer walls and barred entrance gates. They resemble nothing so much as huge fish tanks. And here, I suppose, is where this place gets its name: the Glass House, where everything is revealed. We passed several of these glass chambers teeming with bodies on the way to the one that will be my abode for the next few days, and there are more on the floors above and below. This massive jail houses thousands of prisoners, I learn later. As I enter the unit, I must pass through a gauntlet of flailing brown and black limbs stretching out through the bars of the front gate as prisoners grope for pay phones hung on a panel within reach just outside the unit. A long line of prisoners stands inside, waiting for their turn on the phones.

Bunk beds are stacked around like steel shelving in a warehouse. There are no mattresses, no blankets or sheets—the crazies have burned them all and would set fire to themselves like Buddhist monks if they were allowed matches. All the matches and cigarettes have been confiscated. Everyone is on edge—addicts withdrawing from nicotine, alcohol, heroin, crack, Angel Dust, freedom. The harsh fluorescent lights are never turned off. No one sleeps: they doze, they nod, or they pass out. Drunks reel around bouncing off the walls. Dustheads and dope fiends huddle on the bunks muttering to themselves and gazing at their private hallucinations.

We are all strangers. That's the one comfort—no one knows me here. I don't have to be anything for anyone else. I can simply be who I am, nobody, and hunker down in my corner. In the artificial daylight, time stands still. It's as if the universe stopped expanding. For two more days I'm stuck in the eternal now like an image caught in freeze-frame.

One thing I know: nothing will ever be the same. Life as I have known it is over. I'm slammed, locked up, in custody with nowhere to go and nothing to do but be here now. The world outside is beyond my grasp, freedom vague as the misty LA cityscape glimpsed through layers of Plexiglas. In here is the explicitness of shit. I have pitched my tent in the land of excrement.

There are three open commodes sitting in a bog of piss and floating bits of turd. One would have to wade through the sewage, then hang one's ass over the bowl full-moon-style and shit with the whole world watching, addicts fixated on your ass as if they expected you to shit cigarettes and matches. I piss from a distance, aim for the bowl—a long shot. I'll wait to defecate.

Beefy, baton-wielding, mustachioed hacks patrol outside the unit. The guards are inscrutable, another race of being. They never come inside the unit and even count us through the transparent walls. We rarely see them, but they are always there, watching us with the dispassionate eye of laboratory technicians tending cisterns full of mutant life forms. We exist for them as numbers. I sense that only if they saw one of us lying unconscious in the middle of the tank with the others rooting around in the entrails like a pack of hyenas would they brave the limbs flailing at the front gate and venture into this cesspool.

I find an unoccupied shelf and cling to it like a life raft. Dustheads, young Blacks and Latinos with their synapses fried on Angel Dust—such a sublime name for so hellish a substance—lurk on all sides like zombies. In the corners, Chicano dope fiends crouch together like beaten dogs. I think I spot another white guy in the tank, but like a cuttlefish he disappears in the flow of bodies. During this night that is as bright as day, when I dare close my eyes, I am jerked rudely from my dreams by some demented drunk tugging at my feet, trying to steal my boots. Reflexively, I kick him in the throat and send him sprawling across the slimy floor. Everyone watches, but no one does anything.

In the Glass House, where everything is revealed, no one sees anything.

HOURS PASS LIKE days. As I lie on the steel bunk and stare at the plank above, smudged with burn marks and autographed by former prisoners, I ponder how the Feds were able to set me up and bust me at the hotel. How did they know I'd be there? I narrow it down to two possibilities: either the Captain's phone was wired and he breached security by claiming he was calling me from a pay phone when in fact he was not, or he is a double agent working for the DEA. The Captain is indeed a captain in the US Army. If he set me up, that would mean the arrest was an elaborate choreographed show—the Captain's resisting arrest, the free-for-all and cop pig pile, heavily armed agents dressed up as hotel staff, Deputy US Marshal James Sullivan's claims of C-4 explosives in the Captain's black bag: why go to all that trouble? Why not just bust me as soon as the Captain and I met? If the Captain's phone was tapped and he did in fact bring the C-4, he must possess serious juice to be allowed to walk out on the arrest and take his explosives with him.

It's dismaying; I can't figure it out. Maybe the Captain has been working with the Feds all along. Perhaps he is some sort of active government spook. But his father, Abu Ali, is the biggest hashish and heroin merchant in Lebanon's outlaw Bekaa Valley. How is this possible? None of it makes sense. Or maybe it does, and I'm the sucker. It's like DEA Agent Wolfshein said: *There is a whole other level, a whole other dimension to this drug war.* And while I imagine I know what I'm doing—calling the shots—in reality I am merely a pawn in someone else's bigger, higher-stakes game.

These thoughts vex me; they replay in my head like a video loop. I can't stop thinking about how I got here, who set me up . . . until a drunk falls from the bunk beside me. He lurches to his feet, staggers back toward the wall, stumbles, and then projectile-pukes all over my legs. He spews hot bile and sour alcoholic swill on my pants and boots to remind me that how I got here—the ins and outs of whatever devious machinations resulted in my being in this place, this Glass House—none of that matters. For the truth is, I am here now. This is what's happening. It's swim or drown in the brightly lit shit lagoon. I had better stop fretting about how I got here and deal with the puke on my pants. Deal with the fact that this is my world now, and I have got to survive. That in order to clean my pants, I am going to have to wade through a puddle of piss and shit to get to the sink.

Forget it. The sink is broken. Or maybe they shut the water off to stop the crazies from flooding the tank. I'll just have to live with the puke-stained pants until—what? I can send them out to the dry cleaners? I think not. Face it, Stratton: *You are fucked.* You may have believed you were some hot-shit international fugitive outlaw smuggler with all your cash and exotic stash, your women, your booze and horses and trucks, your homes you were never in, the plush hotel suites, the Lear jets and suitcases full of money. But look around, son. That's all gone, over and done. You're in the jailhouse now, motherfucker. Let's see you get yourself out of this mess.

THE MORNING FEEDING begins well before dawn. I'm still angling my way along the line to get to the phones on the other side of the bars at the front of the tank when guards arrive to slide open the gate. Those of us with the ability and the will to stand up and march three floors below to the chow hall line up to be fed. The guards swing long black truncheons with steel balls in the tips—rib spreaders, they are called—and order us not to speak.

"Shut up! No talking!"

Once we leave the tank, enforced quiet. No talking, muttering, babbling, or screaming during the descent down into the depths of the Glass House. During the feeding, the monastic rule of absolute silence obtains. I move numbly along the chow line and receive my portion: microwave-crusted instant potatoes like a hard mass of unfinished ceramic; a wafer of sausage that floats in a puddle of fat. The fake eggs, like the coffee, are cold. Only a half-starved moray like the huge black dude beside me could eat this shit.

When I go to pass him my tray, the guards bellow at me: "No giving away food! You don't want it, throw it in the garbage!"

This strikes me as unreasonable and wasteful, but I am not about to protest. Maybe the rule is designed to prevent predators from extorting food from the weak, to discourage trafficking in caked potatoes and sausage patties. When you have nothing, even slop has value.

On the march back into the tank, I see my opportunity and make a dive to the front of the phone line. I sit on a bench; stick my arms and legs through the bars like a man in a pillory. I press the phone to my ear; my face is pressed to the bars so I can reach the dial pad on the pay phone. It's 5:30 a.m. in Los Angeles, 8:30 on the East Coast. I reach my attorney, Channing Godfried, at his home in Cambridge.

"Will you accept a collect call from Richard?"

"Yes."

"Hello."

"Rick, where are you?"

At least now I can tell someone.

"In jail," I tell him. "The Los Angeles city jail."

He says he'll call someone and have them come see me. I tell him I'm due in court Monday morning. There is nothing else for me to say, no one else for me to call. I've had my one phone call, and it was all of thirty seconds. I consider hogging the phone, provoking the guy in line behind me, and calling my former partner and ex-girlfriend Val in Maui. But it's the middle of the night in Hawaii, and why chance that they are monitoring these phones and tip them off to her whereabouts?

Anyway, that's over. It's all over, my life before this. I must stay focused on the here and now. I pull my arms and legs, my puke-stained pants and boots out from between the bars, climb down off the bench, and wander back into the depths of the tank.

Someone has taken my plank. Nowhere to sit except on the floor. I wander around, not so much looking for something to do as looking to mind my own business and not get involved in anyone else's craziness. Most everyone dozes in the bright light. You can tell the prisoners who have been here for a while from the fresh fish from the street: the old-timers are dressed out in army-green jumpsuits and rubber shower shoes. Several of the men, I notice, have grossly bloated arms and legs covered with scabs and open sores from shooting junk. Men cough and hack and spit on the floor.

"Cigarettes? Cigarettes?" they ask me as I pass by, hoping against hope that somehow the white guy in the puke-stained suit managed to smuggle in some smokes. I'm thinking about the eight grand in cash, the Rolex Presidential, and my wallet the Feds seized from me back at the airport satellite cop station, wondering if I'll ever see that again, wondering if there was anything incriminating or of evidentiary value in my wallet, if I had any scraps of paper with notes and phone numbers on me when the Heat came down. I try not to think about all the property and money and loved ones I left on the outside. My parents back in Wellesley will be relieved. Godfried will call Mary, my mother, and let her know her son is all right. No one will be surprised to hear that Richard Stratton is in jail, least of all my father and mother. Mary will say, "Thank God he's alive."

THIS IS THE longest Saturday of my life and it could go either way. I could wallow in self-pity. *Poor me! I don't deserve this! Send lawyers, guns, and money. . . . It was only pot!* Big fucking deal. What do I have to do? *Name it.* I'll do anything. I'll rat on all my enemies *and* my friends. Just get me the fuck out of this place, out of the Glass House where even my cowardice is revealed. Or, I could swim through the puddle of piss and shit pooled around the toilet bowls, drop my drawers, hang that ass, and take the biggest crap of my life right here for all to see.

There! How do you like that? Let's see you flush my shit down the clogged toilet of your criminal justice system. I'm like Nixon: *I am not a criminal.* You know we Capricorns are a stubborn lot. Goats. We hate to give in. Muhammad Ali. Elvis . . . well, there is that tendency toward self-destruction. But the truth about me is I don't give a shit. I will not become just another turd in this sewer. I'll fight them to the end and enjoy every minute of it.

Yeah, right. . . . Keep telling yourself that, *Dick.*

I AM so fucking hungry I could chew on a dirty bone like a junkyard dog. I can't even remember the last time I ate before that inedible breakfast. Was it Friday morning? My stomach growls, my bowels rumble. My throat is parched. When they open the gate for lunch, around 10:00 a.m., I line up again and join the march back down to the mess hall on the slim hope for something I can swallow.

"No talking! Shut up!" Different cops, same orders.

Lunch, well, let's just say there reaches a point when a man has got to eat. Doesn't matter what it is. I've been on a strict raw food veggie diet, weight way down. Now, after a day of no food and all the excitement and tension of the arrest, I'm starved. But I'm concerned about putting this greasy mystery meat in my stomach. I nibble on some soggy canned vegetables, drink the Kool-Aid. Eat a piece of white bread, anything to ease the ache in my gut. The guy at the table beside me is laughing, mumbling to himself, and grinning at his food like the madman he surely is. It's the big, hulking black guy I tried to give my tray at breakfast. He has a thick wad of flesh over his brow and heavy sagging jowls, rolls of fat on the back of his neck, hunched shoulders, and a wide, humped back.

"Shut up!" a guard commands. "No laughing!"

There is nothing funny about this. But the guy looks up, flashes the cop a toothy grin. He guffaws. His laugh becomes a bellow.

"Shut the fuck up!" the cop screams at him.

The guard is a white man, couldn't be more than twenty-five, crew-cut blond with a Nazi mustache. It occurs to me that all the hacks are white. The cop leaps over the table and whacks the laughing black guy hard across the back with his truncheon. Another guard approaches from the side and hits him again. They beat the man off his stool and onto the floor. They strike him again and again, a merciless beat-down—for laughing—and then they drag him from the mess hall. All the while, the guy keeps right on laughing.

AT ONE POINT over the endless weekend the guards come, everyone in the tank is roused, and we are all herded out and made to assemble in the corridor while our tank is hosed down. We stand between rows of what look to be single-man units, individual fish bowls arranged like a freak gallery at a sideshow. Hermaphrodites, cretins, men wasting away with some mysterious new disease, transsexuals, predatory peder-asts, and outrageous jailhouse queens—the dangerously infectious, the violently insane, and the brazenly homosexual roost on shelves behind thick glass walls. I see the prisoner the guards beat in the mess hall sprawled in one of the single-man tanks. Fascinated, I stare at these rejects. Compelled to identify their abnormalities, what separates them from us, I study them like exhibits in a chamber of horrors. One guy pulls open his jumpsuit and flashes a pair of girlish tits. Another pris-oner leers at me and slowly strokes his semi-erect cock until a guard raps on the glass with his baton and yells at him to "Put the meat away!" Other prisoners appear so sick as to be near death.

This can't be happening, I tell myself, *not here, not in America. Not to me. There must be some mistake.*

But then something deep inside of me moves. Looking at these poor wretches sequestered from even the dregs of the jailhouse popu-lation, I am ashamed at how good I had it in my life, and how much I squandered and abused and took for granted. I have the fleeting sense that every moment of my past, each event and every decision I made until now conspired to bring me here to this Glass House, into which everyone can look, and there are no secrets—even those secrets I would keep from myself. For to survive this experience and make it through whatever the government has in store for me with body and mind intact, I realize that I must finally come to terms with who I am and what I have done with my life.

The other prisoners jeer at the freaks behind the glass. They seem happy, though they feign anger at the cruel attention. They wave good-bye gaily like children as the guards herd us back into our own freshly hosed-down tank.

Chapter Two

DIESEL THERAPY

FCI Terminal Island, San Pedro, California

MONDAY MORNING, THE hazy light of day filters over the blank fluorescent brilliance of the Glass House, and I am delivered. Two taciturn guards come for me. They dress me in shackles and chains, shiny steel bracelets, and take me down into a subterranean garage where a van waits to remove me with half a dozen other federal prisoners to the US courthouse in downtown Los Angeles. There we are made to wait for hours in a crowded, sweltering bullpen. A criminal defense attorney colleague of my lawyer Channing Godfried comes to see me, and we have a brief, hushed conference through the bars.

"This doesn't look good," he tells me. "It's a bail hearing on a pending extradition warrant. Apparently, you absconded from a federal indictment in the District of Maine. You were released on bond and failed to appear. Is that correct?"

"That's true, yes."

"There's not much I can do," he says with a frown. "Whatever bail they set this time, my guess is it will be prohibitively high. I'll argue for reasonable bail, but since you jumped before and you were a fugitive when they arrested you, I don't have a strong basis for my argument. They're not going to want to take the chance that you'll flee again."

I tell him not to worry, I understand the bond will be high and that I don't expect to make bail or want to fight extradition. "I'm ready to go back and face the charges," I tell him. "Just get me out of the LA City Jail."

"You don't want to go to LA County either," he says. "That's even worse."

Agent Wolfshein and Deputy Sullivan are in the courtroom, seated at the prosecutor's table when I enter. The Wolfman nods to me while conferring with the assistant United States attorney (AUSA) assigned to argue for the government. Sullivan gets up; he takes a position by the entrance with another deputy US marshal as if they expect I might make a break for the door. The prosecutor, an earnest, young, instantly forgettable federal type, addresses the magistrate. He calls Wolfshein, who is sworn in and identifies me as Richard Lowell Stratton.

My attorney admits that is who I am.

"Your honor," the prosecutor states, "this defendant, Richard Stratton is a career criminal, a professional drug smuggler with a long history of violating the federal narcotics statutes."

"Excuse me, judge," my attorney interrupts. "Mr. Stratton has never been convicted of any federal or state narcotics violations."

What narcotics? We're talking about marijuana.

"If I may continue, your Honor," the assistant US attorney fires back.

"Yes," says the magistrate; then, to my lawyer, "You will have an opportunity to speak on behalf of the defendant."

"Agent Wolfshein, you have been investigating Mr. Stratton's activities for the DEA, is that correct?" the AUSA queries the Wolf.

"Yes," Wolfshein says matter-of-factly. "That is correct."

"What can you tell the court about who the Drug Enforcement Administration believes this defendant to be?"

My lawyer starts to object, but the magistrate cuts him off.

"This is a bail hearing, not a trial," he says.

"Mr. Stratton is what is termed within the agency as a Class One violator," Wolfshein addresses the court. "That is, someone who is capable of, and who regularly does, import large quantities of controlled substances—in this case mostly marijuana and hashish—from outside the United States into this country, and then distributes the drugs through a network of wholesalers and retailers all across the United States and Canada."

"Agent Wolfshein, you arrested Mr. Stratton on a previous complaint, correct?" asks the prosecutor.

"I did, yes, in the District of Maine."

"When was that?"

"A little over two years ago."

"What was the result of that proceeding?"

"Several defendants pled guilty. Mr. Stratton failed to appear and was sought as a fugitive."

"And what, to your knowledge, was Mr. Stratton's position relative to the other defendants?"

"Mr. Stratton is the organizer, the manager of the conspiracy."

Manager, my ass. I was a stopgap. I was never meant to be there. Those were other people's doomed trips that I was hired to rescue.

"To your knowledge, what has the defendant been doing while avoiding prosecution in Maine?"

"Our investigation of Mr. Stratton's activities confirms that he has continued to import controlled substances while a fugitive." Wolfshein shrugs and gives his trademark gesture, sliding his glasses back up his nose. "I would say it's been business as usual. We have evidence that he and his organization recently imported a multiton shipment of hashish into the United States."

Shit, so they know about that one, too.

"Thank you."

My lawyer wisely chooses not to question Agent Wolfshein.

"You may step down," says the magistrate.

Wolfshein nods to me as he passes by and takes a seat in the rear of the court. I'm thinking how much I enjoy this mode of communication, this courtroom palaver, damaging as it may be. It's so civilized and pointed. No small talk. No beating about the bush. And when someone speaks, people pay attention. There are real consequences to the dialogue. Freedom is at stake. I could sit here all day and listen to these guys talk about me. It's interesting. Again, it's that feeling of being important. To these folks, I matter. They are on a mission to stop me from doing what I do.

"Judge," the prosecutor continues, "this defendant is known to carry several sets of false identification. He has passports in other people's names. And the government believes he has large sums of money hidden in other countries. While he was a fugitive, he was living for much of that time in Lebanon, beyond the reach of US authorities. Under the circumstances," he winds up his spiel, "the government requests a bond set in the amount of fifteen million dollars."

Wow, from $250K on the Maine beef now up to $15 mil here in LA. My value is skyrocketing.

My stand-in lawyer references the presumption of innocence. He avers that the case against me in Maine involves a "conspiracy to distribute marijuana. There have been no allegations of importing vast amounts of controlled substances."

The judge checks me in my puke-stained suit; three-day stubble growth; hollow-eyed, sleep-deprived gaze. "The government has sent a clear message to the courts that they do not look dismissively on these kinds of defendants," he expounds. "The importation of drugs from other countries to the United States has become a scourge upon our nation. Drug defendants with resources such as this defendant often flee to avoid prosecution, as this defendant has shown he is willing to do. Under the circumstances, I am inclined to accept the government's request and set bond in the amount of fifteen million dollars."

Fine, I say to myself, consoled by the thought that it can only get better from here. *Would you like that in cash or will a check do?*

THE FEDERAL PRISON at Terminal Island in San Pedro, California is like a spa, a semi-tropical resort after the shit-imbued confines of the House of Glass. It's on a man-made island at the entrance to Los Angeles Harbor. It's a real prison, complete with cellblocks, fences, and walls topped with concertina wire. The units are populated with convicts doing serious time. But the prison does strike me as a terminal, a place one comes to for a season, and then one moves on. Yet men spend years here waiting to return to the world.

The hack who processes me in through Receiving and Discharge is a mid-level Bureau of Punishment type, not a lowly turnkey. He tells me he is a retired former investigator from the district attorney's office in Manhattan. He's a tall, graying Brooklynite who claims he knows of me, says he has heard of my case, even followed it, and that he has been prepped for my arrival. I suspect he may be trying to trick me into making some admission of guilt.

"We don't get too many pretrial detainees in here with a fifteen-million-dollar bail," he says. He tells me I should have someone come down and claim my possessions, the watch and cash, before the government seizes them. "It'll take them a couple of days," he says, "but they will come. IRS or DEA. And you'll never get it back."

I'm wondering if this is a setup, a plan to lure one of my co-conspirators in to pick up the money so they can lock them up. But something in this guy's manner tells me he is sincere, that he has no real love for the bureaucracy he has served for so many years. He gives me a form to fill out releasing my property to—whom? A blank space. I fill in Val's alias and call her in Maui, collect, at my first opportunity to use a phone. We are in post-arrest emergency mode. With me in custody, I have no choice but to alert Val and have her take over. There is still a lot of money out there that needs to be collected and dispersed, and she has proven herself adept at evading agents of the law.

"Ah, baby. I'm so sorry," Val laments when I tell her where I am. "Are you okay?" But I sense she is relieved that I am still alive.

"Yeah. Listen, can you come by and pick up my stuff?"

She says she'll be over on the next available flight.

Due to my high bail and the fact that I have not yet been convicted of any crime, and that I am being held in pretrial, holdover status awaiting extradition to Maine, I am afforded what amounts to deluxe accommodations. They assign me to a high-security unit populated with infamous bank robbers and gang leaders, drug kingpins, and the criminally insane, all either pretrial or brought in from other institutions to face new charges.

My first cellie tells me he was arrested for stalking and threatening the TV *Tonight Show* host Johnny Carson. He's a gentle soul, soft and chubby with thinning, sandy blond hair. He says he never meant to cause Johnny any harm, he just wanted an opportunity to get on his show and demonstrate to the late-night viewing audience what he can do, which, he tells me, is a kind of magic, also a calling. He can dematerialize, he claims, and he can conjure the dead. He says he once brought Marilyn Monroe back to life, and she told him she was murdered, her death was not a suicide. "I can prove all this," he says. "And the Kennedy assassinations. I know who's responsible, who did it."

"Who?"

"I'll tell you everything . . . in time. But when I do, when I reveal everything to you, they will take you away and you will never be able to get out. They don't want any of what I know to be made known to the rest of the world." He rushes his speech as if gladdened to finally have an audience, and concerned they may whisk him away before he can reveal his truth.

"A triumvirate of highly evolved spiritual beings sent me here to save mankind," he goes on. "It's a mission . . . and a curse. You see, mankind does not want to be saved. We are the fallen, bent on self-destruction, like lemmings rushing to the edge of the precipice."

I believe him. It all sounds plausible to me, because I am one of those lemmings.

He continues. "This place can't hold me." He claims the walls are an illusion of imprisoned consciousness. They only exist because we believe they exist. We are all as free as we want to be. "I need to be here, for my own good," he says. "And for the good of the human,"—he pronounces it *hu-MIN*—"race. Every great man must spend some time in prison." He rattles off the names of noted former prisoners: John the Baptist. Christ. Saint Paul. Dostoyevsky. O. Henry. Malcolm X. Wilhelm Reich, who died in prison. And the list goes on. "Even Hitler," he adds.

"You too will do great things," he assures me as though this were prophecy. "This is a rite of passage."

THESE THOUGHTS COMFORT me. The guy may be crazy, but I feel better already. Early the next day, however, before breakfast and before my enlightened cellmate can reveal the author of the Kennedy murders, the guards come for him. When I inquire later, the unit manager confides that he was removed to the nut ward for psychiatric evaluation.

My new cellie is a skinny, long-haired failed armored-car robber. He tells me he went to the mall with his girlfriend, and she carried a basket of wash into the Laundromat while he waited in the car.

"I was bored," he says. "The whole idea of it, doing the same boring crap every day—washing clothes, eating, sleeping, and then doing it all over—it depressed the shit out of me. I saw my whole life as one boring, depressing day after another equally fucking boring day. And I just couldn't take it. The idea of it killed me inside."

He was an experienced bank robber who had already done close to a decade in prison. In the trunk of his girlfriend's car he had a Mac 10, and he had a 9mm handgun in the glove box. An armored car pulled up in front of the supermarket. On the spur of the moment, "because I was bored," he grabbed both guns and attempted to commandeer the armored truck. He took one of the guards hostage in the rear of the truck, "with all that money," and ordered the other guard to drive off. But the truck was equipped with LoJack and some anti-theft device that cut the engine a few blocks away from the shopping mall. They were stranded. Cop cars and a SWAT team quickly surrounded the armored truck.

"It was hot as a fuckin' sauna in that truck, man. I couldn't breathe. I had all that money, but nowhere to spend it." He laughs.

The cops brought in a hostage negotiator. News trucks and cameramen flocked to the scene. "I was all over the nightly news. It was like that movie, *Dog Day Afternoon*. I was famous—for a minute."

The heat in the truck became unbearable, and the guard passed out. "I was afraid he had a heart attack. Or heat stroke. You know, he wasn't too healthy, and I didn't want the guy to die on me."

When his girlfriend was located and told him to, "Cut the stupid shit and give yourself up. This isn't funny anymore, Donald," over the bullhorn, several spectators laughed.

"That was it," he says. "I can't stand it when she calls me Donald, like I'm fuckin' Donald Duck. So I tossed my guns and came out with my hands on my head. They went nuts, screaming at me to get down on the ground. Ten cops with guns pointed at me going crazy like they're Dirty Harry. *Make my day!*" He laughs again. "Fuck them. This was my movie. It was the most fun I had in a long time."

Coming back to prison is no big deal, he tells me. It can be boring, of course. But it is expected to be boring. So any variation on the daily routine is a plus. It's a kind of hibernation, a time to gear down and chill out. "I read a lot, mostly crime books. Books about famous criminals. I love crime. But I'm too lazy to be a good criminal, that's my problem. Crime is like anything else—you gotta work hard to be good at it."

Outside, "in the world" one expects to be stimulated, he reasons. So it is a letdown when one day begins to feel exactly like the one before and the one before that and on and on until you die. "It sucks. This life is fucking boring—and meaningless. I should have been a warrior," he concludes. "In prison, I have an excuse to say, 'Fuck it,' and be lazy. So I'm a failure, who gives a shit? It's all bullshit anyway."

This too strikes me as vaguely comforting. I've been mulling over these same thoughts. For a man who needs constant, life-threatening risk to feel alive, the idea of prison as an alternative lifestyle—a life of routine and the concentrated introspection that comes with enforced boredom—this may be exactly what the narcissist in me craves.

IT's MEMORIAL DAY weekend, hot in Southern California. I spend my days on the weight pile, in the sun, doing chins and push-ups, dips and bench presses, getting tanned and cut-up, exercising with the tattooed, heavily muscled gangsters and gangbangers. I sleep, call it rest. I meditate. I read. The food is decent. They bring it to our unit in food carts and we eat in the common area like guests at a convention. The other prisoners have interesting stories. I become friendly with a quiet, ink-sleeve-tattooed convict named Ruben, a Chicano gang boss charged with running a criminal organization—gambling, extortion, narcotics trafficking—from inside a maximum-security federal pen. The new indictment includes allegations he ordered and/or carried out several contract hits in furtherance of the racketeering enterprise. He is facing life with no parole.

"It don't matter, I'm already doing a life bid," he says, "so what the fuck?"

Ruben gives me pot; he offers me heroin, cocaine. "I can get you whatever you want," he says. "Don't let these cops fool you. We run these joints."

I take a couple of joints from him, and we trade books. He is remarkably well-read for a guy who quit school in the sixth grade and embarked on a life of crime. Most of his adult life has been spent in prison.

This is my life now.

VAL COMES TO visit. I tell her she is authorized to collect my watch and the money I had on me when I was arrested.

"You look good, honey," Val tells me. "Sexy."

I could get off just looking at her.

We are in a visiting room filled with prisoners and their families, sad-eyed kids, wives, and girlfriends. Guards and video cameras. Val huddles close and says, "Do you think this place is wired?"

"I doubt it. Too much noise."

She nods. "Your friend Nasif got popped in New York."

I pause while this sinks in. Nasif is the son of Mohammed, my heavy Lebanese connection, the former chief of customs in Beirut, and my partner in the massive seven-and-a-half-ton load of hashish we imported at the Port of Newark, New Jersey, that now appears to have become the subject of an ongoing grand jury investigation. Nasif is also related to the Captain, Ayla Schbley. With Nasif in custody, the government has all they need to indict me.

"Nasif was in New York?"

"Yeah," she says when I give her a baffled look. "Your friend Sammy called me." She refers to Sammy Silver, my other partner in the hash trip. "He's lamming it, took his old lady and is in the wind. Nasif and that other Lebanese dude, the taxi driver Hammoud, they got popped trying to sell ten kis of junk to an undercover DEA agent. They both immediately flipped."

The news nearly takes the wind out of me. I sigh. *Heroin.* Of course. You get in business with people who also deal junk, this is what happens. My karma continues to catch up with me. So this is how Wolfshein knows of the massive hashish smuggle—the fucking

Lebs rolled over and are now spilling their guts to the DEA and US attorney's office.

"Does Biff know?" I ask, speaking of Mailer's friend who came to work for us as a money courier.

"I tried to call him," Val tells me. "But I couldn't get through, and I don't want to leave any numbers."

"Sammy didn't reach out for him?"

"Sammy hates Biff. You know that. He never forgave him for wimping out when the load came in."

"You should keep trying to reach him. He's probably at his place on Long Island. He needs to know. He's in touch with those people—the Arabs. That could be a problem."

"Okay." She looks around impatiently. I feel she is ready to leave.

The shit just keeps getting deeper. Mohammed, that greedy, fat prick. Those fucking Lebs, they can't leave well enough alone. We were making millions importing hash, but Mohammed was determined to get into the junk business. And bring us all down.

"This is not good." I don't know what else to say.

"Tell me about it. They let the taxi driver guy go. He reached out for Sammy like everything was cool. Tried to set him up." She holds my hand and looks up at me with those big, almond-shaped sloe eyes, gives me her pitiful puppy dog look. "I'm so sorry, baby."

"For what?" I want to be hard. I don't want anything to get to me. In this place, at this time, sentiment is my undoing. "It's not your fault."

"Yes, it is. I let you down. I . . . if I hadn't . . . fucked up, you never would have—you know—you never would have left Maui. We'd still be together. They never would have busted you."

"Don't worry about it," I assure her. "I was tired of running. Just take care of yourself."

"I miss you."

I think I'll say, *We'll get through this*, but decide to say, "I'll get through this." I must do this alone. And I go on. "Be careful. I'm sure

Nasif told them whatever he knows about you." It's the only advice I can give her. "Try to keep the damage to a minimum."

We embrace. I give her a loveless kiss. And I know it is the last time we will ever see each other.

WEEKS PASS IN relative bliss. The days are hot, the nights are cool. The air coming in off the Pacific through the barred and ventilated window of my ground-level cell is soft and smells of the sea. I work out in the afternoon and get high in the evening. I read in the morning and sleep peacefully at night. There is nowhere to go. There are no appointments to keep, no panic attacks. For the first time in over a decade, I'm not worried about getting arrested. For the compulsive wanderer I am, this life of compelled confinement brings sustained self-absorption. I turn my travels inward. The outside world fades into memory as memory takes precedence. Survival becomes my new dwelling place in a land of character that I explore minute to minute. It is as though I am walking around always in two minds—one here and now, the other fixed on the past and how I came to be here.

BUT NOW MY little hiatus in the California sun has come to an end. It is time to go back and face the music. I'm hearing the rumblings of grand jury investigations like a distant kettledrum roll emanating from the Southern District of New York. When I reach my attorney, Godfried, he confirms the Lebanese are singing arias. He says he forwarded this information to Biff. He tells me government agents descended on the ranch in Texas and seized everything: horses, dogs, tractors, cars, and furniture. I tell myself that it was never really mine anyway. All I possess is my consciousness, my experience.

One morning before dawn I am trussed up like a stuffed turkey, clamped in leg irons, dressed in shackles and handcuffs and the black box—a hard, molded plastic fitting that immobilizes my wrists. The cuffs are attached to a belly chain looped around my waist. I waddle out of Receiving and Discharge at Terminal Island wearing enough hardware to sink Houdini. I'm outfitted in an army-green jumpsuit and a pair of soft, green canvas slippers the convicts call Peter Pans.

"Name and number," a deputy US marshal barks.

"Stratton. Zero two zero seven zero. Zero three six."

A faded blue Bureau of Punishment bus with tinted, barred windows waits in the sally port. Deputy marshals and BOP guards with shotguns sit in cages, one in front and one in the rear of the bus. Getting up and down the steps, getting in and out of the bus, wearing all that hardware is a challenge. Harder still is to take a leak in the open piss pot at the rear of the bus with hands cuffed and chained to my waist, trying to unsnap the jumpsuit, get the limp lizard out and aim him in the shithole without wetting myself, as the bus lurches, pitches, and sways—this is no simple task. Forget about taking a crap.

We are fed baloney and cheese sandwiches and apples or oranges three times a day. Still maintaining my vegetarian diet, I trade my baloney for fruit. I have a dull, throbbing headache from caffeine withdrawal. I feel like the Tin Man before service with the oilcan. I am bone-weary, my joints ache from lack of movement. At every stop it's the same routine: name and number. A long wait while the restraints are removed. Yet another butthole inspection as new guards gaze up the old Hershey Highway. Lift the nut sack. Check the armpits. Grab a paper bag with a baloney and cheese sandwich and an apple. Lock down for the night in one hole or another.

I think of other bus rides I've taken over the years: as a child to and from school, kids laughing and yelling; as an athlete to and from events, wrestlers sweating it out, butterflies in the gut; as a drug smuggler and fugitive in Mexico, a gringo among the campesinos and livestock. This is a whole new experience. We are shipped like cattle from federal joint to county jail to US penitentiary, all across the nation. It's a meandering coast-to-coast zigzag. There appears to be no thought given to arriving at a final destination. We go up along the West Coast from Terminal Island to the federal penitentiary at Lompoc, California. After a night in the Hole, we are taken with a whole new batch of prisoners to a nearby Air Force base, where a Bureau of Punishment passenger jet awaits. Marshals armed with shotguns surround the plane. I'm seated in the front, directly across from an attractive, butch, young blond female marshal.

"You work out?" she asks.

"When I can," I say.

Is she flirting with me? Is there life after incarceration? Could I take her, on the floor, in chains and shackles? These are the senseless thoughts that meander through my head.

From Lompoc they fly us to El Reno, Oklahoma. A short bus ride to another federal prison where I spend the night sleeping on the floor of a narrow one-man cell with two other holdover prisoners. Then a long haul with several stops along the way to the United States penitentiary at Atlanta, Georgia.

This is it, the Big House. One of the oldest pens in the nation, built in 1902, home to such famous criminals as Al Capone and James "Whitey" Bulger, who did a stretch here before being shipped out to Alcatraz. Yes, Whitey, my savior; after a jam I got into while smuggling hash in through Logan Airport in Boston, Whitey got a mob contract lifted off my sorry ass. I have arrived. One of the big boys now. From Boston's Thompson Island school for wayward boys as a thirteen-year-old juvenile delinquent to the penitentiary, following in Whitey's infamous footsteps.

We are kept in the Hole for several days before another long bus ride, first to Talladega, Alabama, then up the East Coast with stops at prisons along the way in Butner, North Carolina, and Petersburg, Virginia. I am seated on the bus beside a man who tells me he has been doing this for a little more than six months. He has been on the bus, moving from prison to prison, Hole to Hole, more or less continuously since just after the New Year. Marcus is his name, the law is his game. He says he's a "writ writer," known as a jailhouse lawyer who has successfully sued the Bureau of Punishment, and so they retaliate by keeping him on the bus, moving him constantly, never allowing him to land in one place long enough for his property to catch up with him—his books and legal papers, the proceeds of his lawsuit—as a way of keeping him from realizing any benefit from his legal work and holding him incommunicado so he cannot make phone calls or continue to bring new writs in other jurisdictions.

"Diesel therapy, they call it," he says. "There are hundreds, maybe thousands of prisoners on the move on any given day. Men the bureau considers troublemakers, like myself. Pretrial detainees like you who they want to soften up, marinate you with diesel fumes so that by the time you get to where you're going, you're ready to get down on your knees and plead guilty just to get it over with. Then there's the overflow from all the Fed joints, convicts they don't have cells for, so they just keep moving people around while they build new prisons."

Marcus looks like a lawyer. He's bookish, wears thick glasses, has a round, soft body and curly dark hair. Chubby hands swollen at the wrists from the handcuffs. He was convicted of bank fraud in Florida and has been locked up for five years. He wasn't a lawyer on the street; he was a businessman. But he very quickly realized after getting locked up that no one would work as hard on his case as he would.

"The law," he tells me, "is not an exact science. It is more like literature, subject to interpretation, and as malleable as clay. It is a living organism, constantly evolving. *Language* is the key."

"Language?"

"Yes, exactly," Marcus avers. "They say you broke the law, right?"

"Several laws, apparently."

"Have you read the indictment?"

I shake my head.

Marcus speaks like a lawyer, with nuanced accenting on his key pronouncements. "The laws they say you broke, those are *statues codified in language*. Written out *in words*. *Read everything. Study* your case. The government *alleges* you did certain things they have *declared illegal*—this is all done with words. So you counter by saying, 'No, I did not do that. I did something else.' It is called a *theory of defense*. They present their case; you counter with your *defense*. It all comes down to *words*. Most of the so-called evidence is testimony—more *words*. And then there are words used by the lawyers to enhance or under-cut the testimony. That's why it's called *testimony*, cross-examination, and *argument*. Most criminal defense lawyers are useless. They just take your money and try to confuse you with a lot of *gibberish*. Okay? You seem like an intelligent man. So you must *read* the indictment, *study* it, and come up with a contrary argument, a *theory* of defense to present to the jury."

This is fascinating to me. It's beautiful. I never thought of it this way. Words got me locked up, words can set me free. It's like plumb-ing—you need a license to fix pipes—and even medicine. I know when something's wrong with my body, but the experts want to obfus-cate their trade because they don't want us to know how to fix it for ourselves. I recall what the DEA agent told me when they busted my man JD and me in Upstate New York with the empty truck back in '78: "We're gonna get up there and tell our lies," he said. "Then you'll get up there and tell your lies. It's just a question of whose lies the jury believes."

Lies. Statutes. Testimony. Cross-examination. Argument. A theory of defense. Verdict: guilty or not guilty, it's all words. And it makes splendid sense. God created the world using words. He spoke it into existence. I can re-create my fate with words. Marcus reminds me that I have a constitutional right to defend myself. That means the courts have ruled that as a prisoner I must be allowed access to a law library to study my case and learn the language of the law.

I am excited and intrigued with this notion, and I want to hear more, but our conversation is drowned out by the angry laments of a black prisoner riding near the rear of the bus.

"Fuck this shit, man!" he screams when they hand him yet another brown paper bag with yet another baloney and cheese sandwich and apple inside. "Gimme some real food! I'm hungry. Lemme off this fuckin' bus and gimme some damn food!"

"Shut the fuck up!" the lieutenant riding at the front of the bus yells back at him. He's pissed, the lieutenant. This has not been a good day for him, either. We were turned away from one jail because it was already overcrowded, and he had to get on the radio to command headquarters and make new arrangements.

"I'll shut up when you *gimme some damn food!* A man's gotta eat," the convict bellows. "You can't treat a person like this. It ain't right. I been on this bus for days. *I want some damn food!*"

It goes on, yelling back and forth, disrupting the run-down mood on the bus, and winding us up with new tension. No one wants to hear this. No one wants to be part of whatever might jump off. We all feel the same: tired; hungry; longing for a bed, a shower, an end to this interminable bus ride to nowhere; craving real food. But there is an unspoken understanding that the only way through it is to submit. Yelling and pissing these people off will only make it worse.

The angry black convict is beyond thinking this through. In disgust, he throws his lunch bag toward the front of the bus. It hits the back of a seat near the lieutenant and spills out onto the floor—soggy white bread, artificially colored yellow cheese, pale gray mystery meat, and a red apple.

The lieutenant stands. He looms at the front of the bus—a big man, red-faced, sweating rage. "I told you to shut up!" He has a roll of what looks like dull silver duct tape in his hand.

"Hell, no!" the hungry convict yells back at him. "I'll keep hollerin' till you see fit to feed me some real damn food!"

The other prisoners studiously ignore the beef. The bus trundles along a secondary highway in Pennsylvania where a sign reads AMERICA BEGINS HERE. The lieutenant speaks to the driver, who pulls the bus over into the breakdown lane, and we come to a stop.

Marcus tenses beside me. "Don't watch," he warns me. "You don't want to be called as a witness. They'll never let you off the bus."

"You're gonna shut up or I'm gonna shut you up," says the lieutenant, and he lurches along the aisle to the rear of the bus.

"Hell, no I ain't! I ain't gonna shut up until you people feed me! You can't treat a man like this!"

"Shut up!"

"No! *Feed me!*"

No one wants to look. I see it go down in the rearview mirror. The armed marshal in the rear cage comes out and stands behind the black man.

"You gonna shut up?" the lieutenant asks.

"You gonna feed me?" the convict replies.

The lieutenant nods to the marshal, who grabs the guy by his nappy hair and yanks his head back. The lieutenant takes the roll of duct tape and covers the man's mouth. Now the convict's screams are muffled but still audible. Then the lieutenant wraps the black guy's whole head and sparsely bearded face with duct tape until he resembles a mummy from the neck up. The man struggles fiercely, he screams, but the sounds are muted. Wrapped in chains and with his hands cuffed, there is nothing he can do. There is nothing we can do. The lieutenant keeps wrapping his head in duct tape until his screaming is a sucking gasp. The tape over his mouth and nose sucks in and blows out as he labors to breathe.

The lieutenant lumbers to his seat at the front of the bus, and we drive on.

"Now, where was I?" Marcus says.

"Language is the key."

"That's right. Dialectic. Reasoned argument." He shakes his head. "Shouting and screaming will get you nowhere with the government and their functionaries. You have to look to unravel their reasoning, which is perverse and therefore susceptible to challenge. Do you understand?"

I nod. We have the example of the black prisoner with his head wrapped in duct tape. He no longer complains. He's quiet now, slumped in his seat. When we arrive at our next destination, the US penitentiary in Lewisburg, Pennsylvania, the mummified black man doesn't move. Even when they tear the tape off his face, as wisps of his sparse beard are ripped from his hollow cheeks, he doesn't complain or holler for food. The rest of us are hustled inside.

THIS PLACE LOOKS like Dracula's castle set in the middle of the gentle green rolling hills of rural Pennsylvania. The prison is a Gothic, terra-cotta brick structure with elegant arches and ornamental corbels all surrounded by thick concrete walls thirty feet high. Modern-looking, glassed-in gun towers manned by armed guards stand at each juncture in the wall. A tall, elegant spire like a minaret ascends from the center of the compound. The prison was built as part of the WPA project back in the thirties when no brick or laborer's handwork was spared. Al Capone did time here, Jimmy Hoffa, and Whitey Bulger was released from here. Wilhelm Reich, the radical psychiatrist, died in this prison. They found him in his cell at seven in the morning, fully clothed but for his shoes, supposedly dead from a heart attack in the night, just days before he was scheduled to have a parole hearing.

I have come to understand: you don't want to complain; it does no good. You don't want to get sick or let your heart weaken in these places. There is no relief. Steel your emotions. This is a world where there is absolutely no compassion, no empathy. And why should there be? We are the condemned.

I am housed in K Dorm, the holdover unit. It's a long, narrow basement room lined with bunk beds and teeming with prisoners in transit. A gang shower is attached to the end of the block. We are issued a towel and a toothbrush. I take my first shower in weeks. We eat real food in a cavernous, ornate mess hall with a salad bar. I gorge on fresh vegetables. Drink brewed coffee. We get to walk around in a walled-in courtyard open to the sky. Sunshine alights on our flesh. Fresh country air fills our lungs. I sleep on a bed.

This place is a species of paradise after the meandering passage from Terminal Island. Many of the men in this penitentiary are serving life sentences. It is a place long-term convicts come to die, and for that reason the guards treat them with a modicum of respect. The general population dwells around us transients like spirits of the dead. They are of the world but not in it. They are hard-core criminals, East Coast gangster royalty, committed professionals like Jimmy Burke, the alleged mastermind of the six million dollars in cash and jewels hijacked from the Lufthansa Airlines cargo terminal at JFK airport in '78. Jimmy works the yard detail picking up trash, notes, and contraband tossed from the windows of the cellblocks. Herbie Sperling is here as well, another legendary tough guy, one of the first men sentenced to life without parole for drug trafficking under the kingpin statute. Herbie squats beside the window on his way to the yard and tells a friend he was set up and ratted out in a new case by Mr. Untouchable himself, Nicky Barnes, the infamous Harlem heroin merchant who became a government witness. "Nicky Barnes is a *goil*," is how Herbie pronounces *girl*, like *oil* with a *g*. The prison grapevine immediately transmits this information. People get murdered in here, but never for too little.

I lose Marcus in the shuffle at Receiving and Discharge. He's shipped out immediately, continues on his journey to nowhere on the next bus. But his advice has penetrated and set up camp in my mind. The troops are assembling to marshal my defense. Ideas are building the battlements. Once I get to wherever I am going, I am determined to study my case. I will understand this language they call the Law. This has given new purpose to my life.

Each day the bus arrives and disgorges a gaggle of fresh convicts. Most are sentenced prisoners on their way to one of the many federal institutions scattered across the land where they will serve their time. I walk in the courtyard. I do push-ups and crunches on the concrete slab. In the shower room I do chin-ups hanging from a pipe. This is a tense, hectic four-day respite, like living in a busy bus station, so much coming and going, an incarcerated population on the move.

Then, early one day before dawn, guards come for me. I am shackled and chained, hands immobilized by the black box, and then loaded back on the Bureau of Punishment stagecoach. Next stop, New York City, the Big Apple, the Metropolitan Correctional Center—MCC, baby—in Manhattan, just like I remember it from my brief stay here with Jimmy D on the hash importation case that never was back in '78. This time I am just passing through. After a leisurely ride through the hills and back roads of rural Pennsylvania and Upstate New York, with my eyes glued to the outside world as it passes by, the bus comes to a stop in a garage at the base of the high-rise federal jail. We are all removed and locked in a bullpen. Prisoners come and go as their names and numbers are called. Hours later, I am herded back on the bus with several new convicts, and we hit the road again, this time for Connecticut.

The scuttlebutt among the prisoners is that someone died on the bus. There is talk of it in the bullpen and again on the bus. Rumor circulates among the convicts. The guards and marshals are mum. There is a nebulous fear above and beyond the usual dread, some sense that things have reached a point of no return. I hear enough to know that the rumors are all about the black man who had his head wrapped with duct tape. They say he suffocated. I feel like we knew it even as we got off the bus in Lewisburg. The angry black man was angry no more, for he was dead. But we kept our mouths shut. And I keep my mouth shut, remembering Marcus's words, not wanting to be singled out as a witness to an official murder. Hear nothing. See nothing. Say nothing. You are not really here in this place and time. Just passing through.

Yet this fear of speaking out and bearing witness makes me feel cowardly. Despicable. Trying to slip through this experience with the least amount of involvement of conscience, looking out only for myself, concerned only for my own survival. What kind of a man does that make me? A nowhere man. A nothing man. Someone who only cares about his own well-being, his own survival . . . a cockroach.

But this is serious shit. These Punishment people don't play. I could end up on the bus forever. Who would know? My parents? How would I tell them? No one knows where I am. As it is, I have been unable to speak to anyone in the world for weeks. Who would believe me? It is hard to understand that shit like this goes down in America. But I have seen a crazy black man bludgeoned with truncheons in the Glass House. And now I have witnessed an angry black man gagged and mummified on the Bureau of Punishment special. I just want to keep my fucking mealy white mouth shut and get wherever I'm going with the least amount of hassle—lowly cocksucker that I am. I might as well bend over and let the Punishment specialists shove their version of the land of the free up my tight white ass. But then, just maybe I will make it through and live long enough to write about it. That is my secret desire, my solitary plan.

THE FEDERAL BUREAU of Punishment institution at Danbury, Connecticut, is my next stop. After a long and tedious booking-in at Receiving and Discharge, being fingerprinted, mug-shot, asshole-inspected, and degraded for the umpteenth time, I am taken straight to the Hole. My high bail and former fugitive status has them on edge. One of the hacks checking me in looks up and asks, "What the fuck did you do? It says, 'Conspiracy to distribute marijuana'? That must have been a hell of a lot of pot."

Now all of a sudden I am a VIP—Very Important Prisoner. I'm not allowed to mingle with the other convicts. I'm wondering if this is because they know I witnessed the mummification of the black man and are trying to keep me from telling others what I saw, or if they are in fact concerned about my security level. It's impossible to tell with these people. These Bureau of Punishment types are deadpan. They check their empathy at the prison gates. I am reminded of a book I read, *Will* by G. Gordon Liddy. Liddy did time in this joint for refusing to cooperate over his involvement in the Watergate break-in. No rat G. Gordon.

I am locked in a single-man cell, fed three times a day with a tray shoved through a slot in the cell door. They take me out once after two days for a shower. No phone calls. Then, very early one morning before sun-up, deputy US marshals come for me. I'm dressed out in khakis, cuffed behind my back, with chains and shackles at the ankles, loaded into the rear of a plain dark sedan and, lo and behold, who slips in behind the wheel? It's Sullivan, my old pal Boston Sully who arrested me in LA, fresh-faced and grinning, happy to see me.

"Richie boy, how you been?" he says.

"Great, Sullivan. And you?"

"Oh, you know, doin' my thing. . . . Listen, I got a treat for you, one Boston guy to another. You behave yourself and, around lunch-time, we'll stop at McDonald's. How's that grab ya'?"

"Wonderful," I say, though I couldn't care less.

Ah, yes, incrementally, life is getting better even as I get worse.

Chapter Three

GOOD JAIL

Cumberland County Jail, October 1982

AFTER SO MANY nights in jails and prisons, and the endless days riding in the Bureau of Punishment prison on wheels, finally to arrive at the Cumberland County Jail in downtown Portland, Maine is like coming home. There is the comfort of familiar surroundings. No longer a stranger in America's vast prison gulag, I can drop the shield of anonymity and be me. I'm a minor celebrity in this joint. My keepers all but roll out the red carpet. Not so much because of who I am, but due to my notorious connection with the famous novelist, Norman Mailer; and, though only alluded to, for all the cash money I once spread around Vacationland, as the great state of Maine is known.

Mailer's name and picture have been all over the newspapers and local evening news as co-owner of the horse farm I put up as collateral for the bail that got this alleged drug kingpin out of jail—and which I promptly jumped, leaving the government embarrassed, for they had neglected to get Mailer's signature on the bond. I believe this pisses them off more than anything else I may have done. They hate it when you make them look stupid. True, it was their oversight. I never hid the fact that Mailer's name is on the deed as co-owner of the property. It was plain on the face of the document, and the magistrate simply overlooked it. I'm not about to do their job for them.

So Mailer's fame attached to what is being trumpeted as the biggest drug bust in the history of the state of Maine is rich fodder for local media. There are TV cameramen and reporters camped outside the jail when we pull up in the marshal's sedan. I am whisked past the reporters and hustled inside. After a brief, painless pro forma booking-in with no cavity search, the sheriff I know as Gilmore from my previous visit asks me if there is anything I need.

"Not that I can think of at the moment," I say and thank him. "Maybe . . . a shower?"

He locks me up in the same cell I spent the night in when Special Agent Bernie Wolfshein delivered me here on that fateful snowy April eve. To think, it all began when I stopped to help a stranded motorist whose car slid off the road, and who turned out to be a DEA agent. How ironic! I lie in my cell and ponder this sublime paradox: no good deed goes unpunished.

My new dwelling is a single cell in what is known in the jail as bound-over yardside, meaning the cells that are reserved for federal prisoners and prisoners bound over for trial. The cells are located on a tier like a balcony overlooking the enclosed recreation area, therefore yardside. There is a steel slab bunk, a mattress, a pillow, of all things, and a small, shelf-like desk welded to the bars at the front of the cell. The open metal combination sink and toilet, as well as the whole interior space, is painted dark shit brown.

This jail is old and dirty but comfortable; it's like a country inn that has seen better days. No bright lights. No shiny steel surfaces. No Plexiglas walls. It's not noisy as jails go. And just the thought that I will not be roused early in the morning to be strip-searched, made to bend over and spread my cheeks, chained and shackled and constrained by the black box, herded onto the bus to be driven for hours to some other jail, fed baloney and cheese sandwiches, and then locked up for the night only to have the whole process repeated again the next day—that is soothing enough. But to have my own cell all to myself—what luxury! To be marched down the tier to take a hot shower; to be able to hang a towel like a curtain from the bars at the front of the cell for a measure of privacy: these small pleasures are treasures in the life of the prisoner. So that when, on my first evening in my new digs, as I perceive the unmistakable odor of my favorite herb burning, the smell wafting over from the cells on bound-over streetside, I know that I am exactly where I am supposed to be, at least for the foreseeable future.

One of the cardinal principles of doing time is to do it one day at a time. As simple as that sounds, it is profound, and, as I am reminded daily, profoundly difficult to achieve. But the alternative, as I soon realize—to obsess on what the future may bring or agonize and beat yourself up with regret over the stupid mistakes and selfish actions of the past that got you locked up in the first place—that becomes intolerable, for there is no escaping yourself, no way out of your inside, and no getting away from the fact that you now have very little control over what will happen to you at any given moment. I have only been locked up for what—a few months? But I have come to understand, and will appreciate again and again at new levels of understanding, that there is only madness or despair in the life of the prisoner unless you are able to refocus your thoughts and recompose your attitude, for it is all about the attitude you bring to the experience. This can be seen as incredibly liberating. You are free to understand that you control nothing but who you are minute to minute, day to day, until this life plays out. God alone has the key. But to hold on to this thought, to capture this attitude and keep it present in your mind, that is the true challenge of the prisoner's life.

Pacing in my cell, I ponder these thoughts. I think of the black prisoner on the bus who had his head wrapped in duct tape and suffocated because he refused to adapt his attitude to the routine. Or the laughing man who got beat down in the mess hall of the Glass House. Submit, I tell myself. Outwardly conform. This is my jailors' world. I am just passing through. I will hold firmly to the one thing they can never take and never control—my attitude.

The realization of what it means to be a prisoner seeps into my consciousness slowly, in dribs and drabs, and then it fades and dematerializes as, inevitably, I focus on the impending trial. Marcus the writ writer's words are embedded in my thought processes. One must devise a defense. Find the right words. Conceive of an argument. It is not enough to sit there in the courtroom and let the prosecution proclaim you a criminal and hope that their proof is not convincing beyond a reasonable doubt to twelve supposedly unbiased jurors. One must present a proactive defense, an alternative scenario that somehow undermines the prosecution's theory and casts doubt in the jurors' minds.

The very idea of this energizes me. Yes, it is a species of theater. I have seen it play out in courtrooms before, with my arrest for carrying a concealed weapon in Boston and my previous bust for conspiracy to import hashish in New York. I watched my good friend and attorney Hef cajole judges into setting me free with little or no repercussions, simply because he is convincing at speaking his lines, lines he himself composes. I must create a fiction, a good story, something to befuddle, entertain, and dazzle the jurors.

An incipient narrative begins to take hold of my imagination. Lawyers come calling. My first choice is Hef, but he is unavailable, going through some professional and matrimonial difficulties of his own. Hef refers me to Joe Oteri, a legendary Boston criminal defense attorney who has represented any number of men in the marijuana business and who fights cannabis cases with the zeal of a true believer in the fundamental error of the laws against the plant. Oteri and I conference on the phone. He recommends a local attorney, Marshall Stern of Bangor, Maine, who Oteri says has a good rapport with the US attorney's office here in Portland.

"Let Marshall come in and get a sense of the lay of the land," Oteri advises me. "You don't want to come on with out-of-town lawyers at this stage of the game."

The game. Of course, he understands: it is all a game.

Stern arrives at the jail the next day. He's a dapper, plump, short man with big eyewear. "Your reputation precedes you," the lawyer says when we meet in the attorney visiting cubicle. "This case has been the talk of the state for months."

Marshall Stern rose to the top of the criminal bar in the federal District of Maine arena representing a growing number of seafaring pot smugglers attracted to the long, irregular, deep-water coastline and to the relative lack of federal law enforcement presence until recently. That has changed dramatically in the time I was on the lam, Stern advises me. As Maine became a hotbed of smuggling activity, the DEA presence was beefed up commensurately. As we speak, there are two other major pot smuggling cases pending in the district court.

"And you paved the way," the lawyer says. I see him eyeing my gold Rolex Presidential watch that Val neglected to retrieve from my possessions at Terminal Island, though she did collect the cash. Miraculously, the watch survived my odyssey across the incarcerated nation in my property and was returned to me upon my arrival here. "Nice watch," Stern says.

I unclasp the wristband and hand it to him. "Consider yourself retained."

Stern says he has a meeting set with the US attorney for the district, a man named Richard Cohen, to get a copy of the indictment and some sense of what the government hopes to accomplish with this case. "Your codefendants all pled out," he says. "Do you know this guy—?" Stern mentions the man I call Fred Barnswallow by his government name.

"Yeah, I know him."

"And do you know ——? He's cooperating with the government."

"So I heard."

"Can he hurt you?"

I nod. "Yes, definitely."

Stern tells me that Judy, my now ex-girlfriend Val's longtime partner, has been arrested on the West Coast and is on her way to this very jail. The lawyer has a whole list of people who have been arrested and adjudicated. "Many got probation." He shows me the list. "Do you know any of these people?"

The only name I recognize is Barnswallow's. "I never met any of them. I only know this guy, Fred . . . and Judy."

"The government has identified you as the ringleader. This judge, by the way, Edward Gignoux, is a jurist of some repute. He was at one time on the shortlist for consideration to be appointed to the Supreme Court. He's a fair judge. I don't think he has ever given out more than five years on a plea in a pot case. If you should choose to plead guilty and save the government the time and money of a trial, we might be able to make that deal, or something close to it anyway. Of course, there is the fact that you . . . failed to appear. That's also a consideration. Anyway, a plea is always an option, something to consider. If we take it to trial and lose, I would expect Gignoux to give you more time—much more time. But I haven't had those discussions with Cohen's office as yet."

Indeed, a plea is something to think about. But it is never as simple as trying to decide between the lesser of two evils: a guilty plea or a conviction at trial. Because there is always the slim chance of a win, and for a gambler, a risk-taker, the possibility of an acquittal is like taking a shot at hitting the jackpot. The case against me is remarkably weak. Only Fearless Fred can tie me to the series of arrests that took place in the state after the crash landing of the DC-6 on the airstrip near my home, and the successful off-load of thirty-odd tons of Colombian pot from a mother ship offshore. The government apparently has only limited information about these successful smuggles. The weed—or most of it—was shipped out of state. DEA would like to know much more about these successful smuggles: Whose plane was that? And whose freighter? What are the names of all the people involved in these trips? Where did all the pot go? How much was there? Who else was involved in the distribution and sale of the weed? And, most important, where is all the money? Fred Barnswallow cannot answer most of those questions. But I can answer them all.

Several bales of weed from both trips were seized from stash houses that were raided days after the loads were landed and mostly distributed in other parts of the country. At the Barnswallow residence, DEA agents recovered some high-altitude California homegrown pot, cocaine, weapons, financial records, even a few scrawny pot plants Fred was growing in his attic—a trove of damning evidence. And all that evidence will be used against me, Stern explains, as Fearsome Fred is prepared to tell the jury that he was working for me, I was his boss, so, in essence, whatever he did, I am guilty of since he will testify that I put him up to it. Painfully true. Even the cocaine. Yes, it's true, though I am loath to admit it even to myself. Had Fred not met Maria, my Colombian ex-girlfriend, over Halloween in Aspen when we were attempting to clean him up, he wouldn't have had all that blow in the first place. I never approved of him dealing with Maria; I never knew they were working together until it was over. But still, in the eyes of the law, I am guilty; and I'm guilty as sin in my own eyes, for I broke my own fundamental tenet: never do business with anyone who is involved with coke. Maria and her whole family are in the cocaine business as well as trafficking in marijuana. I knew that. For this alone I deserve to be punished. I should just give up now and throw myself on the mercy of Judge Gignoux's court. But I can't. . . . I just can't do it. I must have the drama of a trial.

"If you choose to go to trial, much will depend on this guy's credibility as a witness," the lawyer confides. "And from what I have been able to determine, he has a few large skeletons rattling around in his closet—including the fact that he fell asleep at the wheel of his pickup truck and had a head-on collision with another vehicle. Both occupants of the car he hit were killed."

I shudder recalling this event.

Stern continues, "Apparently, this guy was being followed by local cops and DEA agents when the accident occurred. They had to have known he was driving impaired, under the influence of drugs and alcohol. The whole incident was swept aside and covered up . . . to protect him as a witness, because they hoped he would lead them to you."

"Really? Shit."

"Yes. Shit. *Their* shit. If we can get that in front of a jury . . . you never know." Stern shrugs. "They may decide to discredit his entire testimony." He lets this sink in. "Now what about this so-called corrupt cop, Arnold?"

"I don't really know the guy. Fred told me about him. I met him once briefly at a surprise birthday party Fred threw for me. But I never talked business with him and never discussed anything illegal with him around. If he says I did, he's lying."

Stern nods and considers. "You know he wasn't corrupt at all. It was a setup."

"I'm not surprised."

"He will testify. And again, whatever he says he did with Fred, that will also be used against you." He pauses, refers to his notes on a yellow legal pad. "What about Judy?"

"What about her?"

"Is she a problem? Can she hurt you?"

This I don't know. I suspect she will hold up. But she could seriously hurt me if she decides to cooperate and testify. She could talk about years of illegal activity. She could implicate Val. She could bring in Sammy and the New York people, the West Coast people, any number of other people in Alaska, Middle America, my close friend I call Rosie and the Canadian operation. And she could provide the government with more evidence on the importation of the seven-and-a-half tons of Lebanese hashish in New York.

"She can hurt me, yes. But I don't think she will," I say and pray it is true.

"Can you talk to her?"

"I don't know. Can I?"

"How much influence do you have in this place?"

"Well," I say, "let's find out."

"You know what this is all about, right?" Stern concludes.

"Mailer," I say. My relationship with the novelist whom the government would love to indict and prosecute and lock up as well.

Stern nods. "How well do you know him?"

"Very well. We've been close friends for a long time. Over ten years."

He gazes at me. "And?"

"No 'and.' That's it. We're friends. He has no involvement in my business. Never has."

"I see. But you do own the farm in Phillips together?"

"Yes, we do."

"Any other property? Any other business involvement?"

"No."

"What about the lodge and the airstrip? Is his name anywhere on those deeds?" he asks, speaking of the airstrip where the pot-loaded DC-6 crashed, and the lodge on the adjoining property, all of which was owned in deeds held by bogus offshore companies.

"No. Mine isn't either."

The lawyer nods. "But you own them?"

"In a manner of speaking."

He chuckles. "Just so you understand," Stern says after a few moments, "the fact that you and Mailer own property together complicates matters as far as he's concerned. Did you ever give him any large amounts of cash?"

I don't answer.

"Let me put it another way. Did anyone ever *see* you give him large amounts of cash? Are there witnesses who will say they saw this?"

"No."

"Okay, good. Was he ever present when you were . . . in the middle of something illegal?"

"Not present, no. But he knew what I was up to. Not details. But people close to me knew I made my living smuggling pot. I never tried to hide it."

"Apparently not," Stern says and laughs. "So Mailer knows where your money came from?"

I shrug.

"Did he ever meet Fred or any of the other defendants in this case?"

"No."

"That's good," Stern says. "But, keep in mind, the conspiracy laws are so broad, so vague that merely having knowledge of criminal activity and not reporting it—what the courts call 'guilty knowledge,' if certain other facts are attributed to the individual who possesses that knowledge, such as financial gain and committing an overt act, something as innocent as answering a phone call or going to a meeting—that can constitute an indictable offense under the conspiracy statutes."

"I understand," I say, fully aware of Stern's subtext. "But I am prepared to say that any money Mailer got from me came from my legitimate employment, and that he had no direct knowledge of my criminal activity."

"Can you prove you had any legitimate sources of income?" the lawyer asks.

"That won't be easy. I owned some legit businesses. I'm sure the government will say they were all fronts."

Stern nods. "That's all I need to know."

"Speaking of the conspiracy laws," I tell him, "I would like to conspire in devising my defense."

Stern smiles. "I see. . . . What do you have in mind?"

"I'm not sure yet. But I want to mount a defense. I don't want to simply sit there like a mute. I'll come up with something."

"So you've made up your mind. You are going to trial?"

"I can't say one hundred percent. I'm considering it. Seriously considering it. I hate to give in to these people. Their laws are ridiculous. Pleading guilty doesn't sit right with me at all. Guilty of what? Importing organic vegetable matter that is in huge demand? Fuck that. They are full of shit."

Stern nods, smiles. "A true believer."

"I want to study their case, look at the evidence, and see if I can come up with a creative defense. Some way to answer the charges that makes sense. But we should act like we don't know what we're going to do, as if we're open to discussing options."

Stern nods enthusiastically. "Okay, good," he says and chuckles. "Very good. I like that. Keep our options open. See what the government has in mind. I'll talk to Oteri and see how he thinks we should proceed." He stands. "This is going to be fun."

As he prepares to leave, Stern says there are a number of requests for interviews from representatives of the media: the local newspaper, Boston papers, local TV.

"Are you willing to meet with reporters?"

"Let's figure out what we're doing first, so I have my story together. The main thing is, I want to see my mother."

Stern tells me he spoke to Mary. My mother is driving up from Massachusetts to visit me as soon as tomorrow.

"Good. Thank you."

"How do you get along with this sheriff?" he asks.

"Gilmore and I are okay. I've always enjoyed good relations with local law enforcement."

More smiles and chuckles. Stern says, "So I understand. I saw the evidence report of the articles seized from your place. The sheriff's hat . . ."

He's enjoying this; I am, too, in a perverse sort of way. A lot will depend on how I hold up mentally as I go through this ordeal. I keep telling myself that it is best to make whatever alliances present themselves, and to be creative in an effort to make the journey more bearable. Try to look at it all as valuable experience.

"Maybe I can reach out, get someone to make a call," I say.

"I'm sure that would go a long way."

Marshall Stern goes off to conference with prosecutors in the US attorney's office. The wheels are in motion. My request for access to the law library becomes complicated by the fact that there is no law library in the county jail. Either I must get the authorities to order that a couple of deputy marshals escort me to the law library in the US attorney's office a few blocks from the jail—which they are not wont to do—or I must make specific, written requests for the legal tomes I wish to peruse, and they will deliver them to my cell.

The problem is I have no idea what books I need to review. I'm a novice in this business and so at a loss where to begin my study of federal criminal law. I am like a patient on the ward who is dying but can't determine the nature of his illness and has no clue as to the cure.

As I lie in my cell thinking of all that has happened—the many years of smuggling pot and hash from all over the world into these great United States of America, land of the free and the brave and all that, and the experience of living as an outlaw—and as the smell of the smoke of the weed of wisdom drifts over to my cell from the adjoining tier, bound-over streetside, the very scent of the herb offers a clue.

I learn from the jailhouse grapevine maintained by a crudely tattooed, speed-freak orderly called Cosmo that the cells located on bound-over streetside, from where the secret odors emanate, back up against my cell and are occupied mostly by members of the Ethiopian Zion Coptic Church. They are white Rastafarians. Included in their number is their spiritual leader, known as Brother Luv. Using Cosmo as my courier, I send the Coptics a note. We have a number of business associates and friends in common as well as respect for good herb. The Coptics have made it their religion. They invite me to visit them in their cells so that we can "reason" together, and worship.

After the evening count, a guard comes for me.

"Open number four, bound-over yardside!" he calls, and the loud metallic clanking and grinding sounds that accompany my cell door sliding open echo along the tier. The guard escorts me to bound-over streetside, where I am welcomed into Brother Luv's cell to partake of the holy sacrament—ganja—and commune with the captive church elders.

"Three things you want to stay away from in prison," Brother Luv advises me. "Gambling, drugs, and homosexuals." He passes me the burning spliff. "Do your own time. Don't get caught up in anyone else's bullshit, and you'll be all right. . . . There are a lot of us in the system."

Brother Luv has been down for close to five years. He and his co-defendants were due to be released next year, but the government has hit all the Coptic brothers with a new indictment.

"There's an old saying," another of the dreadlocked Rastas intones, "Don't serve the time; let the time serve you. I got my master's degree last year."

The Coptics are doing their various bids at different joints around the country. Just before they were to be released, they were all brought back to Portland to face new charges for a successful smuggle that took place on the coast of Maine two months short of five years ago.

"Five years is the extent of the statute of limitations," Brother Luv explains. "If they don't indict you within five years of the date of the last overt act, they can't bring the case. They've been holding this case back, waiting till we got short to bring this new indictment."

"Fuckers," another brother says, and they chuckle.

He's a tall man, Brother Luv, six feet, seven inches, with shoulder-length dreadlocks and a full beard. All the Coptic brothers have full beards and dreadlocks. They tell me they do not believe in cutting their hair. They do not eat meat, nor do they believe in engaging in cunnilingus—they are proscribed from eating pussy, which would necessarily preclude me from joining the faithful. They profess ganja as their holy sacrament and have mounted as their defense a First Amendment freedom of religion right to partake of the holy herb, and to import it by the ton if necessary to distribute among the congregation.

"And how has that defense been working for you so far?" I ask.

"Well," Brother Luv smiles, "here we are."

And we share a laugh.

"You know, it's not about winning or losing," he goes on. "It's about objecting to their laws. Civil and even criminal disobedience. This is all political, this drug war. It's a war on the American people, on our rights as Americans. The baldheads know their laws don't make sense. It's about control, power, and money. There's another group of smugglers locked up in here who are all Vietnam vets. Helicopter pilots and Special Forces guys, Lurps. War heroes. Their defense is PTSD—post-traumatic stress disorder. They claim the action they saw in Nam was so horrific it warped them psychologically, so that now only smuggling pot can satisfy their need for excitement and danger to appease their fucked-up nervous disorder. They're in front of Judge Gignoux, too. This has been Gignoux's year for creative pot defenses."

Around midnight the guard comes to return me to my cell. My brain alive with THC, imagination runs wild as I lie on my bunk and chase the runaway train of thought, seek it out, follow it down, burrow into the kernel of an idea until it bursts forth and blooms to become a beautiful conceptual orchid luxuriating in my hyperactive consciousness.

There it is! *I see it all:* my defense. I behold the narrative in all its glory. Yes! And it makes perfect sense. It seizes my mind with the clarity of revelation.

My mother, God bless her, dear Mary, could a man ask for a mother more devoted to her prodigal son? She brings me a portable typewriter, a dictionary, and reams of paper. Home-baked cookies for the guards. She has won them over. Fat, one might say obese, red-faced Sheriff Gilmore is in love with my mother, Mary. She has utterly charmed him and fed him cookies. Certainly she spoiled me as a child, of course she did, and she imbued me with an inflated sense of my own importance, my own value, and with the will to succeed at whatever I undertook—although it turned out to be crime. I was a tyrant as a kid, given to violent temper tantrums if I didn't get my own way, a bad boy. My father couldn't control me, and my mother never really tried. But she loved me unconditionally. Oh, how Mary loved me. And that made all the difference in the choices I made and am still making. I may have lived as an outlaw most of my adult life, and I may have made some stupid choices and behaved foolishly. Selfishly. But all that is behind me now. What matters is how I carry myself going forward—the man I become through this experience. I never want my mother to be ashamed of her only son.

The old man, Emery, she tells me, is still playing golf. That is his passion. His son is secondary, a mystery to him. She hopes Emery will come up for the trial. "You are going to trial?" she asks.

"It looks that way."

"Good. You should. That bastard Fred. How dare he say those things about you?"

She catches me up on family news. My nephew, Carlos, is safely away at sea in the Navy. A few old girlfriends have called, asking if they can come visit. My high school wrestling coach sends his regards. Mary says she spoke to Mailer and to my friend and attorney, Channing Godfried. "You have a lot of support, Rick. We're all behind you. Do whatever you think is right. This whole thing is ridiculous. It's only pot, for goodness sake. You haven't murdered anyone."

No, but people close to me did die—although, I'm sure, even if I had personally killed them, Mary would still find me blameless.

A WEEK OR two slip by. Time becomes a whole new concept when you do it one day at a time. Law books are delivered to my cell. The language seems opaque at first, almost foreign, or like reading Shakespeare. But, once I get into it, I find that at its best there is poetry in artfully worded legal writing, beauty in well-reasoned and articulated dialectic. I begin writing out my argument, drafting it in longhand on yellow legal pads like a real lawyer, then typing it up on the portable typewriter my mother brought me, and which Gilmore has allowed me to place on the steel shelf welded to the bars at the foot of my bunk. I have my own little office here on bound-over yardside where I am occupied concocting my theory of defense. Locked up twenty-three hours a day, with an hour rec time in the enclosed yard, I have plenty of time to write. Soon my legal writing has morphed into a species of fiction. Why not write a novel?

STERN REPORTS THAT an attorney from New York rather than Joe Oteri will join him on the defense team. "I think you know why," he says during a visit.

Indeed, I do. I have learned that a grand jury has been convened in the Southern District of New York. People, close friends and partners, are concerned. I am the linchpin. If I flip, many heads will roll. There is a lot of interest in my case in the Boston office of the Drug Enforcement Administration as well as the Federal Bureau of Investigation, Stern reports. Texas and California as well have requested to be kept abreast of the government's developing conspiracy. Oteri mentioned a couple of names: James Bulger, also known as Whitey, who has a famous politician for a brother. And one Michael Capuana. The Grillo brothers. Uncle George, as Stern names him. How about a Texan named Jimmy Chagra, who has been implicated in the assassination of a federal judge? Do I know these men, Stern asks in confidence. I admit I do. These are organized crime figures, serious bad guys; he tells me what I already know. This could elevate my case to a whole new and ugly level that we do not want to approach with the good citizens of Cumberland County in Portland, Maine who will sit as my jury.

Stern tells me the prosecutor has presented him with their first offer: plead guilty to one count of conspiracy to possess with intent to distribute marijuana, and the government will recommend a sentence not to exceed ten years. When I pretend interest in the plea, deputy marshals escort me to the prosecutor's office to discuss the details of a potential agreement.

Richard Cohen, the US attorney for the District of Maine, is a slight man with thinning, sandy reddish hair; pale skin; and a nervous, officious manner. He is unable to look me in the eye as he informs me that as part of any deal the government would be willing to make, I must agree to forfeit all my property, give up all assets, known and unknown to the government, "disgorge" as he calls it, and to "proffer," to tell agents of the government everything I know about everyone I know who is or has been involved in the illegal marijuana business or any other criminal activity. And then I must stand before the Honorable Edward T. Gignoux to admit my crimes and declare for all to hear that I recognize the error of my ways and that I am remorseful, truly sorry for what I have done. I must then go on to cooperate fully with the government in any future investigations that are initiated as a result of my cooperation, and I must be prepared to testify at any and all trials resulting from my cooperation. My sentencing will be postponed until after my cooperation agreement has been fulfilled. The US attorney's office will then provide the sentencing judge with a letter attesting to the truthfulness and value of my cooperation.

Cohen is accompanied by a young assistant by the name of Groff, who I insist on calling Gorf after my favorite video game—the game I was playing when Wolfshein and his DEA posse first brought me to ground at the pharmacy in Farmington, Maine. Cohen goes on to say that Judge Gignoux is not required to abide by the government's recommendation for the length of sentence. He could go higher or lower. However, in most cases, when there is a plea and display of remorse and full cooperation, the judge will usually go along with the government's suggested length of sentence.

"Who said anything about cooperation?" I object. "I thought we were talking about a simple plea."

Cohen and Groff share a look.

I turn to my attorney. "Marshall?"

"Not me," Stern says and makes ready to leave.

"What about New York?" I ask.

They give me a studied baffled look.

Hmmm. A redheaded Jew from Maine, I'm thinking, what's wrong with this picture? "We know nothing about New York," says Groff, the designated liar.

"Well, I suggest you find out," Stern admonishes. "I mean—how many federal governments are there?"

"We can look into it," Groff says.

Stern says, "It's Richard's decision, but I would be ill-advised to counsel him to plead here in Maine only to have any number of other charges brought in other districts."

The prosecutor nods. "We will inquire," he says and gives me a hopeful look.

"And then there is Canada," Stern says.

Shrugs. Silence from the prosecutors.

Agent Wolfshein is the answer. I ask if I may have a private audience with the DEA agent.

"That could be arranged, of course, if you were willing to cooperate," Cohen says, and betrays a hopeful smile.

"You want me to testify against Mailer? Is that where we're going with this?"

Cohen shrugs. "If—"

"C'mon, Marshall, let's go," I say and stand. And then to the prosecutors, "See you in court."

THESE MEN HAVE no idea how much I secretly enjoy these encounters. Yes, we are talking about years of my life that could well be spent behind prison walls. Be that as it may. The talks I have with DEA agents, deputy US marshals, and federal prosecutors are like forays behind enemy lines, an opportunity to gather intelligence and try to wrap my head around the way government functionaries think. The drug warriors have given new purpose to my life. We are discussing serious matters. This is real life with real decisions to be made. Yes, I have been captured, but I have not been converted. I want to be respectful, a gentleman. I sense the presence of my mother and my grandmother Ba Ba, good women that they are, reminding me that I come from a long line of well-bred New Englanders, and as such I should keep up the tradition and always be polite. Respectful. At least pretend that I am entertaining their offers when in truth I am on a fact-finding mission to determine how much they know as a means of marshaling my defense. It's obvious they are aware that there are other indictments pending in other jurisdictions. Now I know this for certain as well. And it must be factored into any decisions I make.

After we leave Cohen's office, accompanied by the same two deputy US marshals, Stern pulls me aside and confides. "Look, Richard, whatever you decide to do, that's your business. But you should know that I will not continue to represent you if you choose to cooperate. And I—"

I stop him. "Please, Marshall, take it easy. You heard me. I have no intention of cooperating," I tell him.

"Good," he says. "I thought so. But you never know what a man will do when he's faced with many years in prison." He's repeating a line I've heard somewhere before and come to accept as gospel.

"I thought we were clear after our first visit. I intend to participate in my defense. That means feeling these guys out, listening to everything they have to say, studying everything they allow us access to. I don't want to let them know what we plan to do. We're playing chess here. We might as well participate in the process."

Stern smiles, nods, happy now. "I was hoping you would say that."

"*It's only pot, Marshall.*" I flash him a hopeful grin.

"Yes, that's true," he says. "But all these organized crime characters take it up a few notches."

"We've got to keep that out."

"That could be tricky," he says. "They'll want to get it in."

"Where's the relevance," I say, already talking like a lawyer. "They had nothing to do with any of the charges in this case."

Stern nods. "Okay. So we must limit the evidence to what happened here in the District of Maine and try to keep any of these other

. . . allegations from coming in. Which could be difficult. . . . I mean, if you are even considering taking the stand, that would open you up to a whole line of questioning that would inevitably bring in evidence from all these other activities with other individuals."

My lawyer and I are still waiting for the other shoe to drop. The New York grand jury investigation hangs over the Maine case like a guillotine poised to lop off any hope I have of freedom in the foreseeable future.

Sheriff Gilmore pulls me aside when I am returned to the jail. "What do you feel like eating today?" he asks.

He grins and flashes a box of Cohiba Cuban cigars I had delivered to the jail. Gilmore is a lawman who is a slave to his prodigious appetites. We all are, but Gilmore more than most. He loves to eat. He loves booze. He loves cigars. He loves to talk about pussy, though I suspect he's not getting much. His girth strains at the seams of his uniform. His fleshy face and pink neck are flushed with an unhealthy tinge, and his skin glistens with a perpetual sheen of hectic sweat. His armpits are ringed with dark stains. But he's my friend, I like this fat, corrupt cop, and he likes me. We make no pretense of a typical keeper-and-kept relationship. We are buddies, and partners in our mission to eat well.

"How about lobster?" I say. "Maybe some oysters? Shrimp cocktails? After all, we are in Maine."

"Yes! Lobsters! Steamers?"

"Steamers, definitely. And cherrystones. Let's do it right, Gilmore. Life is short. We need to eat well."

The sheriff's eyes light up and he nods conspiratorially. He sends one of his deputies across the street to Portland's finest seafood restaurant for takeout.

"By the way," he tells me with a leer, "Judy is here."

Gilmore arranges for me to have a private visit with Judy in her cell. A deputy delivers me to the women's section of the jail. Judy and I hug, we kiss, and I take a seat on her bunk. She says she has decided to plead guilty to one count of conspiracy and will appear before Judge Gignoux for sentencing in the morning.

I say, "That was quick."

"My lawyer hooked it up while I was on my way here," she replies, then adds, "Don't worry, we're cool."

"I never doubted that."

This judge is known to be lenient on female defendants. Judy's connection to the conspiracy is tenuous at best. Her culpability relies entirely on Fred's testimony with nothing to corroborate whatever he might say.

"He thinks I'll get probation," she says. "All the other women got probation. They asked me about you. I told them I never met you."

"What about Val?"

"No one has mentioned her," Judy says and we both consider this odd deficiency in the government's case. "Fred must have told them about her."

"He never knew her real name or where she lives," I remind her. "Fucking Fred. Without him, they got nothing. We walk on this."

"Oh, God, Fred!" Judy exclaims. "That bastard. I am so disgusted with him. This is all his fault."

"How is Val?" I ask her.

"Okay . . . So . . . you know, I'm worried about her."

"Me, too."

"She's drinking a lot. And doing a lot of . . . this." She touches her nose.

I nod in response. This is a large part of my sadness, my guilt. I feel much more remorse over the women I have betrayed, let down, and led astray than I do over the laws I have broken. My wife, Anaïs, still in custody in Canada, and her sister, Avril, their lives forever altered by a chance encounter. And now Judy, facing possible prison time. And Val . . . strung out.

"How are you doing?" Judy asks. "Damn, guy. You look great."

"Jail as an alternative lifestyle," I say. "It has its advantages."

"Here," she says and palms me some bud. "This should help."

Ah, yes, reefer. Where there is dope, there is hope.

SHE'S A SOUTHERN California girl, Judy, born and raised in and around Laguna Beach, and has the blond, almost white hair and tan skin to prove it even after some weeks in custody. A Brotherhood of Eternal Love chick, purebred hippie mafia, she's faithful, loyal to the cause. I see no need to worry about Judy agreeing to testify against me.

And the reefer does help me cogitate. In my cell at night I get high and continue plotting my defense. Poring over legal tomes high on pot, it is all coming together in my mind. Yes, yes, I see it clearly now. Obfuscate. Bury them with paperwork. Delay . . . delay. Object. Make motions. Demand additional discovery. Ask for oral argument. Words, words, and more words. Bury the facts with words.

There is a young man in the next cell who killed his wife. Nice guy, actually. Gentle and kind. We have become friends. Call him Roland. He's well-educated, a former English teacher at a boys' preparatory school. His father is a noted author. Roland told me his story. He and his wife are both alcoholics. Roland would come home after work each day and they would drink, get drunk, and often end the evening in violent argument. They have two young sons who witnessed their many vicious fights. On his way home from teaching at the prep school one day, Roland stopped at a gun shop and bought a handgun.

"That was the day you decided to kill your wife," I tell him as he recounts the story.

"Yes," he says and nods. "I think you're right—though it never occurred to me at the time."

"Maybe not consciously. But why else would you need a gun?"

He nods, shrugs. "No reason," he admits.

Then it happened. One evening, during one of their drunken fights, Roland took out the gun and shot his wife in the head. She died instantly.

"The boys, my sons—they were there." He swallows hard, and then he cries, he weeps bitterly and prodigiously. I want to hug him and tell him it's all right, but we both know it is not. It is a tragedy he and his boys will live with for the rest of their lives. "They saw me kill their mother," he sobs. "How can they ever forgive me?"

Another man who lives on my tier, bound-over yardside, killed his entire family—mother, father, sister, and younger brother—stabbed and bludgeoned them to death and then set the house on fire. A violent, bipolar psychotic, he's heavily sedated, sleeps most of the time. When he does wake up and is allowed out of his cell, all the other prisoners are locked in as he does what is known as the thorazine shuffle: a slow, zombie-like perambulation dragging his feet as he shuffles up and down the tier. He's heavy and moves like a beast of burden carrying the souls of his dead kin. The other prisoners have taken to calling him Lurch. He pled not guilty by reason of insanity and will soon be transferred to a facility for the criminally insane.

These men are my neighbors on bound-over yardside.

Chapter Four

THE BEST DEFENSE

A TRIAL DATE has been set. Still I refuse to give Cohen and Groff an answer to any of their proposals. I keep my own counsel, put off my response, ask for more information, more time to think, and demand to speak to Wolfshein without agreeing to cooperate. And it is beginning to piss Cohen off. I tell Stern that I operate under rules promulgated by the Beirut school of business. Never let your opponent see your hand, and negotiate right down to the wire, even after the deal is in place, keep negotiating, agree to terms, and then, at the eleventh hour, back out and renegotiate.

My request for an audience with Special Agent Bernie Wolfshein has been formally denied. He refuses to see me unless I decide to "debrief" as they like to say. I say, well, let's talk about it. But I think they know my parrying game, and they are becoming increasingly hard-line. Wolfshein sends a message through Stern. He says he would like to meet with me but he can't; he's the case agent on the investigation and it would be improper—unless, of course, I am willing to cooperate. They float the possibility of the witness protection program if it's my safety I am worried about. Capuana, Bulger, Uncle George—these are bad dudes with notches in their respective belts. But if I were worried about my safety, I never would have become a pot smuggler in the first place. No, it is my conscience I am concerned with, the fact that I have to live with myself for the rest of my life.

I visit with Sheriff Gilmore and write out permission to allow myself to be interviewed by the press. "Why not?" says the sheriff. "This is America. We have freedom of the press. Right?"

"Right," I say, and Gilmore hands me a couple of Cohibas.

First, I have an interview with a lady from the *Portland Press Herald*, the local daily, who says she has been covering the case since the original series of arrests. It has been deemed the "biggest drug bust" in the state's history, she tells me, by the number of people arrested, since there really wasn't all that much dope seized. Still, the government estimated the street value of the drugs at two-and-a-half million dollars. I assure her I know nothing about any of that.

I look her in the eye and say, "I'm a writer," the words rolling off my tongue. "A journalist. I'm working on a book about drug smuggling. I was doing research—nothing more. I was never involved in any of this. Now they're trying to say I was part of some conspiracy because I met a few of these people, really only one, this guy Fred. Now he has implicated me to save himself. That would be like you walking out of here now and being arrested because you interviewed me and I said you were part of a conspiracy. These conspiracy laws are insane. They make no sense in a democracy. They're un-American. If all it takes is someone else's word to say you did something illegal, anyone could be guilty."

Then I feed her back Gilmore's line. "Whatever happened to freedom of the press?"

"You're a writer?" She appears astounded.

"That's right." *Why not?* I'm thinking. Writers make shit up. And it is true. I have been published. A long, two-part interview I did with Mailer in *Rolling Stone*. Short stories in literary journals. I was a writing fellow at the Fine Arts Work Center in Provincetown, Massachusetts, which is how I came to meet Mailer in the first place. I used to tell people I smuggled pot to support my writing habit. In time, however, the outlaw life took over.

"You're writing a book about drug smuggling?"

"Yes, I am."

"Fiction?"

"Fiction . . . a novel, but based entirely on fact, and on my research. All this—including the trial—will become part of my book."

"What's the title of your book?"

I say the first thing that comes to mind: "*Drug War*."

This revelation has the desired effect. It's front-page news the next day along with a photo of me in my cell at my typewriter. Now I am both championed and pilloried in the press. *Time* magazine, *Newsweek*, the *New York Times*, the *Washington Post* all pick up the story because of the Mailer connection. Reporters come to visit, and I present them with my defense. Some like it and paint a sympathetic portrait of the jailed writer. Others see it for what it is: a fiction with little foundation in fact. But if the Coptics can claim freedom of religion and the Vietnam vets can say they were forced to become dope smugglers as a result of their service in the military, what's so outlandish about saying it was all research for a book? *This book!* The book I am writing now. Why not? It makes perfect sense to me. Anyway, it is my defense and I'm sticking with it all the way to trial.

Chief Judge Edward T. Gignoux is not persuaded by my defense, and he's upset by all the media coverage of the case. He's a prickly old Huguenot. Tall, lean, and aristocratic. Clearly, he doesn't like me and thinks less of my trial-by-media offensive. The New York lawyer who has been sent by my friends to represent me loves the defense and the media spotlight it has cast upon the case and him. His name is Sheldon Berlinger. I call him Irving Berlin. He immediately latches on to the energy of the case, though he does next to nothing to prepare. It would appear his only concern is damage control and basking in the media spotlight. When I announce my list of witnesses—to the press and not to the prosecution—US Attorney Cohen is irate. He calls for a hearing before Gignoux and makes a motion for a gag order. Gignoux is flustered. He knows that if he imposes a gag order upon me, he will be generating an even bigger media feeding frenzy. I can see the headlines now: JAILED SELF-PROCLAIMED WRITER GAGGED!

No, they don't want that. Mailer's name is dragged into the fray. And Channing Godfried. And Channing's wife. Who else? My friend and fellow *Rolling Stone* contributor, the inimitable Dr. Hunter S. Thompson. To call Hunter to the stand would be courtroom theater-of-the-absurd at its most outrageous. My list of potential witnesses continues to grow.

As THE DAYS before trial fade into time served, I grow wired and tense with anticipation. I pore over the case materials. I read case law on drug conspiracy. I fashion pretrial motions and run them by Stern and Berlin. I read and consider the "discovery," as the evidence that will be used against me is termed. The government opposes my motions. I apply to the court for oral argument. I come to appreciate the unique beauty to this language of the law. Suppression. Severance. Continuance. All denied. *My motions are all denied.* No doubt with prejudice. On and on. More words and phrases. Recusal. A judge or juror can be recused from a case by reason of prejudice or conflict of interest. I want to recuse Judge Gignoux for his apparent bias against me and my defense. That will never fly. Still, I love this verbal jousting. Legal tomes are piled high in my cramped cell. I work on my novel when not writing briefs or answering motions put forth by the prosecution. I am rediscovering the discipline of writing. Pages are accumulating in my manuscript. Photographers come to take more pictures of me behind bars. I relish the attention. It feeds my vanity. It is all a great adventure.

Will Mailer be testifying? Everyone wants to know. So I ask him. Unfortunately for me—and for him—Mailer's status in the world of letters and courtrooms has taken a nosedive of late, not due to anything he has written but because of another jailed would-be writer he befriended through a series of letters who then got out of prison, published a book, and stabbed to death an unarmed waiter in a Manhattan restaurant. He killed the man simply because the waiter refused to let the ex-con writer use the men's room. Jack Abbott is the guy's name. I recall Mailer told me about Abbott as we stood on the balcony of his home in Brooklyn Heights. Later the same evening, Wolfshein warned me about playing this high stakes game with other players who had a different agenda. Even then I sensed Abbott was no good, distorted by all the time he had done, and I warned Mailer to beware. These convict writers are not to be trusted.

My name is inevitably linked to Abbott. Mailer brings this up when he comes to the jail to visit.

"I may do you more harm than good, Rick," he says.

It doesn't matter. My runaway hubris knows no restraint. In Portland, Mailer is beyond reproach. Let the New York press excoriate him for consorting with criminals; here he is beloved for his many years of taking summer vacations with his considerable brood at rented homes along the Maine coast, for the books he has written, for the literary awards he has been given, and for his general status as a celebrity author and intellectual.

Yes, I announce, I will call Mailer to testify. His picture is all over the papers the next day.

Of course, there are moments, and even prolonged spells as I sit in my cell, when I must question the wisdom of taking on the US government, the Justice Department with all its assets and minions, its laws and punishments. But even when I consider the facts, and when I read of the many defendants who have gone before me and argued against laws that criminalize the use and trafficking in this plant, it becomes clear how intransigent the government is with regard to how they treat violators of the drug laws, and I am convinced that they are wrong and I (we, the many pot prisoners) are right. Fuck these people. They just don't get it. Americans have got to stand up and tell them their laws are wrong.

BACKROOM NEGOTIATIONS CONTINUE up until the eve of the trial. In fact, there are no negotiations. They fuck with me, I fuck with them right back. I keep reminding myself: the best defense is a good offense. It's like football or wrestling or any other competition. You can't just throw in the towel and quit. You have got to fight and never say die.

Cohen brings down Sergeant Terrance Carter of the Metro Toronto Drug Squad and a couple of RCMP officers, who produce transcripts of wiretaps. *Oh, shit, this is real evidence.* My name is all over the tapes, though my voice is heard on only two recordings: one made of the conversation I had with Carter when I phoned and called him a punk for arresting my ex-wife, Anaïs. And there is another, even more damning, X-rated tape made from a bug placed in a hotel room I shared with Val—more damaging to my already fractured relationship with my ex-wife than to the case. I mount a strong argument to keep the Canadian tapes out of evidence.

Judge Gignoux rules on my list of potential witnesses. Norman Mailer will be allowed to testify. Channing Godfried will not be called, as he is protected and excluded by virtue of the attorney/client privilege. His wife, however, who is also well-known and highly regarded in the district, will be allowed to take the stand in my defense. Dr. Hunter S. Thompson is excluded, as are some other lesser-known writers and editors. Everyone seems to suspect that my defense is bogus. I don't let this bother me. I have the good counsel of Brother Luv, who advises that this is political theater; therefore the defenses we mount are no more absurd than the laws the government uses to condemn us.

The Coptics all plead out and receive concurrent sentences. Brother Luv's parole date may be affected, but he leaves the jail and returns to, as he puts it, "a real prison" with no regrets. And the Vietnam War vets also make out well in Gignoux's court. The judge imposes sentences of five years after they all agree to plead guilty. As Stern gleefully points out, I am the only one crazy enough to take my defense before a jury.

Maybe I will look foolish, but that's a chance I must take. To those who can see the hidden machinations, it is not simply a clear-cut case of grandstanding on my part. I have actually entertained the possibility of a plea if the government will agree to bring all their far-flung prosecutions in one proceeding. I'll take the ten years and go away and do the time and keep my mouth shut. With good behavior, I could be out in five or six years. But Cohen and the faceless bureaucrats he reports to are only willing to combine all their cases and accept my plea and recommend the ten-year deal *if* I agree to cooperate and rat out Mailer and everyone I know. Fuck that. That is not going to happen.

Stern and Irving Berlin warn me that I am taking a serious gamble by calling Mailer. "He is their main target," the lawyers advise. I know this, and Mailer also is aware the government wants to take him down so they can smear him with a drug conviction. We have both determined that the best defense is to walk into the Star Chamber and confront the forces of totalitarianism. Engage your fear and meet it head-on, and it will diminish. Run and try to hide, and fear will overtake you and consume you from within.

Judge Gignoux is utterly charmed by Mailer. He requests a private audience in his chambers before trial. Mailer outlines his testimony *in camera*, without the jury present, so the judge can rule on its relevance. Gignoux is obviously a fan, a great reader of novels, particularly those about World War II. He treats the great writer with the deference he deserves. Mailer leaves signed copies of a few of his books to be presented to the judge after the trial. A jury is impaneled. Trial commences.

A WEEK INTO the government's case, I sense the proceeding is going remarkably well. Even the newspapers are commenting upon the paucity of evidence against me. Fearless Fred, the prosecution's star witness, utterly stiffs on the stand. He makes a terrible witness. Nobody likes him. Even Cohen and Groff seem to regret calling him. I feel sorry for Fred. He looks terrible, like he's been dead for years and dug up to testify against me. He mumbles. He can't remember anything. He admits to using large quantities of cocaine daily whenever he had the opportunity.

Early on the second day of Fred's testimony, as I am led into the courtroom by the marshals to join my attorneys at the defense table before the judge and jury have entered, I catch Gorf holding a bag of the California homegrown buds that will be entered into evidence. The dope was seized in the raid on Fred's pad and is from a load brought east by my friend, Goofy John. Gorf holds the bag to his nose, sniffs, and announces, "Hmmm, smells like really good weed."

This astounds me. Gorf is a guy who obviously knows his herb.

"Wait a minute," I say, "so what's all the fuss? Why don't we roll one up and all relax?"

Gorf flushes with embarrassment and changes his demeanor back to that of the loyal civil servant. The hypocrisy of these guys never ceases to amaze me.

On cross-examination, Irving Berlin rips Fred a new asshole. It's sad, actually. His addiction to cocaine, including smoking base; the fact that I brought him to Val's place in Aspen, Colorado, to try to dry him out; and how he met my friend, Maria, who he then did coke business with behind my back—all that is bad enough. But then Berlin brings out the accident when Fred crashed head-on into another car in which two innocent people lost their lives, one a small child. When the so-called corrupt cop, Arnold, testifies and the jury hears that two people were killed when an obviously drug-and-alcohol-impaired driver—fucked-up Fred—was allowed to operate a motor vehicle under the influence while being trailed by police and federal agents—agents who knew he was fucked-up but let him go because they believed he could lead them to me—this does not go over well for the prosecution. Jurors squirm in their seats. They turn their heads in disgust. Fearless Fred Barnswallow creeps out of the courtroom and leaves a trail of slime on the government's case.

The DEA agents called to testify do little to resuscitate Cohen's and Gorf's evidence. The blue-eyed stranger DEA special agent who was stranded by the roadside is only able to assert that, yes, it was the defendant Mr. Stratton behind the wheel of the four-wheel-drive pickup truck who stopped to help him out of the ditch that snowy day in April. And, yes, Fred was with Mr. Stratton. The agent then observed me drop Fred at his home. My lawyers make an issue of the fact that DEA agents shot and killed Fred's dog, Bear, for no reason, as he posed no threat. The jury, though hardly made up of my peers, no doubt includes more than a few dog lovers. Several jurors appear disturbed by this revelation as well.

Wolfshein comes off more like a witness for the defense than for the government. "No," he tells the jury, "after a thorough search of the premises, no controlled substances were recovered from Mr. Stratton's residence." No large amounts of cash. No financial records or anything else to connect the defendant to the conspiracy. He had no drugs on him when he was arrested. He was alone in a drugstore playing a video game. He made no admissions that night on the long drive from Farmington to Portland.

I'm elated as the Wolf steps down from the stand. *We may actually win this thing!*

Wolfshein's testimony wraps up the afternoon session and brings to an end the proposed list of government witnesses. The jury is excused. The judge says he wants to deal with some housekeeping issues as the trial enters its second week of testimony and we still have not got to the defense case. The Court would like to know if the defendant intends to take the stand in his own behalf. Berlin tells Gignoux that I am giving it serious consideration. Gignoux nods but refuses to look at me. He appears angry with Cohen and Gorf. It is clear he does not like the way this prosecution is being handled. My lawyers are cautiously optimistic. They believe Gignoux may actually be considering a dismissal or a directed verdict wherein he rules there is not ample evidence for the jury to convict me.

It's like halftime during the big game and my team is well ahead. I am in the holding cell in the courthouse after the days' testimony, waiting to be removed and escorted back to the jail by the marshals, trying not to feel too good about the way the case is going for fear of jinxing it, when Agent Bernie Wolfshein stops by to pay me a visit.

"I can talk to you now," he says, "since I testified."

"Listen—what can I say? I mean . . . thanks. That was incredible," I tell him.

He shrugs, nudges his glasses back up the bridge of his nose. And then he fixes me with his curious, intelligent gaze. "I told the truth," he says.

"That's what I mean. Thank you."

"They asked the wrong questions," he says cryptically.

"Maybe so."

"Rich, it's simple. I do my job; you do your job. I understand that. You have your reasons for doing what you do, and I respect that. But I should warn you." He looks around as if to see if anyone is within earshot. "I think you know this. It won't come as a surprise. But this is not going to end here, in Portland, Maine, with this trial. The government has a long reach, and an even longer memory." He pauses, smiles. "I wish you luck."

He reaches through the bars to shake my hand.

"We didn't get you right up here," the Wolf contends. "But, whatever happens, take it from me: it's not over, as they say, until the fat lady sings." Wolfshein's smile fades. "Or," he adds, "as the case may be—until the *fat man* sings."

The "fat man" refers to Mohammed, my heavy Lebanese connection, and the fifteen-thousand-pound load of hash we brought in at the port in Newark, New Jersey, that is now the subject of an ongoing grand jury probe in New York City.

The Wolfman knows how to unsettle me.

WHEN TRIAL RESUMES the following week, Cohen asks the Court for a brief recess while he attempts to locate a "surprise witness."

What? Who?

Gignoux is not pleased with the delay. Still, he grants the government until Wednesday of next week to produce their witness. We object. The judge overrules. I'm sure he's hopeful for any opportunity to resuscitate Cohen's faltering prosecution.

Who the fuck? Surprise witness? I am at my wits end. I have heard that agents were scouring the state looking for people who may have worked for me. Among my trusted lieutenants, Father Flaherty is in the wind and JD also left the area and is hiding out in western Massachusetts. The pilot I call Wart Hog? Maybe. That fucker is weak. Who could it be? I spend an anxious weekend wondering what to expect—if anything. Mailer will be my lead-off witness. I have done all I can do to prepare for the first day of my defense.

My friend Roland, the alcoholic prep school master who shot and killed his wife in front of their two young sons pled guilty to one count of unintentional manslaughter in the shooting death of his twenty-eight-year-old wife. At sentencing, his attorney argued there were mitigating circumstances: a history of alcoholism. When I come in from court on the afternoon of Wolfshein's appearance, Roland is being processed out of the jail. He tells me the judge gave him five years' probation. He has also been ordered to undergo treatment for alcoholism. But Roland says he is not relieved or even mollified by the sentence. He's a broken man who must now face his two young sons and live with the reality that he killed their mother.

Facing fifteen years if I lose this case, and the possibility of another prosecution in New York, I would not trade places with Roland even as he walks out of the jail.

"I'M SORRY, RICHARD," Mild Bill apologizes as he takes the witness stand against me.

Yes, it's him, the man with the Abraham Lincoln looks. The finish carpenter who worked in my home, the farm I owned with Mailer, and whose old lady pleaded with my wife to give him extra work unloading airplanes full of pot so they could save his home from foreclosure. And

I did hire him, against my better judgment. Mild Bill is their surprise witness. Now he is on the witness stand to testify against me.

My lawyers have argued strenuously that Bill should not be allowed to appear, as his evidence is not relevant to the current charges. The judge has heard argument from the government that, although Bill cannot give evidence about anything within the purview of the conspiracy as charged in the instant indictment, his testimony should be allowed as proof of "like prior bad acts" under the federal rules of evidence.

Judge Gignoux seems relieved that he will not have to dismiss the case. He rules to allow Bill's evidence in. Berlin objects once again. The objection is noted for the record.

Mild Bill is sworn in and identifies me as the man who employed him some years before to work on my farm as a cabinetmaker. Again, he apologizes to me and tells the jury that I was always good to him, a fair and generous employer. And my wife couldn't do enough to help him and his family through their hard times. But, yes, he was there on the early spring morning when a huge plane, a DC-6, crash-landed on an airstrip in Phillips, Maine, property that Bill believes I own. Under my direction, he helped unload approximately five tons of marijuana from the airplane. He knew me to be the boss of the operation. I was known in the area as a big-time pot smuggler.

This admission gets a sustained objection from Berlin, but the jury has heard it. Bill goes on to tell the jury that he was paid thirty thousand dollars in cash by a man who works for me, and that he used the money to pay off his mortgage and to support his family for months, even years, after I disappeared from the area. Soon after the plane crash, and once Bill had no more work on the Stratton properties, he was no longer in contact with me. Groff enters photographs of the hulk of the crashed DC-6 to bolster Bill's testimony. The government admits they recovered none of the alleged illegal weed from the planeload. Berlin makes the point that the jury has only Bill's word that there was a load of pot on the plane. But, of course, the jury will reason, why else would someone crash a big plane in the wilds of Maine and then abandon it?

Bill comes off exactly as he looks—like Abraham Lincoln. His bearded face is the picture of veracity. Honest Abe would never tell a lie. Nor would Mild Bill. On cross-examination, my lawyers are able to establish for the jury that Bill has only agreed to testify against me because government agents threatened to arrest him and seize his property if he refused. This does nothing to detract from the facts of his evidence. Bill's testimony is crushing to my defense. Did he file tax returns for the thirty grand Mr. Stratton paid him? No. Big deal. Who pays taxes on cash they earn unloading airplanes full of pot? Will he be prosecuted for his failure to pay taxes or for his participation in the smuggling venture? Bill does not know, no promises have been made, but he expects his testimony will protect him from being charged with any crimes.

The truth is out. The defendant, Richard Lowell Stratton, is a lying sack of shit; he has been revealed for exactly what he is: a longtime successful drug smuggler who finally got caught and is now looking to stick it up the government's ass by mounting this cockamamie bullshit writer's-freedom-of-the-press defense. In fact, worse. He has defamed the noble notion of journalistic objectivity, the protection writers who investigate illegal activity enjoy, not only by straying over the line but by refusing to acknowledge that any such line even exists.

Writer—what unmitigated horseshit! I can see it in the jurors' eyes as they leave the courtroom for the day: *You lied to us.*

Not even the erudite, articulate, amusing, and entertaining testimony by one of America's most respected authors can make up for the damage done by Mild Bill. Mailer is essentially a character witness, attesting to my merit as a friend.

"Rick is a stand-up guy," Mailer tells the packed courtroom, which doesn't really help as my character has already been revealed as that of a man who would fabricate a defense to criminal charges and then have the temerity to lie to the federal government and create an elaborate perversion of a time-honored privilege only to try to bamboozle honest citizens into acquitting me of serious crimes I obviously committed.

Cohen is unable to trip Mailer up. He does no better with Godfried's wife. But it is a long way back from the revelatory abyss I have been cast into by Honest Abe's testimony. I am wandering in a valley filled with the dried and bleached bones of my defense. My mendacity now lives on me like a scarlet letter—a curse. I have been undressed and made to stand naked, exposed as a fraud.

Cohen and Groff are smug in their seeming reversal of the tide. They inform Stern and Berlin that if I choose to take the stand, they will have grounds to admit the Canadian tapes, as well as a basis upon which to call the Canadian drug agents to give evidence about my extensive illegal activities north of the border. And that's just the beginning, they warn us. They will call a host of agents from around the country who will testify that the Drug Enforcement Administration has long been aware of and investigating my managerial role in the dope trade as a boss in the so-called hippie mafia. Berlin and Stern both tell me that by taking the stand, I will give the prosecution grounds to ask questions about men named Capuana and Bulger, Chagra, Uncle George, even my partner Sammy Silver.

I decline to testify.

I am fucked.

The defense rests. Closing arguments pound home the utter lack of merit to my defense. Fearless Fred, Wolfshein, Mailer—none of that matters. Only Mild Bill's surprise appearance, his insistence that I forgive him for what he was about to do—and did—his sincere, pained confession, only this lives in the jurors' minds as they listen to the lawyers sum up what has been an entertaining farce. Yes, that's exactly what it is, Cohen even names it such: a farce, he says, a comic play, a sham, but not funny, not at all, more a huge waste of taxpayers' money and the good jurors' time, let alone an insult to their intelligence.

Gignoux appears satisfied as he gives the case to the jury. After a three-week trial, they are out deliberating for six hours before asking for further instruction from the court. The jury requests that Judge Gignoux elucidate that section of the charge wherein he explained the nature of a conspiracy.

This is a hopeful sign. The jury is obviously wrestling with a central question: the nebulous nature of this case, the very nature of conspiracy. How can one be guilty of a crime when the illegal activity exists only in theory based on testimony with no physical evidence to connect the defendant to the crime? Gignoux's explanation, though legally correct, is so broad that anyone who has ever agreed to try a hit of pot could be considered guilty of having conspired to violate federal narcotics laws. The crime of conspiracy, he instructs, is made up of an agreement to commit an illegal act, whether that act actually takes place or not. As long as there has been at least one overt act—a telephone call, a meeting, a drive on a snowy day in a pickup truck to set up stash houses, whatever—the conspiracy is complete.

No one is smiling as the jury files back into the courtroom after considering the expanded explanation of the charge. The foreman hands Judge Gignoux the verdict. He reads it to himself. Nods. Thanks them. Hands it back to the jury foreman, who reads the verdict.

As to all counts, "We find the defendant, Richard Lowell Stratton, *guilty as charged.*"

OH, WELL. To be sure, it was a long shot. For a while there before they trotted out Honest Abe, it looked like I might walk. What a victory that would have been! What a high! Better even than smuggling dope.

Sheriff Gilmore, Cosmo the orderly, the jailhouse staff and regulars are sympathetic. Win some; lose some. We still have our cigars. Gilmore will order in lobsters. There is always the appeal. Mailer comes to visit.

"Hey, Rick . . . you put up a noble fight," he says.

My mother and father come as well. It is the sentencing that is our focus now. Berlin slips me a couple of nips of Cutty Sark he saved from the plane ride from New York. *New York.* That's another concern. Maybe the government will be satisfied with this conviction and leave well enough alone. *Fat chance.*

HANGING DAY. I am pictured in a front-page photo in the local newspaper entering the courthouse wearing a suit, in handcuffs, and smoking a cigar. *What? Still no remorse?*

Judge Gignoux seems more agitated than I am as I stand before him and refuse to make a comment. I would like to say, "Beam me up, Scotty." What the fuck planet am I on? A man walks after killing his wife—because he was drunk. I don't wish Roland any more time; he will suffer for the rest of his life. But how many guys kill their old ladies after smoking weed? It is deemed wise for me to remain mute, given that I might yet be facing another case. And besides, I've been revealed as a charlatan.

Gignoux is apoplectic. He cannot look at me as he imposes his sentence—which is about to become my sentence. His hands flutter over his broad bench like delicate birds taking flight as he rustles through some papers. He looks as though he is about to have a stroke.

"Calm down, your Honor," I want to say. "I'm the one in the dock."

"Has the defendant read the presentence report?" Gignoux intones.

Yes, yes . . . get on with it. All this blather about government resources. Fuck that nonsense. The government spends billions waging this ridiculous, destructive war on plants.

Mr. Stratton, bend over. We would like to fuck you in the ass.

Fifteen years, the maximum sentence allowed under the law.

Thank you, your Honor. *And fuck you, too.*

I AM WHISKED out of the Cumberland County Jail this very afternoon. Highly unusual. Ordinarily, there would be a two-to-three-week delay while the Federal Bureau of Punishment bureaucrats decided upon a suitable penal institution for my sentence. But as soon as I am returned to the jail, my old pal Deputy US Marshal James Sullivan appears with another deputy and teletyped orders to remove me at once. I am not even allowed to return to my cell to pack my belongings. All that has been done for me. My property will be shipped to the prison where I will begin serving my time.

Sully is all business until we are out of the jail and in the marshal's car speeding along the Maine turnpike heading south. He tells me that they received word I was planning an escape. The empty nip bottles of Cutty Sark were recovered from under the pillow in my cell. It was decided I had too much juice with the local Heat and that I was bribing—or attempting to bribe—officials at the jail to let me flee.

I know where this comes from. That sleazy trustee, Cosmo. He was constantly pumping me for information, and he had proposed that he could help me escape for five grand. I never agreed, but I did entertain the idea. And who knows what I might have done once I was returned to bound-over yardside with a fifteen-year sentence to contemplate.

"Where are we headed?" I ask Sully.

He looks at his partner and smiles. "Sending you to Terre Haute," he says. "Rough joint. You better watch yourself out there, Richie boy. Don't let some big buck nigger fuck you in the ass."

Racist Irish prick. If I could whack him on the back of the head, I would.

"Listen, Sullivan," I say, "the only fucking I'm getting around here is from the government."

He laughs. "You got that right."

You gotta love these Boston Irish.

THE MARSHALS DELIVER me to a county jail in Lowell, Massachusetts, where I will pass the night. Jailers inform me that they have no empty cells in the "regular" jail. So they will have to lock me up in the condemned wing.

Whatever. Who gives a shit? Not me.

Oh no? Check this out.

It's a fucking dungeon. Nothing more, nothing less. No bed. No toilet. A stinking half-full bucket of piss and shit to relieve myself in. The walls are damp and scummy; the floor is, too. I sit on the floor, draw my knees up and rest my head on my arms.

Say it again, Stratton. Convince yourself: *I don't give a shit.* I am beyond caring about any of this. Show me the worst you have got to offer. Lock me in a dungeon in the town named for my forebears. No matter how bad it gets, it is all good. For I am exactly where I am supposed to be—in a prison cell.

Chapter Five

THE CRIMINAL HILTON

Metropolitan Correctional Center, New York City, 1983–1984

THERE ARE GOOD jails, and then there are bad jails. The Cumberland County Jail is a good jail—at least it was for me. The LA City Jail is a bad jail by anyone's standards. That county joint they locked me up in for the night in Lowell, Massachusetts—that place was beyond the pale. It will go down along with the Glass House as one of the worst jails in America. And with the hefty dose of diesel therapy I received upon entering the federal system of punishment, I have seen my fair share and more of bad jails.

Then there is the Metropolitan Correctional Center in New York City, known as MCC, a.k.a. the Criminal Hilton. There is no jail in the world quite like MCC; it is in a class all by itself, just as there is no city in the world to compare to New York. MCC is where the criminal elite from around the world gather to bow down before the almighty rule of Uncle Sam's international police force. Any outlaw or criminal worth his or her salt is bound to make a pilgrimage to this Mecca of the notorious.

MCC is a twelve-story, fortress-like structure protruding from Foley Square in downtown Manhattan. The federal lock-up is attached to the majestic Thurgood Marshall United States Courthouse next door by an umbilical-like elevated walkway to feed the accused into the maw of the American criminal punishment system. This joint has such a high caliber of clientele it's like a think tank for professional criminals; a high-security tenement teeming with deviants; an abode for unregenerate dope dealers and squealers, mafiosi, bent correctional officers, flimflam artists and white-collar crooks, bank robbers, IRA soldiers, international arms dealers, and professional assassins. There are spies and terrorists, mob bosses of every stripe, Colombian drug lords, renegade CIA agents, Wall Street cowboys, racketeers, international confidence men, kidnappers, Black Panthers, gang leaders, Russian mobsters, extortionists, Israeli heroin smugglers, Albanian hitmen, Weathermen, armored-car robbers, counterfeiters, Jamaican posse members, Bloods and Crips, Latin Kings, Hell's Angels, contract killers, fraudsters—players and rogues from every dark alley in the international underworld.

This is my kind of jail. There is never a dull moment. Nonstop action from the moment they unlock the cell doors in the morning until they lock us back down at night, and often after lock-down into the early morning hours. Like a bus stop on the way to hell, the place festers with a perverse energy that boils over from the proximity of so many dedicated sinners confined in such close quarters.

WHAT WAS SUPPOSED to be a few days' holdover while in transit to the penitentiary in Terre Haute, Indiana, has turned into weeks of waiting and wondering: *What the fuck?* They pulled me off the Bureau of Punishment bus headed west and booked me into the ninth floor, maximum-security unit. After a couple of days of total twenty-four-hour-a-day lockdown in segregation, I was moved across the sally port to the high-security intake unit known as Nine North. Here is where new prisoners come straight from the street or from other prisons after lingering for hours and sometimes days in purgatory in the bullpens, the antechambers of hell, waiting on the long-drawn-out process of being checked into the Criminal Hilton.

Each evening I sit in the common area and watch the six o'clock news to see who US lawman Rudy Giuliani locked up on that day. Then, hours later, sure enough those same suckers come straggling onto the unit looking dazed and confused, dressed in ill-fitting orange jumpsuits, with bedrolls tucked under their arms. Millionaire captains of industry, their horizons suddenly diminished to a seven-and-a-half-by-eight-foot cell, they wander around like inmates in a mental ward. Colombian drug barons extradited to the US sit glued to the TV, watching their embattled billionaire chieftain, Pablo Escobar, wage war against his government. Domestic and foreign terrorists who would blow up America plot how they will get through the day. White supremacists and Black Panthers stand in line to pick up a food tray or make collect calls from the two pay phones. Militant Zionists and Islamic fundamentalists coexist in this rank hotbed of criminality. International arms traders swap packs of cigarettes for Snickers bars. Radical Puerto Ricans, millionaire capitalists, bankers and loan sharks, intelligence agents who strayed from the reservation—all have been stripped of external plumage and defenses, reduced to their attitudes.

Ah, yes, jail: the great equalizer.

Or—maybe not. For I have discovered that there is one whole tier, D tier, known as Mafia Row where things are not as they seem, where the vaunted rules and regulations of the institution apparently do not apply. The guests housed on Mafia Row have made discrete accommodations. Some of these guys have little TVs in their cells. They dine on takeout from the Italian restaurants on Mulberry Street and from the restaurants of nearby Chinatown. They puff on cigars that are not available from the commissary. They sip on aperitifs or after-dinner brandies. They hire stiffs to stand in line and wait for a turn to use the pay phones. The other prisoners rarely venture onto Mafia Row. The hacks leave them alone.

I have carved out my own unique niche here on the unit and in this singular jail. Because I am being held in some kind of legal limbo with no set transfer date, and, more importantly, because I can read and write with some proficiency, I have been assigned the position of unit clerk. It's a good gig. I maintain what is known as the bed board, a clipboard with a form attached to keep track of who is in which cell. Many of these correctional officers are lazy, a few are corrupt; but they all leave when their shift ends. We live here. The cells were designed for single-occupancy, but with the drug war raging in the nation and on the streets of New York, the prisoner population is booming, so the cells have been converted to two-man dwellings with the installation of bunk beds. We still have the standard plumbing fixtures: open, seatless steel toilets two feet from the bunk, and a sink. The cells are cramped and there is no privacy. This is a transient unit; most men do not stay here long. But some of us remain on Nine North for weeks or months while our cases wend their way through the federal legal labyrinth. So, who one lives with is of the utmost importance. By controlling the bed board, I have a certain power. Within reason, I can sway the shift CO to assign convicts to the cell and cellmate of their choosing. And as the unit clerk, my cell is always last to have double occupancy.

We are counted six times a day. For the 4:00 p.m. stand-up count, the guards lock down the entire unit until the count clears, and then the cells are opened to release prisoners for the evening meal. The evening-shift cops open my cell first so I can update the bed board. I go from tier to tier checking the names on the form with the bodies in the cells to make sure they match. Then the kitchen workers' cells are opened and they set up the food trays, zap them in the microwave, and feed the hungry convicts as they are released tier by tier. Once or twice a week the guards are supposed to take us up to a caged-in area on the roof for a little outdoor recreation, but that rarely happens. Between counts during the day we are allowed to wander freely within the unit. At ten o'clock, they lock us back down for the night.

Days turn into weeks, and then months slip past. The days are so similar they blend into a kind of timeless pause in real life. Routine becomes the saving grace of doing time; uncertainty undermines any measure of peace. It is now over two months since I was sentenced in

Maine, and I am still here with no idea what the government has in store for me—no, that's not true, I do know. I know the grand jury is still convened, still in session and considering evidence against me for new charges. Irving Berlin has come to see me twice, with no real news other than that there are new charges pending.

At night before lockdown I stand in the common area and look out through the steel-barred windows at the city of New York—so close, so real, so enticing, and yet a reality away. Gazing from my cell on the Fourth of July, I watch the fireworks over the East River. America is out there celebrating its independence while I am locked up. Life goes on out there; in here we exist in a state of suspended animation. Out there, millions and millions of people come and go in freedom. Yet they are subject to the constraints of work-a-day lives: having to pay rent or make mortgage and car payments; having to buy food and clothes; having to hold a job, keep appointments, and keep up appearances. Here we are *in custody*. I don't have to do shit. I pay for nothing except my mistakes, and pay for them with an abstraction—time—and a feeling—guilt. I try to wrap my head around the whole idea of what it means to be a convicted criminal and a kept human being serving time—as if time were something tangible that could be cooked and served and consumed like a meal.

I'm subject to the constant control and scrutiny of my keepers, yet there is a subtle perversity to being in custody. If they tell me to do something and I refuse, what can they do? Lock me up? I'm already in jail, so it's liberating. I remind myself almost hourly that the one thing they cannot control is my mind, including my mental attitude. For the first time in my life, I may be totally free, free from the precepts of society, already a convicted deviant and facing more charges. I am never bored. Beside the constant action on the unit—the coming and going of the most intriguing crooks and gangsters—I am fascinated by what is going on inside my head.

I think of the man I was when I was free: obsessed with risk, an ingrate who did not appreciate or use wisely my freedom and the vast amounts of money I made. A profligate. An unfaithful husband. A seeker after cheap thrills. Let me pay now with my time for my mistakes. Let the pain of loneliness compensate for some measure of the karmic debt I owe for the pain I caused others. Let this isolation sustain me as I come to grips with who I was and grow into a different, better person. Out there, the game was a constant distraction. I thrived on the action. All that exists in here, too. But there is a time when the cell door closes and is locked and the unit goes quiet, and I must accept that I cannot run away from my better self. I cannot drink or smoke myself to sleep. I must face the reality of how and why I fucked up my life and abused my freedom, and I must come up with a plan to win it back.

Fifteen years and a new case pending! This is serious. Yes, it's true, as Special Agent Bernie Wolfshein warned me: these *federales* don't play.

"YOU GOT A lawyer visit," the hack says as he unlocks my cell door after the 4:00 p.m. count. It's Officer Martin. Cool. I get along with this cop. He's a tall, slim, studious-looking black man who wears glasses and looks like he should be doing something else, dressed in a suit instead of the Bureau of Punishment uniform, carrying a briefcase instead of a walkie-talkie and body alarm. He scribbles out a pass and hands it to me.

"Everything cool?" he asks.

"We're good," I say.

Martin hands me an orange. Fresh fruit is a cherished commodity, an antidote to scurvy. After weeks and months in prisons and jails, my skin is so pale I glow in the dark. I'm transparent. You can see my heart beating in my chest, watch my lungs suck in and expel recycled air.

"On the door," Martin speaks into his radio. An electronic door release sounds and he opens the gate to the sally port. The cop operating the elevator checks my pass, speaks briefly with Martin.

On the way down to the lawyer's visiting room on the third floor, we stop on the fifth floor to pick up additional prisoners on their way to visit with their lawyers. A woman prisoner gets on the elevator. *What? Females, you say?* Yes, as if this place were not enough fun, there are women here. Lady criminals, girl gangsters, chick outlaws, a whole unit full of bad girls, so naughty as to merit federal charges. A teenage fantasy has in a sense become true. We used to drive up to the women's prison in Framingham, Massachusetts, park on the perimeter road, and gape at the caged females. The women would call to us like sirens from the windows of their cellblock. "Hey, big boy! C'mere and let me show you what I can do with that little thing between your legs!" Sometimes they would show us their tits. They taunted us with lurid intimations of their wet, hairy pussies. We were stunned, too scared of these hell-cats even to call back to them. I would lie awake at night and try to imagine what it would be like to be locked up in there with a whole prison full of sex-starved women and to let them have their way with me. Now I lie awake at night in my cell and fantasize what it would be like to be locked up on Five South, the women's unit.

And here getting into the elevator is the woman prisoner of my dreams. She is attractive in a punked-out sort of way. Wild, frizzy, two-tone hair. Even with her dressed in the pale blue slacks and smock that is the women prisoners' uniform, I can see she has a good, full figure. We share a quick look. A glimmer of recognition passes between us. Not that we have ever met, but we sense an affinity. We are both white, so-called sophisticated criminals. I make her for a dope dealer who partook of her product and may be going through mild withdrawal.

A guard unlocks the attorney visiting room door and we are herded inside. Irving Berlin waits in one of the small cubicles spaced along the back wall. The attorney visiting room is like a fish bowl with glass walls so the guards outside can keep an eye on what goes on inside. Criminal defense lawyers swim around like sharks in expensive suits looking for fresh meat to feed on. Berlin comes out from the cubicle and greets me—and my female fellow prisoner, the woman I just encountered on the elevator.

"You two should know each other," he says.

Now I know who she is, the so-called Smack Goddess, dope dealer to the stars whose picture was plastered all over the tabloids a few days ago as a gang of dope cops led her in handcuffs from her Upper West Side apartment building. Allegedly the street where she lived would be choked with limos while her rock star customers popped in for a quick score. Berlin introduces us. Then he takes me into the cubicle for a hurried private conference.

The government, he tells me, has dismissed the grand jury. A true bill was returned. The indictment is being prepared as we speak. A new prosecution is to be mounted against me and as yet unnamed co-conspirators here in the Southern District of New York, brought by an assistant from the office of that champion of law and order, United States Attorney Rudy Giuliani. This comes as no surprise. We knew it was in the works. Rumors and reports of a grand jury meeting in New York and calling witnesses to be questioned about a massive load of hashish imported through the port of Newark, New Jersey, have been relayed to me for months—from lawyers and from people called to testify. I had hoped the fifteen years I received in Maine would satisfy the Feds. But it is clear they feel there are more important deviants out there, and they assume I might be the one to lure them in.

"I've been in touch with the assistant handling the case," Berlin concludes. "They want to know if you are willing to take a meeting."

"A meeting? With who?"

"DEA. The US attorney's office."

"What for?"

Berlin shrugs, smiles. "Well, what for? What else? Cooperation. They're interested to know if you're . . . perhaps . . . more amenable to the idea of . . . helping them."

"Fuck that. What more can they do to me? I already got the maximum."

"They could cut your time. Or they could give you more time. Both possibilities exist, depending on what you decide to do." He stops, looks around. We are alone in the cubicle.

"You know how I feel," I say.

"Of course, I do. This is your decision."

"I'm not caving in at this point. That makes no sense."

He nods. "I can't advise you on this, Richard."

"Don't they get it? I won't go there. Tell them they can shove their cooperation up their collective government asses. I'm not interested."

Pissed off is how I feel. Even though I knew this was a possibility, it feels like overkill. Enough is enough already. Let me go to the penitentiary and do my fucking time. They want to turn me into a rat? What is this, Nazi Germany?

"You can understand where they are coming from. People change their minds," Berlin reminds me. "Fifteen years is a lot to think about."

"Yeah, it's a lot to think about. But I already made up my mind."

"That's what I should tell them?" he persists. I'm wondering if he gave them some indication I might be willing to roll over.

"You should tell them to suck my cock."

Berlin laughs. He loves it when I go convict and talk tough. We both laugh.

"Are we having fun yet?" I ask. "Tell me about her," I say, meaning the lady dope dealer in the blue smock.

"Ah . . . I'll let her tell you about herself."

"Let's play their game," I say, giving the proposal some consideration. "No harm in having a meeting, right? Let's hear what's on their mind. At least it will get me off the unit for a few hours."

I know somewhere deep inside this is wrong. I must not even entertain the notion of cooperation. To meet with the enemy is a breach of honor, a show of weakness, but I can't resist.

Berlin shakes his head. "There's only one thing on their mind, Richard: cooperation. You need to think about this. Fifteen years, that's one thing. You would be eligible for parole after five. If they give you

THE CRIMINAL HILTON **91**

another ten or fifteen, you're looking at well over a decade in prison—
and possibly a lot more."

BERLIN CONFERS IN private with the lady prisoner, then he leaves us
alone to sit together and chat like normal people for as long as it takes
for the guards outside the attorney conference room to realize that our
lawyer has departed. There's a curious, awkward feel to the moment.
We could be on a blind date. We're convict chic, she in her baby blue
smock and slacks, me in my blaze-orange jumpsuit. I wish I could wave
to a waiter and order cocktails to break the ice. But it is prisoners and
criminal defense lawyers who surround us, not wait staff. Still, there is
the feeling of a potential relationship in the mood, like there might be
a second date.

The guards announce, "Movement!" They pull heavy curtains
closed around the glass windows, cutting off our view of the hallway
outside.

"What's happening?" she asks.

"They're moving a rat. Someone who is in the witness protection
program. They have a whole unit full of high-level protected snitches
here on the third floor. Whenever they move one of them, take them
to court to testify, they put a hood over the guy's head and lock down
the whole place so no one sees them."

"Really? Dear God, I can't imagine living like that."

She's a Brit; her name is Frances, says they call her Frin.

"The reporters asked me how I was finding this place," Frin tells
me. "I said, it's easy: I just wake up every day and here it is and here I
am. All I must do is look around."

"Are you okay?"

"Yes, catching up on my rest. Actually, it's no worse than an English boarding school."

She wants to know if I have access to any "gear," dope of any kind.

"Let me see what I can do."

"I prefer to go *downtown*," she says. I take that to mean barbiturates or smack.

The cops soon cotton to the fact that Berlin has left us alone and move us back upstairs. I leave Frin on the fifth floor with a quick squeeze of her hand and the promise that we will see each other again . . . somehow.

Life in the Criminal Hilton just got a whole lot more interesting.

THEY COME FOR me in early morning.

"Court," the graveyard-shift hack says as he unlocks my cell door.

It's 5:00 a.m. I while away the hours in the bullpen on the third floor. They dress me out in a clean suit my mother delivered to the jail. I'm handcuffed to another prisoner. We are attached to a chain of criminals and pulled across the elevated walkway to yet another suite of bullpens in the basement of the federal courthouse. More hours of sitting around on steel benches listening to criminals complain. I have come to appreciate the stoic men who journey through this inferno, those convicts who keep their mouths shut and accept whatever inconvenience the keepers see fit to impose, unlike that loudmouth, now dead guy who kept bitching on the BOP bus. He didn't get it. The keepers despise us, which is clear from their attitude. As a prisoner, one must submit outwardly while maintaining a reserve of inner fortitude. For clearly their objective is to demean us, degrade us, humiliate us, and bully us into total submission, often by the subtlest means, simply by making us wait.

Two DEA agents come to the marshal's bullpen and pull me out. I don't recognize either of them but they claim to know me.

"That bust up in Orange County. Remember? We were on that one."

"Oh, yeah," I say. "The empty truck bust. The load you guys stole and sold. How could I forget?"

"Looks like we got you this time," the agent gloats.

I say nothing but smile so as to let him know there are no hard feelings.

We repair to a conference room in the US attorney's office. Berlin is here. And the AUSA who has been assigned to handle my new case, a guy named Stuart Abraham. He's slight, pale, in his thirties, and has curly red hair. Where do they find these guys? One to two percent of the population of the entire world has red hair. Jews make up a small portion of that tiny segment of humanity. Two of the four redheaded Jews on the East Coast and they both end up prosecuting me? I will call him Stuart Little. No doubt he's using this stint with the federal prosecutor's office as a stepping-stone to private practice at some white shoe Park Avenue corporate law firm, where he'll be pulling down the big fees representing the kind of white-collar crooks he's now prosecuting.

The door opens and in walks my old pal, Agent Bernie Wolfshein, a.k.a. the Wolfman. He looks harried, slightly rumpled, as though he slept in his suit.

"Rich," he says, greets me like an old friend. "How have you been?" And to the assembled group, "Sorry I'm late. My flight was delayed," he adds and looks directly at me. "You know how that goes."

I nod. I sense he's trying to tell me something, but I have no idea what.

"Coming from that part of the world," Wolfshein goes on cryptically and keeps looking at me, nodding his head slightly, adjusting his glasses. I'm struck by how much I have come to like this guy. Clearly, his whole agenda is to destroy everything I have spent the last fifteen years of my life pursuing and to topple the freedom I have labored to bring about, yet when he walks into the room I feel relieved. I'm sure he would count it a victory if I were to agree to give in and cooperate with the government. But there is an unspoken respect I sense from the way the Wolf sizes me up, and that I welcome. I believe he secretly applauds my refusal to become a government rat. He clearly has a larger initiative in mind.

Now I get it. Wolfshein is hinting that he just returned from a trip to the Middle East. The Wolfman loves playing this game of psychological warfare with me. All along I'm thinking, *What do I care? The hash is long gone. I'm already locked up. It's all over.* I keep asking myself: *What more can they do to me?*

Stuart Little lays it out. One of the DEA agents, whose name I learn is McNeil, went undercover posing as a drug dealer. Hammoud, the taxi driver who acted as my heavy Lebanese's connection, Mohammed's translator, got busted along with Nasif, Mohammed's son, as they attempted to sell ten kilos of heroin to an undercover DEA agent—this same guy, Special Agent McNeil. Both Hammoud and Nasif immediately flipped and began working for the Feds. Hammoud introduced undercover agent McNeil to Mailer's friend Biff and told him McNeil was interested in buying large quantities of hashish. Biff and the undercover had several meetings. There are tapes of their conversations. This happened after I got a message to Biff that the Arabs were cooperating and that he should have nothing to do with them, a warning he ignored, this fucking idiot. Now the Feds claim they have gathered evidence from the stash house on Staten Island, where we stored the seven tons of Lebanese hashish. *What evidence?* That has got to be a lie. The hash was sold and that place was emptied and vacated more than a year ago.

I'm dubious of their whole scenario. To me it reeks of an elaborate bluff to try to scare me into implicating—who else? Norman Mailer.

The prosecutor carries on. This is clearly his show. The DEA agents are extras. The government, he says, can produce witnesses who will testify regarding the seven-ton importation of hash into the port at New Jersey. My partner in that trip, Sammy Silver, his father, his brother, Sammy's driver, Fat Bobby—everyone connected to that smuggle will be located, arrested, and prosecuted for conspiracy to import and distribute fifteen thousand pounds of hashish. Biff has already been arrested and made a number of incriminating statements to the agents. As the prosecutor continues, I get an uneasy feeling from the way he says this that Biff may have gone over to the government's camp. No surprise there, either.

"Special Agent Wolfshein has just returned from Beirut," Stuart Little says, and he lets this statement hang in the air. "There is a sealed indictment about to be handed down once some of the other co-conspirators have been located and apprehended," he goes on, and looks at Berlin, and then at me. "Mr. Stratton, you appear to be the organizer and manager of the conspiracy. This could result in a significant sentence in addition to the sentence you are already serving."

Now everyone looks at me.

"Rich," Wolfshein breaks the silence, "you're still a relatively young man. You don't want to grow old in prison."

"What do you have in mind?" I ask Stuart Little.

"Any agreement the government would be willing to enter into will require your complete and truthful cooperation. Names, dates, and activities." And once again I hear the names: Michael Capuana, James Bulger, Jamiel Chagra, the man I call Uncle George.

"Norman Mailer," he says.

"Mailer had nothing to do with my business."

"We know he was involved."

"No," I say. "You're wrong."

"C'mon, Rich," Wolfshein interjects. "Your boy Biff already spilled the beans. And we have the kid, Mohammed's son."

"So?"

"So . . . the dinner party. Mailer was there," Wolfshein says. "Who introduced you to Biff? Who introduced Mailer to Mohammed?"

I let the questions go unanswered. Obviously, they already have that information.

"These . . . events constitute overt acts in furtherance of the conspiracy," Stuart Little adds.

I had forgotten all about that evening at Biff's apartment on Riverside Drive, the dinner party. Indeed, Mohammed was there, and Hammoud, his driver and translator. Mailer did stop by with his then very pregnant wife. Biff may have even displayed a slab of hashish and bragged about the successful smuggle.

"You could walk out of here tomorrow," DEA Agent McNeil offers.

"But I'd be wearing a leash."

"Call it what you want," he says. "It's not handcuffs."

"You want me to set up Mailer?"

No one answers. I take this to mean they don't have enough to indict him. I look at Berlin, and then back at Stuart Little. "I'm not following. Tell me exactly what you want me to do."

I want them to say it.

Stuart Little says, "I told you. The government would expect your complete and truthful cooperation. You would be required to testify at any and all trials resulting from your cooperation."

Now I see their play. The US attorney's office is covering their ass. DEA is going out on the limb. That's why the agents are here.

I ask Wolfshein, "How do you fit into this?"

"Good question. Special Agent McNeil would be your control. I'm his supervisor."

Control. So they have a scenario in mind where I would be a *confidential informant* working undercover in the business to set people up for arrest. Mailer would be my first target. Then, after Norman, whomever else I can lure into the government's trap.

"You want me to agree to set up my close friend Norman Mailer, lie to him, falsely incriminate him, then perjure myself. Right?"

"No, that is not right," the prosecutor says. He suddenly appears angry, as though he has figured out that I have no intention of helping them. "Absolutely not. We have evidence—"

I cut him off. "I don't care what you think you have. It's bullshit. Some people will say and do anything to save their own skin. But that's not who I am. I won't be involved in any attempt to put Norman Mailer or anyone else in prison to save my ass just so you can hang his scalp on your trophy wall."

A brief stunned silence. Now they all glower at me—except Wolf-shein, who shows nothing. I'm thinking this guy would make a good poker player.

"You gave the man money," Stuart Little pushes back. "We know that for a fact. You paid him cash for the property in Maine, and more besides. His name is on the deed. That place was used to store the proceeds of illegal activity. You gave him money on any number of other occasions. He knows how and where you got that money—smuggling drugs. He introduced you to Biff. And he urged you to use him to facilitate the conspiracy."

"Says who?"

Fucking Biff! That's who. What else has this weak fuck told these people?

"That makes him a member of the conspiracy," Stuart Little concludes.

"Him and thirty-five thousand other people," I say. "That's a crock of shit and you know it. This is star-fucking. If his name wasn't Norman Mailer you wouldn't give a damn about him."

"How about your pal Rosie in Canada? He's pretty chummy with Mailer, too," Agent McNeil adds.

"I don't know anything about that."

"The RCMP does."

I look at Berlin. "Let's go. This meeting is over. I want to go back to my cell."

Stuart Little addresses Berlin. "Then we will be proceeding to trial?"

I answer for him. "Yes." I stand. "And if you think my defense in Maine was wild, wait until you see what I do here."

Snickers from Wolfshein. Stuart Little shakes his head and gathers up his paperwork.

"Can I have a word in private with Mr. Stratton?" Berlin asks.

"I don't like the sound of this," he tells me after they leave the room. "Organizer. Manager. Sounds to me like they're going for an 848—CCE. You know what that is?"

"I've heard, yes."

"The kingpin statute. . . . This is not good."

"No, it's not. It's bullshit, and I'm not going for it. Fuck them."

A long pause as the lawyer looks at me.

"Okay. That's your decision. But you should know," he continues and gives me a sad look. "If I'm going to try this case, I'm going to need more money. A lot more money."

Yeah, right. Money. Everybody wants money.

My unit, Nine North, is awash with dope. I swear people come in to the jail, to the visiting room, to score from the prisoners. What can you expect? You lock up fifty or a hundred of the top drug smugglers in the world, put them all together with any number of relatively affluent junkies with nothing else to do but get loaded, they are going to come up with ingenious ways to ply their trade and keep everybody high. The jail administrators would have you believe the dope comes in through the visiting room, passed surreptitiously from visitor to prisoner. Certainly, some of the low-level dopers swallow balloons full of dope, shit them out in the morning. *That is the real shit!* But it's slim pickings. The professionals, the wiseguys, the kingpins, they own the cops or enough of them, anyway, to get whatever they desire. The big packages are smuggled in by staff. At least half the fun is figuring out how to stay high in jail. It's a matter of concentration. In here, in this POW encampment well behind enemy lines, there is more dope of higher quality than one could ever find in a similar space on the street. The secret is to learn who the players are and then control the flow.

Recently, I was invited to take up residence on Mafia Row, an honor of sorts, and of course I took the wiseguys up on their offer. I now occupy a cell all to myself at the end of D tier. It is remarkably quiet here compared to the rest of the unit. A few of the men sit at a table at the far end of the tier near the window, where they play pinochle and tell war stories. Most of the wiseguys stay in their cells and come out only to make phone calls or to go down to the third floor for visits with their lawyers. Angelo Ruggiero is here; he's said to be close to the ranking member of a faction of the Gambino Crime Family at odds with the boss, Paul Castellano. The name whispered among the good fellas is Gotti, John Gotti. Watch that name, a rising star in the world of organized crime.

As the unit clerk in charge of the bed board, I am apportioned some of the swag that comes onto the unit in exchange for my job of making sure the prisoners assigned to cells are agreeable to each other—in particular on D tier, but throughout the whole unit. This makes for a better atmosphere all around. I am like the concierge of Nine North.

Frin got a job in food service. She and a hot Colombian woman deliver the food carts from the kitchen in the basement to the various units, and this is how much of the contraband gets distributed within the jail. A package will come to me smuggled in the food cart—street food, drugs, cash money, whatever it is—and usually it goes straight down to D tier, to my cell, where the wiseguys whack it up.

Now I get to see Frin twice a day. She comes sashaying onto the unit dressed in tight-fitting kitchen whites rolled up to the knees, tied with a sash at the midriff. Braless. Her ample tits are free even in jail. Depending on which cop accompanies her, I might get a kiss and a quick hug. That's enough to make me tumescent.

MOST OF MY days are spent in the law library located in the education department in the basement of the jail. My study of the law has advanced to analyzing the intricacies of double-jeopardy rulings as I prepare a motion to block future prosecution on the grounds that I have already been tried and convicted in Maine. Then, as my sojourn in the MCC approaches a year, there are speedy trial considerations to factor into my plea. I read all I can find on the so-called kingpin statute recently enacted as part of the government's stepped-up war on drugs, known as 848, the continuing criminal enterprise statute, which includes a punishment of life in prison with no possibility of parole.

All sorts of high jinx go on in the law library besides the study of law. A few weeks ago a rogue CIA agent who was busted for allegedly selling plastique explosives to Colonel Muammar Gaddafi of Libya approached me as I stood between the stacks looking for a volume on double jeopardy. Edwin Wilson is his name. He confided that he wanted to hire a hitman to whack the US prosecutor and the federal judge presiding over his case. Did I by any chance know someone who might be interested in taking the contract?

"No," I said, and I warned Wilson against soliciting murder from within these walls. "This place is full of rats," I told him. "And not just the four-legged variety."

Sure enough, Wilson made the contact. The whole deal was recorded on a wire worn by an FBI snitch, a black guy who lives on Nine North. The CIA agent's twenty-three-year-old son was arrested on the street as he delivered ten thousand dollars cash to an undercover FBI agent posing as the hitman. Now Wilson is in solitary confinement on Nine South and facing new charges of conspiracy to murder a federal judge and prosecutor. This jail is a breeding ground of intrigue, double-cross, treachery, and corruption. Twice in the now ten or eleven months that I have been here attempts have been made to set me up in wholesale drug deals. A rich Pakistani rajah asked for an audience. He came to my cell and wanted to know if I could help him distribute a massive load of Afghan hash he claimed to have already landed in the country. Tempted, I declined. I can smell these rats. Another guy approached me in the law library and claimed to know Biff and Mailer. He wanted to talk about my case, but kept asking questions about Norman. No doubt the guy was wired.

The other day I rode up from the third floor on the elevator with Anthony "Fat Tony" Salerno, alleged boss of the Genovese Crime Family. Fat Tony hobbles around the jail on a cane, has a choice cigar stuffed in the side of his mouth, looks a little like Winston Churchill. Tony banged his walking stick on the food cart on the elevator and said, "Rats! Rats! Watch out for the rats!" He's right. The wiseguys know how to do time. Fat Tony and the bosses and hierarchy of all five New York Mafia families have been swept up in a massive new racketeering prosecution, Rudy Giuliani's magnum opus, the so-called Commission Case. The government brought an indictment charging the ruling council of the Mafia with a plethora of crimes, including dozens of murders in furtherance of the criminal enterprise known as La Cosa Nostra. They are all facing life with no parole. Fat Tony told me he was caught napping in court the other day. The judge ordered him to wake up and pay attention to the proceedings.

"What for?" Salerno quipped. "Judge, the last time I woke up, you gave me *a hundred years*."

These organized crime guys, many of them don't give a shit. Jail for old-school gangsters is a retirement home. They are treated with respect even by the guards and the administration. Once you are in with the wiseguys, doing a bid is a different experience. They have made this life their own. They are firmly entrenched in food service. They make it their business to keep them and their friends as well fed as possible. At least for the present, the traditional mob gangsters hold sway against an onslaught of young, hotheaded, loud, uneducated junior criminals who have no respect. These kids are buried with unbelievably long federal sentences—twenty, thirty years—for dealing relatively small amounts of crack cocaine while wholesale dealers caught with much larger amounts of powdered cocaine get half that time. It makes no sense. Nothing about this war on drugs makes sense. No attempt is made on behalf of the Bureau of Punishment to give the gangsters-in-training any kind of schooling except the advance courses in criminal behavior they get from their elders.

My own new case, whatever it is, lingers in a tortuous indeterminate legal state. The indictment has yet to be unsealed, therefore the terms of the speedy trial act are not yet in effect. Sammy Silver is on the run. The other co-conspirators have yet to be arrested and charged. The clock is ticking, but not for me. I busy myself studying the speedy trial procedural rules, hoping to get the case thrown out if the government fails to take me to trial within the allotted time. But it's a futile effort, just something to occupy my mind, as the jailhouse lawyers who are my mentors tell me the government has all sorts of ways of getting around their own rules and regulations.

But it says it right here, they have seventy days from the filing of the indictment to take me to trial.

So? You've been indicted, yes. But they haven't unsealed the indictment yet. And if they go over the allotted time, they simply impanel a new grand jury and come down with a superseding indictment. There will probably be a superseding indictment in this case anyway as they capture new conspirators, and people roll over and give them additional evidence.

The rules of criminal procedure are made to appear fair, and they are. But it is in the artful application of the rules by lawyers, prosecutors, and judges, and in the establishment of exceptions to the rules that the defendant gets fucked. Of course, it is also true that we are all guilty, if not guilty of exactly what the government has seen fit to charge us with, then guilty of something equally illegal. The Feds know I'm not going anywhere. The clock will continue to tick, ever so faintly, on my fifteen-year sentence. The Feds have as long as it takes them. They can do whatever they want, or whatever some judge in the employ of the federal government rules they can do. I don't mind this; believe me. I'm not squawking. It's their game. They make the rules; they break the rules. I didn't abide by their rules to begin with, so I won't start bitching now. But I'm not going to just bend over and let them stick it up my ass with no Vaseline. What fun would that be? I love to match wits with these guys —the guys in the suits, the guys with the bank accounts who get a paycheck every week, guys like my new pal Special Agent Bernie Wolfshein. I suspect he's just as interested as I am to see how this whole drug war plays out. After all, he's spent as much of his career as I have caught up in the conflict.

Bottom line, I'm still alive. Life, in a sense, is doing time. It's all about how you do that time. My method for getting through and using the time has become my ever-expanding study of the law. As this study continues, the deeper I get into it, the more I look for metaphors to understand what I am up against—or rather, what I am involved in, for I have chosen to immerse myself in the process. It is too simple to say this is a game of chess. In chess, the rules regarding what moves the players can make are clearly defined. Even the king and queen must move within set parameters. The law exists in word alone. It is constantly evolving, changing, even devolving as new rulings come down from higher courts undercutting established rules and laws and procedures. The letter of the law is plastic; written law is a theory more closely related to fiction than to fact. It is a story told by men and women who are highly educated in the finer points of how to give a word several nuances of meaning.

Okay, I like that. I can play that game. Where there are likenesses to chess, it is in the realm of devising a strategy. To have a strategy is in itself a strategy. One must meditate and plot and plan. Watch your opponent and figure out your next move based on his anticipated moves. To occupy the brain is half the game. And I have the secret weapon—THC. Recently a friend of mine from the West Coast straggled onto the unit. I have begun to call him Smog Monster because he looks like one of those creatures in a Japanese horror movie. He hasn't shaved or cut his hair for months to protest a grand jury he's been called before, and before which he refuses to testify. Wherever he parks himself, once he departs he leaves a trail of litter. When he arrived fresh off the BOP express from California, he had a cigar tube full of tightly packed Thai bud tucked up in his *suitcase*—also known as the anal cavity. The dope reeks so high we have to blow cigar smoke to mask the smell.

Already, as I continue my cerebration, I am roughing out and then fine-tuning a scenario for my new, improved defense. This one is a whopper.

"You think this is funny?" Smog Monster says to me when I share my plan.

"No," I say, "not funny. Amusing."

"STRATTON! LAWYER VISIT!" the hack shouts and hands me a pass.

I walk in the attorney visiting room expecting to see Irving Berlin and hopeful for a liaison with sweet Frin. Instead, a tall, very tall, maybe six-foot-five-inch impeccably dressed criminal defense attorney greets me. I recognize him as one of the top trial lawyers in the city, maybe even in the country—certainly in the area of criminal law.

"Richard Stratton," he says and offers me his large hand. "Ivan Fisher."

"I'm honored."

"Likewise."

He turns and whisks me into one of the private cubicles.

Fisher's hair is fashionably long and perfectly groomed, tucked behind his large, pendulously lobed ears—a sign of wisdom. Every accouterment of his wardrobe speaks of sartorial elegance, more Brooks Brothers than Brioni. The shoes are English leather. The tie is silk, muted, tied to perfection in a slim, casual knot. Intelligence bubbles from his brain in short, succinct sentences.

"You are in a heap of shit here. You know that?"

"I kind of figured."

"My first bit of advice to you is don't discuss your case with anyone. And I mean anyone. Other than your lawyer."

"Got it," I say, though I have already been sharing my plans with the Smog Monster, whom I will soon refer to Fisher.

Fisher smiles and nods. "Here's how I fit in. That scumbag, if I may use the word, that idiot, Biff—I represent him! Thankfully, he is now a co-defendant. Previously, before I was his lawyer, he was a cooperating witness."

"No shit."

"Yes. DEA set him up in a phony cocaine transaction. Hammoud, Mohammed Bero's lackey, contacted Biff once you were in custody in California, and he introduced Biff to an undercover DEA agent named McNeil, who posed as a wealthy dope dealer hoping to buy quantities of hashish, which Biff claimed to have access to."

"Yes, I know. I met McNeil."

"You did? When?" Fisher asks.

"Weeks, maybe a month ago. They offered me a deal, which I declined."

"Then you know there was no hashish," Fisher continues. "I'm not sure what Biff had in mind. He's not saying. Perhaps he thought he could swindle this guy for some down payment cash and then rip him off. He was playing drug dealer. Biff and the agent were both posing as drug dealers. Absurd, but true. In any case, the agent offered to front him kilos of cocaine, which turned out to be harmless white powder. The moment Biff took delivery of the package, McNeil identified himself as a DEA agent. Other agents appeared and Biff was arrested. They immediately took him up to his apartment and told him, 'Call your friend, Norman Mailer.'"

"This fucking asshole."

"Biff did call Norman. He made a lunch date with him. And to that luncheon, Biff came wearing a wire."

"You're kidding me."

"No. But here's where it gets even more interesting. Norman said nothing during that taped conversation that would give the government any basis to charge him as a participant in the conspiracy. He admitted to knowing you, of course. He called you his good friend of many years, but said he never totally understood where and how you got your money, said he never asked and didn't want to know.

He admitted to meeting Mohammed, but said he got an unpleasant vibe from the man and left the party early. The tape of that lunch meeting, for the prosecution's purposes, is useless; it probably has more value to the defense. The government's reaction was to accuse Biff of tipping Norman off that he was wired. And they terminated him as a cooperator."

Fisher's eyes light up. He grins. Shakes his head. His hair comes unglued and falls from behind his ears. "Yes!" he practically shouts. "He failed as a rat! Can you imagine? And that's where I come in. I am now this failed rat's attorney."

I love this guy. He's a showman in a Brooks Brothers suit. He's Perry Mason on speed.

"Now, here's the bad . . . possibly good news. Your pals have all been arrested. Sammy Silver—they found him in Amsterdam, his father, and Bobby. They all made bail and are represented by outstanding lawyers with whom I am in close contact. So there are now five defendants in this case including you. And that is not a random number the government pulled out of a hat. There are undoubtedly more people they could arrest and bring into this case, and perhaps they will. But for now, for their purposes, five is the magic number. *Five*." Fisher holds up five long fingers, and then points his trigger finger at me.

"Five conspirators, with you singled out as the organizer, the manager—in other words, the boss, or the kingpin. In the indictment that has just been unsealed, you have been charged under the continuing criminal enterprise statute, also referred to as 848, or CCE. Do you know what that means?"

"I'm familiar with it. Berlin seemed to think that's where they were headed. I've been reading up on it."

"Then you know there are various elements to this statute which the government must prove in order to secure a conviction. The good news is I don't think they have ever charged a marijuana smuggler with this statute, at least not in this district. Ordinarily, it's reserved for organized crime heroin kingpins. But all that is changing daily as the government gets more aggressive in these big marijuana cases. Nevertheless, given the circumstances, to me it smacks of prosecutorial overreaching," Fisher surmises, and he becomes quite serious. "You do know what you're facing? A minimum of ten years, and up to life with no possibility of parole. As well as forfeiture of all your assets."

I nod.

He combs his fingers through his long hair. "It doesn't get any heavier than this, Richard," he says. "Unless, I suppose, you were facing a death sentence."

I take a breath. It's one thing to contemplate serving fifteen years with a parole eligibility date after serving one third of that time. But it's a whole other world of pain to conceive of doing life with no possibility of parole. Especially when the message is delivered by someone who knows intimately the lengths and expense to which the government is willing to go to make their charges stick.

"Fuck. Life. For smuggling pot—or hash . . ."

"Yes, I know. It's excessive. It's doubtful they will go there. But you never know. So much will depend on what judge we get."

"What about double jeopardy?" I ask. "Isn't this like trying me twice for the same criminal activity?"

"Precisely!" Fisher yelps and practically leaps out of his seat. "I haven't had the benefit of reading the transcripts of the Maine trial yet," he goes on. "But this is exactly my thinking. From what I have been able to gather, you were charged with conspiracy to import and distribute marijuana."

"No, charged only with conspiracy to possess with intent to distribute marijuana. Tried and convicted," I say. "Sentenced to fifteen years. The maximum. No importation. No hashish."

"Hmmm, that does add a different wrinkle. Here they are charging importation of hashish as well as possession with intent to distribute. But hashish is also cannabis, and in fact a by-product of marijuana, correct? A condensed form of the same substance?"

"It is, yes. Absolutely."

"And we are talking about the same period of time when all this alleged criminal activity took place, are we not?"

"Yes, it was all going on simultaneously," I concur.

"Excellent. Therefore, I believe, you should argue that the government is precluded from bringing this new indictment on the grounds that you have already been tried and convicted of in essence the same offense. The double jeopardy clause of the United States Constitution bars the government from trying a defendant—you—twice for what is essentially the same crime."

"How should I go about doing that?" I ask him.

"I'll speak to Berlin. He is still your lawyer?"

"He was as of yesterday, though he's looking for more money to try the new case."

A moment of silence as we both contemplate the subject of money.

"Of course. This could be a lengthy, difficult, and expensive trial. But you seem to know what you're doing," Fisher says. "You could prepare and file the double jeopardy motion yourself. You really don't need Berlin or anyone else. That might be a wise tactic. You file your motion to dismiss right after you are arraigned on the new indictment, which will probably happen as soon as next week. File your motion pro se before the district court judge assigned to preside over the case. We don't know who that person is yet. But there will be ample time to file your motion in district court. Ask for an evidentiary hearing. Lay out the facts of both cases showing how they are all part of one overall conspiracy. Back that up with any and all case law you can find to support your argument. In particular, look for case law out of the Second Circuit, which is the appellate court for the Southern District. And any Supreme Court rulings you may find that are on point. I'll have my office send you some citations. As I mentioned, this is fairly new legal territory we are venturing into. The CCE statute has been on the books less than a decade. And again, it's not commonly used to prosecute marijuana smugglers. The government is using it more and more these days. In particular, they love the forfeiture clause."

I have already been doing all of what Fisher advises. In fact, I have been drafting a double jeopardy motion and editing it with help from some of the resident jailhouse lawyers. Carmine Persico, alleged boss of the Colombo Crime Family, and himself a jailhouse lawyer of some repute, has read my draft motion and offered his suggestions.

Fisher stands. He towers over me and offers me his hand once again.

"I'm happy to help you and to advise you in any way I can," the lawyer assures me. "I will have my assistant send you copies of similar motions for you to reference." Fisher's eyes light up. "This could be very interesting."

Fisher scans the outer area of the conference room. "Now, I must confer with my paying clients," he says and starts for the door. "Of course, you know who the real target is here?"

"They made that very clear."

"Norman."

A pause as we both consider the stakes.

"If we get a sympathetic judge," Fisher concludes, "he may just throw it out."

"Let's hope so."

"It's certainly worth a try," Fisher says and leads me from the cubicle. "Norman sends his regards. He wants to come see you. But under the circumstances, I have advised he wait until after we see how this shakes out. The government would certainly make an issue of his coming to visit with you."

I make my way back to my cell on Mafia Row. So much to think about: continuing criminal enterprise, *the kingpin statute*—it's insidiously flattering. I have never thought of myself as a kingpin. *Life with no parole*. For pot? That doesn't seem possible. I never imagined such a fate. *Double jeopardy*. I like the sound of that, and working under the auspices of renowned criminal defense attorney Ivan Fisher. Now there is new purpose and direction to my study of the law.

As SOON AS the 4:00 p.m. count clears, the evening-shift hack comes to my cell and unlocks the door. We call this cop Sly Stone. He's a hyperactive wild man with greasy Jheri curls and lots of gold jewelry. It's going to be a festive night in the rock'n' roll jail with this hack on duty. Anything goes. Anything can happen.

I take the bed board and make my rounds, never knowing what I'm going to find as I peer in through the rectangular windows in the cell doors. One morning I came upon a humping beast of two backs, some big black guy mounting his white cellmate. Another day on my post-count rounds I found a young Dominican kid hanging by the neck from a bedsheet tied to the post of the upper bunk bed. I ran to get the CO to unlock the door, but the kid was already dead by the time we cut him down.

Sly opens the kitchen workers' cells, and they begin setting up for the evening meal. I make sure to be hanging out near the sally port when the food cart arrives. Frin and the Colombian girl wheel the cart onto the unit. The girls look sexy in their kitchen whites altered to show off their figures. Sly escorts them in and then ducks back into the hack's office—a closet really, just off the kitchen. I suspect he's in there doing lines of coke. I get a quick hug and a kiss as Frin slips me a bundle.

Once Sly has opened all the cells and the convicts are lined up to get their food trays, he withdraws back into his office. He's the ideal guard—a cocaine addict wholly owned by Ernie Boy, a big-time, mob-connected junk dealer with the East Harlem Purple Gang. There is another count at 9:00 p.m. Sly doesn't even bother to lock us up. I make the count for him and he calls it in. He's sweating, agitated. I don't know what's wrong until Ernie Boy pulls him aside, calls me, and the three of us huddle in the hack's closet.

"What the fuck, Sly?" Ernie demands. "Where's my fuckin' package? You holding out on me?"

"No, no, hell no, Ernie. You know me better than that. The guy never showed!" Sly says and throws up his hands.

"What d'you mean he never showed?"

"I was there," Sly pleads. "I waited half an hour. I couldn't wait any longer or I'd be late for work. He never came, honest."

"Stay right here. Let me call this fucking guy," Ernie says and charges from the office.

Ernie makes a collect call from one of the pay phones. He comes back and tells Sly the guy got held up, but he's on his way—now. We go down to D tier, outside Ernie Boy's cell. Through the barred window at the end of the tier, Ernie points to a phone booth on the corner of an intersection nine floors below. "See, there he is," Ernie says as a guy gets out of a car and enters the phone booth.

Sly's blinking, quivering. "Wha' da ya' want me to do?"

"Go down there and get my fuckin' package."

"Ernie, you know I'd do anything for you. But I can't leave my post. If the lieutenant comes up here and I'm gone, that's it. It's all over. I'm fucked. I'll lose my job."

"Listen to me. Lock the fuckin' unit down and run across the street and get my package. It'll take you five minutes."

"No, no, I can't."

"C'mon, Sly. Wha' da ya' mean you can't? Don't fuck with me. I'll give you a thousand bucks plus what I already gave you."

"Shit, Ernie boy, what if I get caught?" Sly protests. "What'm I gonna tell 'em downstairs?"

"I don't give a fuck what you tell 'em. Just go get my fuckin' package. I don't want to hear no more about it."

Sly is tongue-tied, practically gagging.

"I'll give you fifteen hundred," Ernie says and turns to me. "Richie, go get the bag."

I retrieve the bundle Frin slipped me from the food cart. It contains a pint of Courvoisier, half a dozen Cuban cigars, and fifty $100 bills—Ernie Boy's money with which to pay Sly.

Sly shakes his head. "I can't do it Ernie. There's no way—"

"I'll give you two thousand." Ernie takes the wad of bills out of the swag bag and starts counting. "And a couple a' grams for your head."

"Oh, shit, Ernie, please. Don't do this to me! You know I want to help you. But I can't leave my post! What if the lieutenant comes up here?"

"Fuck the lieutenant. He's a moron, too. Lock the fuckin' unit down. Leave Richie out here. If the phone rings, Richie'll answer and tell 'em you had to take a shit."

I have to laugh at this. Ernie laughs, too. Locking the unit down and leaving me out to deal with any calls that might come from control or the duty officer is taking my position as unit clerk and elevating me to a whole new level.

"I can't do it, Ernie! You know me, if there was any way—"

"Okay, listen to me, you greedy fuck. Twenty-five hundred! And an eighth! My final offer!"

Sly swallows, wipes the sweat dripping from his brow. Then he bellows, "LOCK DOWN! LOCK DOWN! Everybody in the cells! NOW!"

He runs around locking the doors. "If the lieutenant comes, tell 'em . . . you know . . . I'm takin' a shit," he says and leaves my door unlocked.

This is insane. What, I'm supposed to just come wandering out of my cell, answer the cop's phone, which is a shot in and of itself, a violation of the rules and regulations of the institution, as the cops like to say, and then tell the lieutenant that Sly has gone to use the bathroom? And he left me unlocked, a prisoner in charge of the unit? That won't work. No way. I'm staying in my cell no matter what happens.

Through the barred window, I see Sly leave the building. He runs across the street to the phone booth, meets Ernie Boy's connection, and then nips back to the jail. A few minutes later he delivers Ernie's package: two ounces of un-stepped-on blow and a bag of Valium pills. Ernie pays Sly $2,500 cash, and we whack up the coke in my cell before Sly unlocks the unit. Ernie gives me five hundred bucks and half the coke to hold. He gives Sly an envelope with a few grams of blow and dismisses him.

"All right. Now unlock the cells and go back to your office and shut the fuck up." Ernie pats Sly on the back. "You're a good cop. You got a future in this business."

Ernie laughs, shakes his head, and looks at me. "Richie boy," he says, "do you believe this? It's the fuckin' Criminal Hilton all right." And he snorts up two little mounds of cocaine.

I don't understand why anyone would choose to do coke in jail. This is MCC, not Studio 54. Hardly a party atmosphere. I didn't much care for coke when I was on the street. After the first couple of lines, it's all downhill. But Ernie loves it. And then, on the other hand, there is something to be said for pretending we are somewhere else. When in the Criminal Hilton, I have come to believe, it's best to go with the flow. When Ernie offers me the bag, I do a couple of hits. You never know what might develop.

A few of the female hacks are running a prostitution ring. There is one who is definitely fuckable. I've had my eye on her. She has a dancer's body with great legs and a firm, round ass. For a hundred bucks, I'm told, one of them will stop by your cell after the evening lockdown and give you a blowjob. As the coke hits, that gives me something to think about. Ernie and I light up cigars, he pours shots of cognac, and we play poker until lockdown.

Once I get my nose in the bag, I keep thinking, *Well, maybe just one more hit.* There is some idea, some notion I can't quite capture, and I feel that one more blast to the brain might just enlighten me. I'll experience a breakthrough. I'm alone, I have no cellmate unless and until all the cells are full and they bring up more new prisoners from the bullpens in the middle of the night; then I am the last guy to get doubled-up. I've been here so long, the cops all trust me. I help them by maintaining the bed board, so they rarely shake me down. My cell has become the depository for all D-tier Mafia Row contraband. Except weapons, I refuse to hold weapons. To what end? The only violence I have witnessed in the time I've been here has been cop-on-prisoner beatdowns, as in when the goon squad invades the unit to do a cell extraction. Man, that's hairy, some kinda SWAT team shit. The cops march along the tier in their black riot gear, helmets with plastic facemasks, carrying shields and truncheons. They open the cell door and gang charge the recalcitrant prisoner who, for whatever reason, refuses to come out. They mow him down. Give him a few whacks with their batons for good measure. Sit on him, mash his face into the floor, chain the sorry motherfucker up, and drag him out of his cell. I saw that go down once with a very serious guy, a professional killer who was charged with over a dozen gruesome murders for one of the crime families. He was coked up and wouldn't leave his cell. The cops were afraid of him. So they locked the unit down and the goon squad came and got him. They beat him into submission and then dragged him out by his cuffed wrists.

The Criminal Hilton—*You can check out anytime, but you can never leave.*

Yes, I'm thinking, I'm so horny a nocturnal visit from one of the female hacks is looking good right about now. I have an X-rated vision of her kneeling on the floor in her correctional officer's uniform. I'm sitting on my bunk with my blaze-orange jumpsuit down around my ankles. Her cop head bobs up and down as she polishes my knob. Now that would be a step toward true rehabilitation. Hmmm . . . I have the dough, the five hundred Ernie boy gave me. Let me do another line and see who comes on duty for the graveyard shift.

After lockdown, suddenly feeling paranoid, I unscrew the towel rack and stash the bag of blow inside the hollow handle. Alone in the cell, locked up with nowhere to go, and already buzzed on coke, nico-tine, and cognac, I check my reflection in the scratched plastic mirror mounted on the cinderblock wall above the sink. I'm looking at the man in the mirror, but I don't know the guy looking back at me. He's thin and looks haggard, his face ghostly pale with a stubble of red beard going gray. New wrinkles have etched latticework around his eyes. He's thirty-eight years old and facing decades in prison. Perhaps the rest of his misspent life locked up. No, no, no . . . that must never happen. They wouldn't do that to him—would they? He's not a bad guy, really, just a fool who fucked up his life. You know, people do that. They lose their way. They forget about what really matters and go after symbols, illusions, myths they think will make them happy and give meaning to their lives. But it all adds up to nothing. Maybe someday he'll change . . . and become a better man . . . more concerned with what really matters. There is still time. He's been locked up now for a couple of years. . . . There is still a whole lot of time.

This jail cell is like a sleeper car on a train going nowhere. We are motionless as the world outside rushes past. Nowhere man is going nowhere, very slowly. He's a real nowhere man, sitting in his nowhere land, making all his nowhere plans for nobody.

To rat or not to rat? That is the question.

He has to think about it, certainly. Facing a whole shitload of time, nowhere man has to at least consider the alternatives. Escape? Tough but not impossible. The problem is you spend the rest of your life on the run until they catch you again. Become a stool pigeon and help them make a case against Norman Mailer and whomever else they want? It could be done. People do it all the time. Nowhere man just has himself to answer to. But what if there were children, little kids waiting in the world. Good thing the ex-wife had the good sense to refuse to have children. Perhaps she saw this day coming.

That guy in the scratched-up mirror gazing back at nowhere man was brought up to believe there is no life form lower than the rat, the informer, the snitch. When he was kid, as president-for-life of the Pink

Rats—the first and only juvenile delinquent gang in his hometown of Wellesley, Massachusetts—he and his fellow gang members determined they were pink because they wouldn't fink. Don't do the crime if you can't do the time. Hold your mud, motherfucker. Accept the consequences for your own fucked-up choices. At least get that part right.

But what if you are faced with *life with no possibility of parole?*

Can you do the time? You, the man in the mirror: *Can you do the fucking time, motherfucker?*

That guy unscrews the towel rack and does another blast of cocaine in each nostril. *Last one! This is it! No More!* There is an idea hidden somewhere in this bag of nose medicine—maybe even a revelation. *No, no, no.* Put the fucking shit away and stop! Stop thinking. Stop obsessing. *Impossible.* Just let the man in the mirror, the nowhere man in the cell, figure this out, capture the fugitive thought, and then we can rest.

Mailer. They want Mailer. Norman Mailer. For fuck's sake, give them Mailer and you walk. This is the era of government star-fucking in drug cases. Just weeks after Stratton was cracked in LA, maverick automobile designer John DeLorean was busted in a federal cocaine sting operation at the very same hotel where nowhere man was brought to ground. Mailer has long held a prime position on the Fed's hit list. J. Edgar Hoover pegged him as an enemy of the state back in the day when he was flirting with leftwing politics. *Radical conservative,* Mailer would call himself. Opposed the war in Vietnam. Arrested marching on the Pentagon to protest the war. Nixon had Mailer on his enemies list. Fucking hero, if you ask Stratton. Nowhere man loves Mailer like a father, like a brother, like a kindred soul. But what does the man in the mirror think? The guy who will end up doing the time?

That guy lies down on his bunk and tries to sleep. It is all here, somewhere in the whirling dervish of consciousness trapped in this cell: the key to unlock the door, the nugget of gold to trade for freedom. *But it must not be another man's freedom.* That would be fool's gold. No, there is a pure essence somewhere in this man's life that must be preserved to have real value and worth beyond the experience, beyond the physical, for the body dies and fades away, the spirit, the soul, the character lives on. And who is this man, Richard Stratton? What does he really stand for beneath all the posing? The wads of money, the dope, the women—who is he? The answer lies somewhere in the connection, the relationship, the friendship. What brought these two men together in the first place, Mailer and Stratton? An affinity. Both stood for something. *But what?* Honor. To have the courage of one's convictions. Yes, yes, we're getting there now. Courage, yes, certainly. Grace under pressure. "Look for the risk," Mailer wrote. "We must obey it every time. There is no credit to be drawn from the virtue of one's past."

Does any of that have real meaning when faced with life with no parole? Perhaps the answer lies in the bag stashed in the towel rack. Just one more whiff! . . . and we may have a revelation.

But, wait. They are counting. The midnight count. It's her! Lord God above, it's the hack with the great ass. She looks in at the prisoner and nods, glances at the vacant upper bunk. Counts. "Just you in there, huh, Stratton?" She doesn't recognize that there are three of us in the cell now: the outlaw prisoner, the initiate, and the observer.

I am the observer who is observing.

In a few minutes, the prisoner is back up, unscrewing the towel rack. This is going to be a long night. The prisoner sees the years stretched out before him like the white lines on a road through a tunnel with no end. That pathetic asshole with no future hunched over the magazine cover sucking up flaky crystalline white powder, and the adult juvenile delinquent Lucky Luciano Al Capone Bugsy Siegel wannabe big shot. Those two have got to have a conversation and a meeting of the minds. Between them, they can figure this out. For the answer lies somewhere in him—the fool, the outlaw, the egotist, the man who would be infamous, kingpin! Organizer and manager, boss, ringleader, gangster, criminal mastermind, pirate—that guy and the other one, the humbled man who falls to his knees and marvels at the beauty and glory of all things in God's creation and who feels crushed by the sight of those who have been expelled from the family of man, the lover of fat girls who wanted to dance with all the wallflowers at Miss Erickson's Dancing School in sixth grade, hold their chubby, sweaty hands, feel their gratitude in the awkward, halting steps, and make them his own, make them feel good. That guy! . . . The guy who felt bad for the girl in the woods getting fucked by a gang of stiff cocks—but not bad enough to stop it. And don't forget the noisy black guy who got his head wrapped with duct tape. No, forget them all, just run away . . . and duck the other guy, the compassionate one who has strength of character.

But wait, those two, if they can just put their heads together even for a minute, they will discover an answer to everything. Then the free-floating entity observing it all will take note, and finally we will have the essence of a workable plan.

On the soundtrack, J. J. Cale sings *Cocaine*.

She don't lie, she don't lie, she don't lie . . . cocaine.

Stratton sings the *Outlaw Blues*:

This is my story
This is my song
Can't do right by doin' wrong . . .

Now all three of us know what those lyrics mean. My whole life plays out before me in moments. There is no getting around it, I see the climax: I am a failure at crime. I squandered a fortune, blew any chance I might have had for a family and a decent, productive life. By the time that miserable fuck sucking up the coke gets out of prison—if he gets out, if he survives with body and soul intact—he/I will be too old and too crazy to start over. I'm lonely. I want a wife. Kids. A family. Say it again, motherfucker: *Prison is the loneliest place in the world.*

But that other guy is far from being rehabilitated. Look at him, asshole that he is, still doing the same stupid shit. His cell is full of contraband. He's still dealing drugs, even in prison. At this rate—the man in the mirror, the convict, and the higher self—none of you will ever get free.

One more trip to the towel rack and I am ready to face the Big Question: How did this happen? How did a well-educated, middle-class WASP boy from the gentle, tree-lined streets of Wellesley, Massachusetts, end up in a place like this? Charged with being a drug kingpin?

Facing life in prison. Are you happy now, Dick? Have you fulfilled your childhood fantasies? All that trash you watched on TV as a kid. You should have been reading the classics. All that devil's weed with roots in hell you smoked. You should have been drinking martinis. All that rock 'n' roll music you listened to. You should have tuned in to Lawrence Welk. Now lie down in the darkness of the prison cell and feel the shallow breathing, the rapid pulse. Watch the movie of your life play out in hyper-speed on the backs of your eyelids.

Wait. *I have it!* The answer.

Let those two fight it out, the convict and the man in the mirror. I know the answer. I sit up. I stand and once more face the man in the mirror.

There is only one of us here now. Evil weed, the war in Vietnam, the Kennedy assassination—I wasn't ready to suck up and swallow their shit then, so why should I break weak now?

This is only about me, no one else. *To rat or not to rat?* That was never the question.

Chapter Six

KINGPIN: A CONTINUING CRIMINAL ENTERPRISE

It is the Orwellian year of 1984. My mind is twisted. I am ripped to the tits on high-altitude Humboldt skunkweed, and soothed, riding above the fray on Sicilian white heroin.

That would be fine except that I am standing before Chief Judge Constance Baker Motley in federal court in the Southern District of New York. The government has charged me with being the kingpin of a far-flung dope smuggling ring that has been importing large loads of marijuana and hashish into the United States and Canada since the seventies. If convicted, I face a minimum of ten years and up to life in prison with no possibility of parole.

Judge Motley is a heavyset, no-nonsense African American woman in her sixties. She peers down at me from her lofty attitude on the bench. The Honorable Motley had been chief counsel for the NAACP before Lyndon Johnson appointed her to the federal bench—the first black woman so named. Judge Motley is a lady of firsts: first African American woman to argue a case before the US Supreme Court; first African American woman elected to the New York State Senate . . . the list goes on. And today will be another first: first time a pot smuggler indicted under the dreaded kingpin statute will appear pro se in her court.

"Mr. Stratton, where is your attorney?" the judge inquires.

"I let him go, your Honor."

She glowers at me. "You *what?*"

"I dismissed him."

Title 21, United States Code, Section 848 is known as the continuing criminal enterprise (CCE) or kingpin statute. Federal law defines a criminal enterprise as any group of five or more people. Where one of the five occupies a position of organizer, a supervisory position, or any other position of management, he or she is deemed the kingpin. The enterprise must be shown to generate substantial income or resources, and to have been engaged in a continuing series of drug law violations.

Guilty as charged! Yes, that description fits. But whoever thought of what we did in those terms? Criminal enterprise? We were just a bunch of hippies smuggling weed.

However, why let inconvenient truth get in the way of a good trial? United States Attorney Rudy Giuliani's lackey, Stuart Little, is upset. He believes I am determined to turn this prosecution into a circus, a showcase trial, a farce, like I attempted in Maine. He wouldn't budge on any sort of plea deal without cooperation, and in particular they want me to rat on Mailer. No fucking way. My double jeopardy motion was soundly denied, first in the district court by Judge Motley, then by a three-judge panel of the Second Circuit appellate court after a lengthy interlocutory appeal that delayed the trial for more than twenty months.

Yes, it took them twenty-two months, almost two full years to say: *No, you lose. Yes, we can and will try you again here in New York because the charges are different from the charges in Maine. In Maine, you were charged with conspiracy to possess with intent to distribute marijuana. This is a different conspiracy. Here you are charged with conspiracy to import seven tons of hashish from Lebanon to the United States and distribute it throughout North America. Different co-defendants. Different criminal agreement.*

True, but as I argued in my motion, the government was aware of the hashish smuggle at the time they tried me in Maine. All of the substantive acts in both contemporaneously. Therefore, it was all part of the same series of drug law violations. Hence, it was incumbent upon the government to bring all of their charges together in one proceeding instead of piecemealing them out as they have done, taking in essence two bites of the apple. Otherwise they could try me twenty or thirty times for all of the different smuggles I participated in over my career.

That argument the appellate court simply ignored.

Try the bastard again! Fuckers . . . Oh, well, it is theater, after all. And having previewed my production in the provinces, so to speak, here is my opportunity to take the show to Broadway, New York City, baby! Southern District. This is the Big Time.

"Will you be retaining new counsel?" The judge casts a quick look at AUSA Stuart Little. "Or are you requesting that the Court appoint a lawyer to represent you?"

"Ah, no, judge," I say. "I'm petitioning the Court for your Honor's permission to represent myself."

It is not purely drug-fueled hubris that motivates me to want to act as my own lawyer. Though I will admit the skunkweed I've been smoking and the tiny mounds of junk I've been snorting each morning before court are having a salutary effect on my state of mind. The cannabis high causes me to be endlessly fascinated by the minutiae of the criminal proceeding against me and to enjoy leaps, if not bounds, of perception that at the moment seem brilliant. At the same time, the heroin emboldens me to the point where I don't give a fuck. Yes, it's a heady combination. I stand outside myself. It's like watching a play where the main character looks and sounds like me but is someone with whom I share no emotional connection. *There goes that maniac, Stratton. He has such confidence! Now he wants to act as his own lawyer! Oh, man, what will he think of next?*

I produce the brief I wrote citing the relevant Supreme Court and Second Circuit Court of Appeals decisions granting criminal defendants the right to act as their own lawyer at trial, and I hand a copy to

Judge Motley, a copy to the judge's clerk, and one to Stuart Little, who closes his eyes and shakes his head with a weary *oh, no* expression.

The heroin kicks in. *Fuck him. We are not here to please this wimp, this government lackey. We are here to kick ass. Cause a ruckus.* The cannabis agrees. *This is a brilliant maneuver! They are totally flummoxed now!*

Judge Motley gathers all her judicial gravitas. "Mr. Stratton, are you an attorney?"

"Ah, no, your Honor, I am not." Nascent jailhouse lawyer, perhaps. And maybe the first person charged under the kingpin statute to appear as his own attorney—who knows?

"Do you understand the seriousness of the charges you're facing?" Motley enquires. She seems concerned. "You could be sentenced to life in prison without parole. Forfeiture of all your assets, and significant fines if convicted."

Heroin says, "Yes, judge. I have read the statute."

Cannabis questions, *Does she think I'm stupid, or has she figured out how smart I am?*

Motley addresses the prosecutor. "What is the government's position on this?"

Stuart Little bristles. "The government strenuously objects to Mr. Stratton representing himself. We see this as yet another attempt by this defendant to delay the proceedings and turn this court into a theater for Mr. Stratton's self-aggrandizing antics aimed at attracting publicity so he can promote himself as some kind of author or showman when in fact he is a sophisticated criminal with ample means to retain competent counsel."

Heroin and cannabis in unison: *Man, this guy has me pegged. Author manqué. Showman! Still, this is our venue. We are in control.*

The judge leafs through the brief. She is already familiar with my legal writings. With guidance from Ivan Fisher's office, I wrote and filed pro se my motion to have the New York indictment thrown out on double jeopardy grounds. I also wrote the appeal and the answer briefs submitted to the Second Circuit. I discussed my self-representation strategy with Ivan Fisher, who still represents that sorry fuck Biff. Fisher is lead counsel on the case. He loves the idea. He agrees that if I sit mute in the courtroom and let the prosecutor trot out a bunch of witnesses who will testify that I am the boss, the jury is bound to find me guilty. But if they get to know me, if they get a glimpse of my production and entertain it for what it is—theater—without me being subjected to cross-examination, I might just win them over.

Besides, I have concocted another novel defense.

"He cited the relevant case law," says Judge Motley, setting aside my brief. "The defendant is a literate, educated man."

She looks up. "I see no grounds for me to deny the petition."

Motley then levels her imperious, dark-eyed gaze upon me. "However, Mr. Stratton, I will require you to present to the Court in camera your theory of defense. With that you must submit a list of potential witnesses. I will consider your proffer before I allow you to proceed to trial. Do you understand that?"

"I do. Thank you, your Honor."

"I will also appoint stand-by counsel to assist you. Motion granted. Good day, gentlemen."

Heroin says, *Damn right you will grant my fucking motion, you old bag.* Cannabis chirps, *Fooled ya'!*

Two DEPUTY US marshals handcuff me and escort me to a holding cell. I'm starting to come down.

What the fuck have I done? The reality of the situation hits me as hard as the steel bench my skinny white ass is resting on. Now that I am my own attorney, I am forced to consider the prospect that I have a madman for a client and a lunatic for a lawyer.

Please, take me back to my cell. I've had enough excitement for one day.

Two years I have been a guest at the Criminal Hilton. Over two years! Most everyone else passes through, but I have moved in and made MCC my home. There is only one other prisoner in the building who has been here longer than me. IRA soldier Joe Doherty has been fighting the British government's attempts to extradite him back to Northern Ireland where he stands convicted in absentia of murder. Joe is kept in seclusion on Nine South, the supermax isolation unit. I see him occasionally when the doors to both units are open and we are allowed to meet in the sally port to exchange greetings and observations. He is as pale as I am, two long-term white prisoners in this multihued population.

My new friend, Frin, shipped out well over a year ago. But that was not the last I heard of her. She too was indicted under the continuing criminal enterprise statute, one of the first women ever to be so charged. Irving Berlin negotiated her plea agreement. No cooperation. She got the minimum, ten years, and was transferred to the women's maximum-security prison in Alderson, West Virginia. Before she left MCC, we had a last meeting in the attorney visiting room.

"I'm going to escape," Frin told me. "There is no way I will go without sex for ten years."

"Oh?" I said. "So you are going to break out? Just like that?"

"Yes. Just like that."

And she did. Several months after she shipped out I received a postcard. On the face was a picture of The Rockettes kicking up their heels. "Just had to hightail it," Frin wrote. "Good luck. I hope we meet again someday."

The US marshals' fugitive task force paid me a visit a few weeks ago, wanted to know what I knew about Frin's disappearance.

"Listen," I told them, "even if I knew anything about where she is, do you really think I would share that information with you?"

The woman made such an impression that, in my spare time when not working on my own case, I have begun writing a novel based on Frin's story.

THE RESIDUAL HERO in the heroin in my bloodstream wants to know: *When are these people going to get hip to the fact that we don't give a fuck what they do to us, we will not rat? That simply is not in our DNA.* THC elaborates: *We have drawn a line in the sands of time and the dimension of character across which we will not tread.*

Back in the cell, I break out the bag of heroin. There's that feeling again: *None of this really matters. It's all just bullshit anyway, their absurd war on drugs. Sometime in the future, perhaps before I die, this war will be recognized for what it is: a war on the American people, a war on freedom and justice. I am immune to their punishment. No one can hurt me, no one can touch me in my cocoon, my cell, the cells of my brain now happily embraced by the hero in the heroin.*

Here is how this happened, how I became a minor god in this ever-entertaining Hades. It was the other night, what may have been two weeks ago—I have lost all track of time. Only my court dates keep me on any kind of schedule beyond the daily round. I was in my cell, asleep in the early morning hours, when the graveyard-shift hack opened my door. Another prisoner dragged his tired ass in and took the vacant upper bunk. I rolled over and went back to sleep. This happens from time to time; I get doubled up. Then the new guy will be moved to one of the other units, depending on the status of his case, or I will move him to another cell, and I'm alone again. Which is how I prefer it. This is a really small space to be inhabited by two grown men. MCC is operating at 150 percent over capacity. Even the TV room has been converted into a makeshift dormitory. In this war on drugs, the captured far exceed the government's capacity to house them. New prisons are opening all over the country. America, land of the free, now has a greater percentage of her population locked up than any other country in the world.

A few hours later, I awoke once more to sounds of moaning and labored breathing. My new cellie was perched on the toilet bowl maybe eighteen inches from my head and taking what appeared to be the biggest, most painful shit of his life. He was sweating, his face was red. He might have been giving birth. He flashed me a pained expression.

What could I do to help? I try to be helpful, that is part of what gets me through the days—being helpful to my fellow prisoners. It makes me feel good. Necessary. With all my experience here, I can help new prisoners adjust to life in the Criminal Hilton. I do my best to assign them to a cell of their choosing. I've been here so long, I'm no longer just the concierge. I'm like the mayor of Nine North. My co-counsel and now confidante, Ivan Fisher, and I have become friendly with the gay Bureau of Punishment Nine North Unit Manager. I call him Harmless. He likes to act like a big shot, but he's really a pussy and would like nothing better than to suck my cock or have me enter him from the rear. I like him. He's smart for a Bureau of Punishment type. I'm sure the only reason he stays on in his position here is because he likes to be surrounded by big bad men.

So now I am also Harmless's clerk as well as the unit clerk. And that gives me the run of the whole rock 'n' roll joint. I get to travel around from floor to floor, unit to unit, on a special pass without a cop to escort me. This degree of freedom within the jail for a prisoner with my security level is unheard of; Harmless has gone out on a limb.

Getting back to my new cellie and the Big Shit: What could I do? There are some things one simply must do on one's own.

I could see he was embarrassed as well as in pain.

"You okay?" I asked.

He groaned. Then he reached down into the bowl and fished out— not a turd but a shit-smeared cylinder. It looked like a cigar tube only bigger, wider, bullet-shaped, like a giant suppository. I sat up in my bunk and immediately took charge of the situation. The guy was still hurting. His asshole was bleeding. As the mayor of Nine North, with this newcomer, whatever was in that cylinder was going to come under my authority. I would decide how it should be managed. This guy doesn't know his way around. If he gets busted with that, whatever it is, he'll be in even more trouble. And since he's in my cell, I'll be in trouble as well. I need to determine what to do with the contraband. I have experience in these matters.

"What is it?" I asked.

He seemed reluctant to fess up.

"It's okay. You can trust me. Whatever it is, I don't want to get caught with it in my cell."

"Heroin," he admitted.

"Ah . . . okay. Give it to me."

I took a roll of toilet paper and wrapped the cylinder, then washed it in the sink, careful to make sure no water got inside.

"How do you happen to have a tube of heroin up your ass?" I asked.

Turns out the guy was on his way into the country from Italy with what amounts to four ounces of uncut junk he got from a relative in Sicily. He was smuggling it in to give to another relative here in New York. But he got stopped at the airport and arrested on an old warrant that had nothing to do with smuggling heroin; it was on a credit card fraud case he claimed to know nothing about. They locked him up with the goods still in the internal suitcase.

That evening my new cellie was transferred from Nine North to the seventh floor. I insisted he leave the heroin with me for safekeeping. All those years on the street, urged and cajoled by Mohammed and the wiseguys to get into the heroin business, I had refused. I had to come to prison to become a junk dealer. Seems about right. With four ounces of uncut heroin in a place like MCC, something like that falls in your lap, you cannot ignore it. You must come up with a plan. I called a meeting with the latest Nine North resident wiseguy boss, known as Ronnie Las Vegas, and his friend and cellmate, Patsy, who is a junkie.

Patsy does not resemble any stereotype of the wasted, skinny, zoned-out addict. For one thing, Patsy is fat. Not obese, but chunky. Big shoulders and chest. Big, hard, round belly. He's covered with battle scars from knife and gunshot wounds, and his legs, arms, and torso are illustrated with crude India-ink jailhouse tattoos that resemble primitive cave drawings. He's been in and out of jail most of his life. Patsy is from the neighborhood, East Harlem, and he knows Ronnie

Las Vegas and some of the other wiseguys on the unit from the street and from prison. He's a knock-around guy, an associate, never made and never could be made because he's a flagrant junkie and a maniac. Heroin doesn't affect Patsy the way it does most people. It's almost like speed for Patsy. He becomes even more uninhibited and will say or do virtually anything when he's loaded on junk. He's a performer; he jumps up on a table in the common room and sings, does impressions of Elvis or Sinatra. It's like he's drunk but without the sloppy stupid side of most drunks. He's witty, brash, and fearless.

Patsy was immediately struck by the purity of the heroin and warned that it would be easy to OD on the stuff. Ronnie Las Vegas, who was a heroin merchant on the street, had some cut smuggled in and they whacked up the four ounces, made it half a pound. Now, for some time the entire jail has been hit by this blizzard of Sicilian white. It is like the place is under a soft, white, downy comforter. The noise level is down several decibels. Anybody so inclined is in that state where nobody gives a fuck. Even the hacks seem sedated.

A day or two later, I arranged to meet with my former roommate on the medium-security unit, Seven South. Ronnie Las Vegas got him a mob-connected lawyer and they posted his bail. I made two grand and kept a small bindle of the uncut goods to keep me relaxed through my trial. A tiny match head is all I need to start me up and sooth my nerves. Heroin and a cup of black coffee in the morning, a few hits of skunkweed, I tuck my file folder under my arm, and I am off to do battle with the US government.

My mother drove down from Wellesley to visit and left me a whole new wardrobe for court: a conservative blue suit, white shirt, muted tie, and dress shoes. No cowboy boots in the Southern District. Mother Mary is such a trooper. Does she question her son's latest mad endeavor? No, she's behind me all the way. Says she will be in the courtroom cheering me on when the day of reckoning comes. While in the city, she had dinner with Mailer. They both feel I am taking a huge risk by defending myself, but they understand my tactic to approach the jury on a personal level. Mailer has met with Ivan Fisher. They subscribe to my theory of defense.

Judge Motley, Stuart Little, and my stand-by counsel—a good-looking, dapper playboy-type member of the New York criminal bar, Robert Leighton—and I convene in Judge Motley's chambers. I address her Honor. "Judge, I must ask that the government's attorney be excused from this meeting. I don't want to reveal my defense to the government at this stage in the proceedings."

I love even speaking in this tongue.

Stuart Little objects. He feels the government has a right to know what I am planning. Judge Motley agrees but sends him from her rooms. She says she will review my theory and, if she approves, share the basic elements of my plan with the US attorney's office. It is clear we are entering new territory. Motley, Stuart Little, my stand-by counsel, and I are all making this up as we go along.

"Proceed," the judge tells me once the prosecutor has left the room.

"Your honor, it is my belief that the government was well aware of the facts of this conspiracy, and that they waited to prosecute me for a second time—"

"Just a minute, Mr. Stratton. I will not allow you to re-argue your double jeopardy issue before a jury in my court. You argued that before the Court of Appeals and were denied."

"No, that's not what I'm saying, your Honor. I will show that this is a vindictive, coercive prosecution brought solely to force me to cooperate with the government. I will admit that I was a professional marijuana smuggler, but I will show that the hashish smuggle the government alleges I masterminded *never took place.*" A lie, of course. "I will prove that the government created this case as a fiction designed to exert additional pressure on me, and to manipulate me, and to have me implicate certain individuals who were not and have never been involved in my illegal activities."

The judge looks to Bob Leighton. "What's he talking about?"

I answer before Leighton gets a word in. "I'm saying, this is an affirmative defense, your Honor. I'm admitting I was a pot smuggler, just denying this particular venture ever happened under my leadership, and also denying that I was in any way the organizer or manager of this fictional hashish smuggle. I will ask the jury, just as I ask you: Where is the hashish? Where is the evidence? They have no proof."

She shakes her head. "I'm not sure this is remotely plausible."

Leighton interjects. "He's saying, basically, Judge, that the government is overreaching, a kind of overzealousness on the part of the US attorney's office in an attempt to get Mr. Stratton to implicate certain government targets who he will assert and prove are not and never have been involved in his drug smuggling ventures."

"But he's admitting to the facts of the case?"

"No, no. Absolutely not," I announce straight-faced. "I will show there is no evidence this alleged hashish smuggle ever took place. I will leave that up to a jury to decide."

Judge Motley looks confused—precisely the desired effect.

"Do you have a list of potential witnesses?" she asks.

"I do, your Honor." I hand her the list.

"This case has been on my docket for years," she laments. "Are you ready to go to trial?"

"I am."

"No more delays?"

"No more. Ready when you are."

She shakes her head, shrugs her mighty shoulders bearing the burden of judicial impartiality. "Well, I suppose . . ."

"Thank you, your Honor. Thank you, Judge Motley," I say and gather up my papers.

"She went for it," I say to Leighton as the marshals cuff me and ready me for the return to MCC.

"I don't think she has any idea what she agreed to," he says.

We shake hands. "See you in court."

JURY SELECTION TAKES a week. I want to empanel as many Jews on the jury as possible. Since all my co-defendants and all but one of their lawyers are Jews, and since the main rats testifying against me are Arabs—Nasif and Hammoud—I assume having Jews on the jury will work to my benefit.

Out of the twelve regular jurors and two alternates finally empaneled, over half are Jewish. Good . . . and not so good, for they are hardly a jury of my peers. These folks are conservative Westchester types, or Upper East Side Jews, retirees, professionals, solidly middle-class. Not the radical dope-smoking Brooklyn Jews I would have chosen. There is no one more conservative and law-abiding than a conservative, law-abiding Jew. Hard to say how these good citizens will respond to my show.

"Where is the hashish?" I open with this question, and it becomes my refrain. "*Show me the hashish.* The government alleges that I imported over seven tons, fifteen thousand pounds, of hashish from Lebanon. And yet they are unable to produce even one gram of the alleged hashish. How can this be?"

I expound on this theory to the jury: there was no hashish importation. "The witnesses you will hear from, and the government agents and prosecutors, have concocted this alleged hashish smuggling conspiracy to try to force me into implicating others in a blatant case of government overreaching and prosecutorial overzealousness. I ask you again and will remind you as the finders of fact, ask them, ask the government witnesses to show you: Where is the hashish?"

In his opening, Stuart Little says it all comes down to greed. Stratton, the government will prove, is just a greedy pig who smuggled dope so he could live like a rock star and thumb his nose at the government, which, by the way, he is still doing as he sits here in this courtroom with his bogus defense.

True that.

In the government's main case, the most damaging evidence against the defense is the tape recordings of Biff's meetings with Hammoud and DEA Agent McNeil. In those recorded conversations, brought in to shore up Hammoud's guttural, inarticulate testimony, Biff talks about the seven-ton load of hash, about Mohammed, and about me, whom he dismisses as a paranoid jerk for warning him that the Arabs were cooperating. We even have the benefit of hearing him on tape ask Hammoud, "Are you working with the DEA?"

"Of course not, Mr. Biff," Hammoud responds dutifully. "Mr. Richard is crazy."

Biff then tells undercover DEA Agent McNeil that Mailer was an investor in the smuggle! Fucking asshole! Why would he say such a thing? Why invent a story like that? It could only be because he hoped to impress the agent and lure him into a fictional drug deal. Was Biff that desperate for money? Fucking guy received close to two hundred grand from the hash trip. He had to know the hash was all sold by the time he met with the undercover agent. Yet still he played the role of drug dealer to get the undercover to give him money. And then what? Was he going to rip the guy off? It is all so bizarre; I can't imagine what Biff was thinking. It smacks of some kind of subconscious desire to do himself in—and me, and all of us—to fuck us over and get everyone busted and locked up.

Biff is shunned like a leper at the defense table. Sammy and his father, owner of the trucking company and bonded warehouse where the hash was unloaded, and Fat Bobby, Sammy's driver—we all ignore Biff, we act like we don't even know he exists. Ivan Fisher, as his attorney, questions undercover DEA Agent McNeil and pursues the line: Did Mr. Biff so-and-so ever produce a sample of the so-called hashish? No, McNeil answers. So you never actually saw any hashish? That's right, McNeil admits.

Where is the hashish?

The prosecution then calls my Austin, Texas, real estate agent, the guy I call Herbert Humbert. Fucking weasel testifies he knew me as Paul Quinlan. And that I bought a total of three ranches and a florist shop through his offices, and that I paid cash. *Cash?* Cash. Briefcases full of packets of hundred dollar bills.

On cross, I could strangle the little runt. Did you ever see any drugs or drug paraphernalia in Mr. Stratton's possession? I ask him. No. Did Mr. Stratton, or Mr. Quinlan, as you say you knew him, ever intimate that he was involved in any illegal activity? No. I make the point that Humbert cheated the IRS and state taxman with regard to the large cash transactions he claims he took part in, and that the records of those transactions were fudged to mislead the government as to the amounts of money paid for the properties.

"So . . . you misled the government then, you lied, and you are attempting to mislead this jury now, is that correct?"

He's stymied. I point out that the overages all went into Humbert's pocket. The little rat probably made a few hundred grand. Does he expect to be prosecuted for his financial indiscretions? No. As part of his agreement with the government, in exchange for testifying against me, he expects he will not be charged. Isn't that good reason to lie? Objection. Sustained.

Okay, fuck Herbert Humbert. He doesn't really hurt me since I am not denying that I was a dope smuggler or even that I made a lot of money. And the jurors certainly picked up on his motive to testify and possibly lie. Next the government calls some guy who moved into the stash house on Staten Island after our crew moved out. Stuart Little produces a large clear plastic bag that he instructs the jury contains "sweepings" from the stash house basement. Those sweepings, a government chemist testifies, contain microscopic traces of tetrahydrocannabinol, THC, the active ingredient in hashish. *What?*

Yes. But, upon close inspection of the sweepings in the plastic bag, defense counsel takes note of a seed, and I ask the government chemist if he can identify the seed. No, he says, he cannot, not without laboratory analysis.

One of the defense lawyers asks, "Could it be a marijuana seed?"

"I couldn't be sure."

"Does it look like a watermelon seed?"

Laughter causes Judge Motley, who has been dozing on the bench, to rouse herself.

"That's enough, counsel," she says. "Move along."

"Does hashish have seeds?" the lawyer continues.

"I don't believe it does, no," the chemist admits.

We have already established that the young man who rented the stash house after Bobby moved out admitted to smoking a joint from time to time, possessing marijuana for personal use. The microscopic traces of THC therefore could be attributed to his droppings.

To me—and I hope to the jury—the plastic bag of sweepings is a pathetic showing. What, fifteen thousand pounds of hash and all you can produce is an empty bag supposedly containing microscopic traces of THC? Fucking ludicrous.

Where is the hashish?

The representative I met with from Bordo Foods, the legitimate company we used as an unwitting cover for the load of hash smuggled in mixed with half a million kilos of Iraqi dates testifies he did business with me under the name Richard Lowell. I facilitated an approximately 1.1-million-pound date shipment from Baghdad to the port of New Jersey through Beirut, Lebanon, he recalls. The bill of lading and other documents are admitted as proof the shipment landed in Newark on the date in question after a lengthy transshipment through the port of Beirut. On cross, I am able to establish that the war in the Gulf had made it nearly impossible to buy and ship dates directly from Iraq, which was why I had arranged to have the dates transported overland to Beirut, where, I establish, the Lebanese civil war created additional delays before the dates were shipped on to the port of Newark, New Jersey. I am also able to show that three of the seven shipment containers full of dates were escorted from the docks by US Customs agents, and that the shipment was given a thorough secondary examination at the bonded warehouse in Jersey City.

The prosecution rests. Mohammed's son, Nasif, is never called to testify. Word is he has returned to Lebanon and is being used by the

DEA to set up other heroin dealers. Nasif did testify against Tamer, a heroin dealer from Detroit, whom I met in a sit-down in the Bekaa Valley in Lebanon. Tamer was convicted and sentenced to forty years in prison. The government feels confident that with Hammoud's testimony and the tapes, they have proved their case against my co-defendants and me despite the fact that they have been unable to produce any of the hash.

As our first witnesses, the defense calls one of the customs agents who inspected the load.

"Was any hashish detected in the shipment of dates?"

"No."

"Were trained dogs used to aid in the inspection of the shipment of dates?"

"I believe so. Yes."

"And did the dogs detect any odor of hashish or any other illegal substances?"

"No."

"Then you are saying the shipment of dates passed inspection and was legally landed in the United States?"

"Yes."

This is actually not correct, though the customs guy wouldn't know it. The dates were rejected by the US Department of Agriculture as having had too high an infestation rate—after all I went through in Baghdad to get quality dates! We had to ship them to Canada where they were sold after all seven tons of hash was removed at the warehouse in Jersey. But the jury will hear none of that. Again, I am struck by how what a jury actually gets to hear and to consider as the so-called evidence in a criminal proceeding is in fact conflicting, often apocryphal versions of events that only approximate what really happened.

On cross-examination, Stuart Little gets the customs guy to state that the smell of the dates could have made it impossible for the dope dogs to pick up the scent of hashish. The defense objects as the answer calls for speculation. Overruled. The customs inspector also admits that of the seven containers and hundreds of cartons in the shipment, only two containers and perhaps twenty cartons were actually opened and inspected.

"So there could have been seven tons of hashish hidden in the containers—" Stuart Little begins only to be interrupted by Fisher's objection.

"Calls for speculation."

Motley overrules.

"It's possible, yes, and that we could have missed them."

On redirect, Fisher drives it home. "But you testified that you used dope-sniffing dogs as well in this secondary inspection, correct?"

"Yes, it is my understanding—"

Fisher cuts him off. "Your understanding? You were there, were you not?"

"Yes."

"You saw the trained dogs used to inspect the shipment?"

"Yes."

"And did the dogs indicate that they smelled hashish?"

"No, but—"

Fisher turns away. "No further questions."

BOBBY'S MOTHER IS called to testify as a witness for the defense. She establishes that her son had moved out of the house on Staten Island even before the government alleges it was used as a stash house. Not true, but as a precaution, we did backdate the termination of the lease to make it look like he had moved before we used the place to stash the hash.

The mother is believable, a good Jewish mother who obviously strikes a chord with a number of the jurors. In all the visits she made to her son, she says, when he was living in that house, she never saw any sign of seven tons of hashish. Her son showed no signs of a sudden windfall to his finances. He's a good boy, a hard-working welder. Stuart

Little objects when she says her son could never have been involved in anything like this.

Once again, I begin to entertain the dazzling concept that I might actually win this trial. It's like the Maine case all over again. The evidence against me simply does not reach the threshold of guilt beyond a reasonable doubt. One sees it in the jurors' eyes, the shifting of their gaze from the prosecutor and his minions to the defense table, and a certain softening of their stare. Judge Motley, Stuart Little, and the DEA case agent, McNeil—they all appear to sense a shift in the mood. I'm elated, high on junk, weed, and the prospect of victory.

Then, midway through the defense case, as I am gearing up to call Norman Mailer as my first witness, Judge Motley halts the proceedings. She excuses the jury, sends them from the courtroom. Then she addresses me.

"Mr. Stratton, I am not going to allow you to call Mr. Mailer."

"What? Judge—"

"No. You heard me. Furthermore, I will not allow you to proceed with this defense. I think this is a red herring and you are using it to confuse the jury."

Fisher gives me a startled look. I glance back at him.

"Object," he hisses under his breath.

"Your Honor—"

"I have ruled. Do you have any more witnesses?"

"Yes, but they are all being called to prove my theory of defense."

"Then I will not allow them to be called. Do you have any other witnesses?"

Stuart Little is gloating.

"Judge, this is not fair. I object!" I bellow.

"Your Honor—" Stuart Little is on his feet, looks like he's ready to approach the bench and kiss Judge Motley.

"You object to what? On what grounds?" Judge Motley demands.

"I object . . . to your ruling!" I say. "I object to this whole proceeding! What is this? What kind of kangaroo court—?"

"Mr. Stratton, sit down!" she booms from her lofty perch.

"No!"

"I will hold you in contempt."

"Your Honor, you have stripped me of my defense! I outlined this defense before trial and you gave your permission for me to proceed with this defense!"

"That's it," Fisher whispers under his breath. "Make a solid record."

"Now you're telling me . . . halfway through the trial, when I am about to call my first witness, that I can't go forward with my defense?"

"That's correct. This defense is inappropriate. And one more thing: I will not allow you to mention to the jury that you are already serving a fifteen-year sentence for your conviction in Maine. That will be unduly prejudicial."

"Prejudicial to whom? Judge, this is outrageous! How am I supposed to defend myself if you won't let me—"

"Mr. Stratton, I have ruled. If you don't like it, you may take it up with the court of appeals. You seem to enjoy writing briefs. Now, bring in the jury and let's proceed."

"Proceed with what? This is unbelievable. I can't understand why you are doing this to me."

"Proceed! Or I will hold you in contempt."

This is the way these federal fuckers are. As soon as it looks like you might actually win at trial, they come up with some ruling that cuts you off at the knees. My co-counsel are equally flabbergasted. The wind is utterly sucked out of my defense. Judge Motley goes on to refuse to allow me to call nearly all of my witnesses, including Mailer. When he shows up in the courtroom as a spectator accompanied by a close mutual friend, the professional boxer, former light-heavyweight champion José Torres, the judge banishes them from the courtroom, claiming their presence is meant to intimidate the jury. The next day, Rudy Giuliani makes a brief appearance in the courtroom as if to give his imprimatur to the proceedings. Talk about influencing the jury. Of course, all this is done with the jury out of the room. They have no idea what's been done to defuse my defense.

I am fucked. I don't know what to do. My theory of defense has been cast aside. I feel helpless. Adrift in uncharted seas. Can she do this to me? Fisher and the other lawyers assure me that I have solid grounds to have the case overturned on appeal. Yeah, okay, great.

But what do I do now?

IN MY SUMMATION, I have no alternative but to revel in defiance.

"Where is the hashish?" I declare once again to the jury. "The government would have you believe that I am the organizer, the manager of a conspiracy to smuggle *seven tons, fifteen thousand pounds*, of hashish into the country, enough hashish to fill this entire jury box. And all they are able to produce is *an empty bag containing microscopic traces of what they say is the active ingredient in marijuana*. Do you know why they are unable to produce any hashish? Because there *never was* any seven-ton smuggle of hashish from Beirut, Lebanon. The seven containers contained dates, dates, dates, and more dates. A million point one pounds of dates from Iraq. Exactly as shown on the bill of lading and the manifest and all of the customs paperwork submitted to you as evidence in this case. Submitted to you *by the government*. They certainly proved that seven containers full of Iraqi dates landed and were inspected and cleared by US customs agents using trained drug-sniffing dogs at the port of New Jersey. But they failed utterly to prove that any hashish was imported."

And then I lose it, and go ethnic.

"This whole case is preposterous," I declare. "You are led to believe that I, some WASP from Boston was the ringleader of a gang of New York Jews. Please . . . what, because some taxi driver from Lebanon who was caught trying to sell heroin to an undercover DEA agent says so? I think not. Hammoud—should you believe anything that man says? Why? He's *a heroin dealer*. And he never saw any hashish either.

It's ridiculous. I submit this whole fiasco is an affront to your intelligence, ladies and gentlemen. This really is 1984, when the government can concoct such an Orwellian case and hold a trial based on no physical evidence whatsoever and expect the good people of this jury to convict an innocent man based on what? The word of a heroin-dealing taxi driver who was set free to implicate me! No, no, no. I am certain that you will not convict me when the government has failed to prove their case. What they have proved is the lengths they will go to try to make me 'cooperate'"—I hold up my fingers in quotation marks—"to lie, to give false evidence against an innocent man."

Stuart Little objects. He sees where I am going. I ignore him.

"Mr. Stratton," the Motley judge says.

I ignore her, too.

I am veering very close to violating Motley Crew's order that I must not present my so-called red herring defense to the jury. But there is no holding me back now. No compromise. No middle ground. I am on a tear. The hero in me, if any such exists, must stand up and make himself heard.

"And, if you find me *not guilty*," I say and throw myself on the mercy of the jury, "as I am sure you will, based on the government's *utter failure* to prove their case, nevertheless, I will not walk out of here a free man. No. I will go back to prison *to finish serving the fifteen years the government has already sentenced me to for—*"

"Mr. Stratton!" the judge thunders from the bench. "Stop! Bailiff, remove the jury."

"*—for smuggling marijuana!*"

The jury is hustled from the courtroom. I'm still standing at the podium facing her Honor.

Her Motleyness is enraged. Her black face has turned a deep blue with fury.

"I specifically instructed you *not* to mention to the jury your prior conviction and sentence in the District of Maine!" the judge warns me.

She is seething. I don't give a fuck. I'm ready to tell her to kiss my Anglo-Saxon ass.

"I'm sorry, you Honor. *I forgot.*"

Titters from the spectators and co-counsel.

"I find you in contempt of this court, and I order that you serve *an additional six months* in prison for contempt."

"Thank you, your Honor."

"Sit down, Mr. Stratton!"

"It was worth it," Ivan Fisher says as I take my seat beside him at the defense table. "You got it in."

Easy for him to say. I'm the sucker who'll do the time—including the extra six months.

GUILTY AS CHARGED.

I am 0 for 2 in this trial game. It did take the jury a few days to reach a decision. Ultimately, it was an eleven-person panel that returned the guilty verdict—another anomaly of this case. Judge Motley dismissed the alternates once the jury withdrew to deliberate. But at the outset of the trial the judge had promised one of the jurors that she would be excused and allowed to leave town over the Jewish holidays. Despite defense counsel's objection, Motley ruled she would allow an eleven-member jury verdict. Yet another issue to be taken up on appeal.

Only Bobby is acquitted. Just goes to show, if at all possible you should always call your mother to testify. The judge sets different dates for sentencing. I will be sentenced last after the other defendants, who are all allowed to remain free on bond pending the outcome of their appeals.

THE HEROIN IS gone, the trial is over, and I am going through withdrawal. I can't sleep. My legs cramp up at night, and I lie in my bunk staring at the cinderblock wall. I'm constipated. I seem to have lost my mojo. I am afraid of what the judge will do to me, though I will not show it or admit it.

Mailer comes to visit. He too is utterly stunned by the outcome of the New York trial.

"Rick, buddy, tell them whatever the fuck they want to hear," he says. "I don't want you to do all this time for me."

"Come on, Norman. I'm not doing it for you. Fuck these people. They don't get it. It's a fucking plant. It will be legal someday if these fuckers ever wake up and get real."

My mother comes to visit. She's irate. No one can believe it. She says the old man, my father Emery, is taking it hard. He's afraid he won't live long enough to see his son get out of prison.

"Let's not give up yet," I encourage her. "There is the appeal. Let's see what Judge Motley does to me at sentencing."

In the presence of others, I keep up my pretenses. In the solitude of my cell at night, I face the harrowing prospect of the prime of my life being spent sucking ass in the Bureau of Punishment.

No! I'll escape. I'll . . . I'll . . . I'll do something. But no way am I going to do decades in prison. That must not happen.

SENTENCING DAY ARRIVES. I'm rehabilitated. Clean and sober. Got my wits about me. I've been working out every day in the little exercise area off the common room. I'm in love with the sister of an Iranian guy who has become my best friend here in the Criminal Hilton. His sister lives in Boston. She drives down with my mother to visit. She is absolutely stunning. Long, thick black hair. The features of a Persian princess. And charming. And she seems to like me, attracted to the hopelessness of the situation. So we write to each other; we talk on the phone. I write her poems. She sends me photos. Diana is her name. There is something tragic about her I can't quite put my finger on until I learn from her brother that their father was a suicide, hung himself in the basement. Then one day it is over. She comes no more. I stop calling. Stop writing. Hard to sustain these long-distance jailhouse romances.

ON SENTENCING DAY, I stand before the good judge, Honorable Constant Baker Motley Crew. Somehow, through it all, I sense the old bag kind of likes me. She makes it clear that she does not see why a man from my background would resort to criminal activity when, obviously, with my education, my intelligence, I had so many other options in life.

Okay, be that as it may, I say, and then I invoke the sixties. C'mon, Judge, you were there. The civil rights movement. The antiwar movement. I was a card-carrying member of SDS. Like you, your Honor, I believe in social justice and an American citizen's duty and right to oppose those laws that are wrong. And furthermore, I make note of the fact that possession of two ounces or less of cannabis in the state of New York is not even considered a criminal offence.

"What are several tons of cannabis but many, many decriminalized ounces?

"Judge," I say, "you sat here and heard heroin dealers testify that Stratton would never touch cocaine or heroin, that I was strictly a marijuana smuggler. Mohammed Bero and his son were never prosecuted for attempting to sell ten kilos of heroin. They are allowed to go free in exchange for implicating me. How is that right or fair? Surely you are aware that it is hard drugs such as heroin and cocaine that are doing so much more harm to our neighborhoods than marijuana. You were a product of those same times I came of age in. You must see how inconsistent our drug laws are and how little sense it makes to let heroin dealers go free in exchange for testifying against someone like me. This whole case, Judge, I mean, I'm already doing fifteen years! How much more time do they want me to do?"

Once again I detect that Judge Motley is feeling unsure of herself. The woman has a heart. And she is also known for making bizarre rulings. In fact, she is the district court judge who has been overruled by the appellate court more than any other jurist sitting in the Southern District, which bodes well for my appeal. My stand-by counsel, Bob Leighton, is beside me. He likes where this appears to be heading. The judge is feeling my allocution. She's unraveling and traveling down those mean streets with me, seeing the needle and the damage done. She's remembering those marches on the Pentagon. "Mailer was there, your Honor. The great man you would ban from your courtroom and accuse of trying to frighten the jurors into doing—what? Come on, that too was a foolish move on your part, Judge, and it will not go over well with the Second Circuit Court of Appeals, either. I may be a difficult defendant, willful and arrogant, but I had a pretty good defense going there for a minute. And then you rammed this conviction down my throat—or up my ass—by trashing my defense midway through the trial."

Now dear Motley seems to be searching around for some solid evil upon which to base her sentence. I wonder if she has even predetermined how much time she will give me or if she is flying by the seat of her judicial robes. Making it up on the spot. She is strangely moved, and a little nonplussed by my meditation upon the sixties. I love it when Lady Motley looks confused. She becomes stern, statuesque. Her black skin is as smooth as obsidian. She has a wide, straight nose like the prow of a ship, and high cheekbones as though she might be descended from some Ethiopian tribe. She seems humorless, but I bet when she gets loose and lets her hair down she's got a funny bone or two. Come on, Judge, remember those good old days, and don't hate me too much. Are you going to tell me no one ever blew a stick of reefer back in the early days of the NAACP? Yes, it's true, I am a spoiled white boy from the wealthy suburbs of Boston, and I never should have become a criminal. Okay, I watched too much TV as a kid. But, please, hear me: I was an outlaw, your Honor. I was selective in the laws I broke. I only violated laws that are stupid and anti-American to begin with, laws that never should have been enacted in the first place. These laws have caused much more harm than the cannabis plant itself.

Oh, yeah, yeah, sure, Stratton we have heard all your self-serving pleas and excuses before, too many times to count. The fact is: *You don't give a fuck! That is your real crime. You are defiant. You won't knuckle under and kiss Uncle Sam's ass. You have shown that to be true time and time again. And for that, you must be punished.*

"I will agree with you," Judge Motley declares as she pronounces her sentence. "I don't think that marijuana is as dangerous a substance as heroin or cocaine. And for that reason, I am going to give you the minimum allowed by the statute. *Ten years.*"

What did you say? Ten years! Holy shit!

A long judicious pause. A shudder and a fleeting gasp of relief. She gazes at me imperiously. And then she continues.

"However, I think that your sentence probably should be made consecutive for the reason that it might convince you that cooperation with the government is in your best interest; and so I intend to make your sentence consecutive for this reason: that is, I expect that you will reflect on your conduct since you are in a reflective mood at this time, and I understand that the government can benefit from your cooperation in respect of other people who were involved in this, so if you are interested in getting out of prison soon and really rehabilitating yourself, the best way to demonstrate that is to cooperate with the government with respect to this matter.

"Now, Mr. Stratton," she continues, making her intent perfectly clear, "if you decide to cooperate with the government in this matter, you have 120 days to apply to the court for reduction of your sentence, and the court will consider reducing your sentence based upon the nature and the extent of your cooperation with the government. So that in addition to the fifteen-year sentence you now have a sentence of ten years to follow that."

The final tally: twenty-five years, plus six months for contempt.

I am a bit shaken by all this. Ten years sounded great until the judge decided to run it consecutive to the fifteen I am already serving. As we leave the courtroom, I query Bob Leighton, my stand-by counsel. "That doesn't seem right. She proved my defense. This whole prosecution was about trying to force me to cooperate. Can she do that?" I ask him. "Can she give me more time for refusing to rat?"

He shrugs. "They do it all the time."

"BACK IN YOUR cells, *motherfuckers!*" the fat cop yells. "This ain't no *motherfuckin' hotel!*"

Ah, but it is, and he knows it.

It's the Criminal Hilton. And the time has come for this unlucky guest to check out.

Chapter Seven

A SKYLINE TURKEY

FCI Petersburg, Virginia, September 1985

Twenty-five years plus six months. Fifteen paroleable with ten non-paroleable running wild, and six months for criminal contempt on top of all that. What an unwieldy sentence!

Once again, there is so much to think about, and so much time in which to think about it. I need to come up with a new plan.

From MCC, at long last I am delivered first back to the US penitentiary at Lewisburg, Pennsylvania, to K Dorm, that transit hub in the federal gulag, that way station teeming with travelers on the highway of the condemned. There I get stuck again, kept much longer than normal as Bureau of Punishment paper pushers try to come up with a suitable real prison in which I am destined to serve my burdensome sentence. My security level has actually dropped, even with the additional time I picked up in New York, due to the now three-plus years I have been locked up. Instead of sending me to the pen in Terre Haute, Indiana—my original destination, known in the system as a gladiator school—or keeping me here at Lewisburg—an elite finishing school for professional criminals and my preferred designation—in their infinite wisdom, my BOP masters decide to ship me here, a day's ride on the punishment coach, to the Federal Correctional Institution (FCI) at Petersburg, Virginia.

I got lucky. This is a sweet stop, a mellow high-medium–security prison in the mild climes of eastern Virginia just south of Richmond. There are manned gun towers at the corners of double, chain-link fences spooled with shiny coils of razor wire surrounding the compound. We are subject to controlled movements; convicts can move only on the hour during a ten-minute period when we must make our way from the housing units to the chow hall, or to the prison industries factories, known as UNICOR, or to various work details, and then back to the cellblocks at count time. But otherwise I might be enrolled at an all-male college where the curriculum is an experiential course in how the federal government wastes taxpayer money. Waste, waste, and more waste dominates. Waste of lives. Waste of precious resources. Waste of time and energy. Waste of manpower. Waste of food. One cannot imagine the amount of food that gets thrown away here, enough to feed an entire starving Third-World nation.

For the seasoned convict, doing time in prison is all about figuring out how to get by and get over. You keep your mouth shut, you look around, you get a feel for the joint, you determine who has the juice, who controls the action, and then you make your moves. I had the best possible training in prison life during my long apprenticeship under my jailhouse gurus at the MCC. Like the song says, if you can make it in New York, you can make it anywhere. I am determined not to waste this weighty time. And with a shitload of time, FCI Petersburg is not a bad place to do it.

I live in a large single cell, practically a condominium compared to the cramped quarters I am accustomed to, with an actual bed—c'mon now, tell it—with a pillow, *fucking sheets!*— yes, brother—and a blanket; a locker for my meager possessions; a desk and chair; a ventilated window. Now get this: my cell has an actual door. We're not talking bars here, no sir, a door with a narrow, rectangular window and an actual doorknob I can use to open and close the door—except, of course, when I am locked in at ten o'clock at night until around six in the morning after the early count clears and they let us out for breakfast. When not locked in, I am free to wander around the unit. Take a shower in a shower stall. No gang showers to get buggered in while bending over to retrieve a bar of soap. (I love these jailhouse clichés.) Watch TV. Play pool. Sign up to use the phone. Can it get any better? Oh, yes it can. There's commissary. One can buy ice cream! Fucking Häagen-Dazs or Ben & Jerry's in several flavors. And sneakers. A tennis racket can be special-ordered. You call this punishment? Please. For a compulsive wanderer and guilt-ridden ambitious outlaw, this is an enforced vacation, a time to meditate upon my misspent youth, and try to come up with a way to make sense of it all.

AT FIRST I am assigned a job in the education department cleaning toilets, which sucks. Twenty-five years of cleaning up someone else's piss and shit. No, of course not. We can't have that. Nothing lasts forever. After a few weeks, my mafia connections from MCC get me a much better gig in the recreation department, working—if you can call it that—outside in the recreation yard. I am not required to report to my work detail until after lunch. I spend my mornings working on my novel, now titled *Smack Goddess*. I wear athletic garb to work, shorts, T-shirt, and sneakers. I pick up a few cigarette butts and then spend the rest of the afternoon playing tennis. What, you say—tennis? In prison? Yes, because we are at the inception of the renewed get-tough-on-prisoners mindset, a reversion to the pre-Attica penal philosophy that will soon strip these so-called correctional facilities of any semblance of rehabilitation, take away the weights and the tennis courts, end the education programs, and turn these joints into what they were intended to be in the first place: factories behind walls.

My days are unremarkable. Say it again: routine is the prisoner's succor. We live by rote. When not writing, I pass my mornings in the law library consuming legal tomes, digesting appellate court decisions, further refining my study of the language of the law, and looking for the right words to continue fighting my case. One must never give up. Persistence is its own reward. The soul lives where hope abides.

I live in anticipation of legal mail, answers to my various post-conviction remedies. The appeal of my Maine conviction has been denied by the First Circuit Court of Appeals; no relief there. The direct appeal of my New York conviction is still pending in the Second Circuit Court of Appeals; a breath of hope there. In the afternoon, I play tennis or work out with weights, do chins and dips, walk around the yard in the hot southern sun. I read or write letters in the evening.

LIKE PRISONERS THROUGHOUT this vast penal system, I do my burdensome sentence one day at a time, day in, day out, week after week, month upon month with little or no variation until one day—any day, a day like this day—there is an event. Something out of the ordinary happens. Someone does something unusual to throw everyone else's routine out of sync.

No one witnesses the actual ascension. Big Bird—a huge black convict well in his fifties—just appears there in the morning, roosting on the catwalk atop the lofty water tower in the middle of the compound. He makes a nest of blankets and parcels like a bag lady, settles in for a long siege with magazines and a portable radio, perched in his rookery like some daft old crow that suddenly moves into the neighborhood.

"Reminds me of when I was in Texas," says the Old Con at breakfast.

We sit at our usual table in the front of the chow hall. In the limpid early-morning sky the water tower is silhouetted high above the buildings of the prison complex. We can sit, sip coffee, and watch Big Bird through the window. It is an occasion, something to distinguish this day from hundreds upon hundreds just like it.

"Texas? When was you ever in Texas?" asks Red, who's done almost as much time as the Old Con. They'd been together at the penitentiary in Marion, Illinois, before that joint was locked down and turned into a control unit. They'd been together at Lompoc in California when that institution became a maximum-security penitentiary. They have seen the Federal Bureau of Punishment expand and morph into a virtual secret society with its own esoteric methods and mores, its primitive rituals, and its encyclopedia of rules and regulations. Red has been locked up so long his full torso and arms are covered with intricate tattoo work that has faded and sagged like a wrinkled old paisley shirt.

"They had them turkeys out there," the Old Con goes on. "Big old turkey buzzards they called 'em."

"You was never in Texas," Red insists. "Old fool's been in jail all his life."

"So? They got jails in Texas, don't they? An' prisons, too. Lots of 'em. You never heard a' Huntsville? Rough stop. An' federal joints. La Tuna. Bastrop. Seagoville. I got out one time in Texas. Went to work out there in a place near San Antone. Turkey ranch, they called it. Had all these turkeys runnin' around a big fenced-in area—jus' like us in here. All day they'd hang out in flocks waitin' for food. Then at night—I never seen 'em, but somehow they must a' hopped up in the trees, them scrubby little trees, live oaks, they call 'em, an' mesquite—'cause in the mornin' when the sun come up, that's where I'd see them turkeys, sittin' in them trees all along that big ole skyline."

The Old Con lifts his coffee mug and points out the window, and all our eyes follow back to the water tower. "Jus' like that fella there."

WHEN THE WHISTLE blows at 7:30 and the prisoners come streaming out from the cellblocks and living units and head for their work details, Big Bird still hasn't moved. Groups of prisoners linger on their way to the factories and stand around laughing and pointing up at the water tower. Word circulates with the speed of rumor. Big Bird, whose feet are so big his shoes have to be specially ordered, is an eccentric, wild-eyed man who wears trench coats or overcoats and a knit wool watch cap in the dog days of a Virginia summer, and he carries on heated arguments with himself, or he sings and laughs lustily as he walks about flapping his arms. A refugee from the streets of Washington, DC, he is forever in and out of prison, doing life on the installment plan. This is the kind of convict who in your worst prison nightmare ends up being assigned to bunk in your cell, and you live in fear not just because he's so big his hands look like oars, but because you know at a glance he's completely insane and you have no idea where he's coming from or what it might take to set him off.

He has a few nicknames: Camel—because of his loping stride and a hump high on his back caused by bad posture; the Strangler—because he supposedly strangled a guy at another prison. But upon his occupation of the water tower none seems to fit so well as Big Bird. The Punishment staff know all about him, as they know about all of us, and they treat him with the kind of amused indifference reserved for those whose names are on the "Pay Him No Mind" list with the rest of the malingerers, charlatans, and stir-crazy old jailbirds. With the recent closing of many state-run mental institutions, a host of these eccentric, aberrant types have found their way into the Federal Bureau of Punishment system.

As the compound clears and most of the convicts begin their work-day, I watch as two lieutenants stroll casually to the base of the water tower to see if they can convince Big Bird to come down and join the rest of us. By lunchtime the Bird still has not flown. The Old Con, a prison archetype who has mysterious sources of information and knows everything that happens not only in this joint but throughout the system, tells us that Big Bird sent word to the warden that he does not intend to jump. Groups of convicts have been standing around the water tower heckling Big Bird and yelling at him, urging him to take off and dive. But he has his radio, presumably the reception is good up there, he has some food, and he has his overcoat and his knit cap and a blanket or two even though it's early September and the temperature is still in the high eighties. He told the lieutenant he's just sitting there and come count time at four o'clock they can count him on the water tower. I wonder how that might sound when the count is called in to Bureau of Punishment headquarters in Washington. "We have one thousand eight hundred and eighty-one inmates in their cells, and one on the water tower."

"He wants somethin'," says the Old Con at lunch as we sit watching the distant aerie. "He ain't up there for the view."

The water tower stands behind the vocational training shops and looks over the rec yard and weight pile on one side and, on the other, the complex of buildings that make up UNICOR, the prison cable factory, printing plant, and warehouses where most of the prisoners work. They walk to and from the factories past the water tower day in, day out without giving it a second thought. I pass the tower every day on my way to work in the rec yard and never look up. Now it is an attraction.

As usual, the Old Con is right. Big Bird wants something. By 3:45 when the whistle blows to end the workday and the compound is cleared for the afternoon count, Big Bird has sent a list of his demands to the warden. The list consists of one item: he wants a job in UNICOR.

"They'll never go for it," says the Old Con as we congregate out on the rec yard after work. From where we sit we can hear tunes from Big Bird's radio carried on the evening breeze. He is still up there, like some brooding god pondering life from above the fray, his thick legs like logs dangling over the edge of the catwalk, his cap pulled down over his forehead, his arms folded across his wide barrel chest.

"His name's been on the list for over a year," Red says and lights another generic cigarette. "I guess he finally wised up to the fact that convicts been comin' in after him and gettin' hired in the factory, an' the Bird's name jus' don't seem to move up the list."

"Damn, that's pitiful." The Old Con shakes his bald, wrinkled head. "Imagine that—bein' too crazy to work in UNICOR."

"Well, they got a lot a' tools down there," Red says, his watery blue eyes watching Big Bird. "The Bird's all right. But sometimes he gets his ass in an uproar for no reason. They're probably worried he might club somebody over the head with one a' them tools."

"Whatever happens, I can tell ya' one thing," the Old Con says. He looks up at the Bird and strokes the gray stubble on his chin. "No way they gonna let him spend the night up there. Somethin's gotta give. He may be a nut job, but I can guarantee ya', these people'll come up with somethin'. They'll have that turkey off the skyline by the nine o'clock count if they have to shoot him."

Red chortles and waves a hand toward the gun towers looming at each corner of the prison. "Talk about a sitting duck!"

No one knows exactly what Big Bird is in prison for, but I know he's from DC. That means his crime need not be a federal offense. He could be in for anything from petty theft and cashing forged welfare checks to rape or murder. DC prisoners are farmed out to federal pens whenever the massive prison complex at Lorton, Virginia, runs well over capacity, which it does all the time. The DC prisoners are the most despised element in the federal punishment system. New York blacks, and blacks from Baltimore and Philadelphia, are quick to point out that they "ain't no DC nigger." Most of the DC blacks are unruly young men who've been doing time since they were kids. Many band together for protection and because they know each other from the streets of the Capital and from doing time together in other prisons. Like most prison gangs—the Colombians, the Mexican and Italian mafias, the bikers, the racists, the Puerto Rican street kids—in numbers they might make you tense with anger and fear, but individually, if you can ever break through their studied pose, they can sometimes amaze you with their intelligence and the complexity and depth of their character. Some of them know so much about the vicious world of street gangs and prison life and little else. They might be talented, daring, and enterprising, but they recognize only the scruples of survival. They come to prison not because they are failures at crime but because in their contempt for society and the law they are not trying to get away with anything. Many are functionally illiterate. They simply do not have the language to understand that they are as much the victims as the perpetrators of crime.

Big Bird is different. He's a loner and a mental case. Whenever I saw him before he took up residence on the water tower, he bounded around the compound with that lunging stride of his as though his feet were so big and heavy he had to heave with his whole body to move them, his arms flapping winglike at his sides. And he was nearly always alone and carrying on a heated discussion with unseen companions. Whites avoided his wide-eyed gaze and cleared out of his way. His homeboys teased him unmercifully and tried to provoke him. Big Bird would laugh at them with his booming guffaw that was scarier than any threats. He grinned at them with a mouthful of huge gleaming teeth that look strong enough to chew off your arm.

Only once did I notice the Bird buddy up, and that was with a kid we called Dirt Man or the Janitor because he ate dirt, dust balls, pieces of trash with the voraciousness of a billy goat. I knew that Dirt Man understood what he was doing wasn't normal because he would do it on the sly. His favorites were the old mop strings that get caught and break off beneath the legs of the tables in the chow hall. I used to watch him when he stood in line, waiting for chow, but really on the lookout for mop strings. When he'd spot one, I could see a little quiver of excitement go through him as he sized up the situation. He'd leave the line and sidle up to the table. Then, in a swift series of moves, he'd catch the piece of mop string with the toe of his work boot, drag it out, reach down and snag it, roll it into a ball, and nonchalantly pop it into his mouth.

Big Bird took Dirt Man under his wing. Dirt Man also wore a lot of heavy clothes even during the hottest weather. I would see them out in the rec yard playing chess, the Bird with his radio, Dirt Man snacking on debris between moves. For a while they even celled together.

The Old Con said Dirt Man was the ideal cellmate because he would lick the floor clean and eat all the trash. But really he was a sad case, and finally a couple of us grabbed the prison shrink, who was also a whack job, and asked him how they could let a young man walk around here all day eating cigarette butts and mop strings. Soon Dirt Man disappeared, which was also sad because then Big Bird was alone again.

And now, Big Bird is bivouacked alone on the water tower, nesting like some giant swallow. But I know the Old Con is right: somehow or other they will get him down by nightfall, even if they have to shoot him.

SURE ENOUGH, BY morning Big Bird has flown. There is all sorts of speculation as to how the cops had enticed him to come down. But those of us who've been here a while know only the Old Con will have the real story, and so I wait until he comes shuffling into the chow hall for his morning coffee, sits down, and gazes out at the now oddly empty water tower.

"Well, they negotiated a settlement," says the Old Con and he blows on his mug of steaming coffee. "Ole Big Bird, that fella's got a appetite. He ate up all his food in the first twelve hours of the sit-in. An' sure enough, come nine o'clock the Bird was hungry. Lieutenant tol' him if he'd come down they'd send out and get him any kind a' food he wanted. Big Bird said he wanted to know about that job in UNICOR. Lieutenant tol' him, 'Don't worry about that job now. Your name's on the list.' Well, Bird wasn't goin' for that. He knows what list they got his name on. Still, the fella was hungry. He needed to eat. So, finally he said he'd come down if they promised to send out and get him a Big Mac."

"A Big Mac!" Red exclaims in disbelief. "You serious? You tellin' me this fool could'a asked for anything he wanted, an' he tells 'em to get him a Big Mac!"

"What can I tell ya'?" the Old Con says. "Doesn't much matter what he wanted. Sure, that's what the fella ordered—a Big Mac. Said if he couldn't have a job in UNICOR, he'd settle for a Big Mac an' some fries."

Everyone at the table is silent. We look at the Old Con, who sits sipping his coffee and stroking his whiskers.

"So?" Red says at last, curiosity getting the better of him, though we all know the answer to his question. "Did they get him the Big Mac?"

Now everyone is laughing.

"Well, c'mon, now, Red. You know how that goes. Give one a' these convicts a Big Mac this week, an' next week you'll have fellas up there demandin' Kentucky Fried Chicken. In no time the *I*-talians'll be up there sayin' they want Mama Leone's pizza. Chinamen wantin' egg foo young. Mexicans, Colombians, all them beaners holdin' out for arroz con pollo. There'll be no end to it."

He pauses, nods sagely. "No, Red. No Big Mac. That ain't the way it works. I'll tell ya' what they did give him, though."

The Old Con smiles and sips his coffee.

"They give him a baloney an' cheese sandwich when they come 'n got his ass from the Hole this mornin', an' shipped him out to Butner, that nut joint they got over there in North Carolina."

Chapter Eight

THE GREAT ESCAPE

COUNT TIME.

Here sounds the mournful bleat of the horn announcing the 4:00 p.m., stand-up count. We convicts trudge back to the cellblocks from the various shops, factories, and work details to stand in our cells and be counted. The guards must make visual contact with each standing prisoner to confirm that they are not counting dummies or corpses. Once the count is complete and the number verified through Control, we are released for the evening meal. Usually this takes no more than half an hour.

Halloween the count fails to clear. I know there is a problem when I see the white-clad Food Service work detail return to the cellblocks. Ordinarily the evening-shift kitchen crew is counted in the mess hall so they can begin serving dinner once the count is clear. Sending them back to the units for a recount means the Food Service out-count is bad. Someone who should be working in the mess hall isn't there. Once all the workers have returned to their units and the compound is again closed, a new count commences.

"COUNT! COUNT!" the guards in the cellblocks bellow as if we didn't know what's happening. "STAND-UP COUNT!"

We stand in our cells with that practiced look of boredom and resentment that comes from being reduced to a number. Soon the insults begin: "These fools are so stupid they can't even count." It's our way of delaying hope. Still that lonely whistle that announces a clear count won't sound. It's six o'clock and we're getting hungry. The guards conduct a picture-card count. Hacks run around with a clip-board and a fist full of eight-by-ten-inch cards with our mug shots stapled to them. They check the face of the prisoner against the face in the picture.

"Name and number," the hack demands. He looks from the pic-ture card to my face.

"Stratton, Richard, zero-two-zero-seven-zero—zero-three-six," I say for the millionth time since I took up residence within the confines of the Punishment Bureau.

Rumors that someone has escaped spread through the units. As the guards become more anxious, our optimism soars. A prisoner is defi-nitely missing. The hacks are searching high and low. We fantasize that one of ours has succeeded in outwitting the keepers.

In the early evening, a party of administration brass and security honchos heads out onto the compound to check for breaches in the secure perimeter. They inspect the double, chain-link fence strewn with coils of razor wire arrayed with barbs that glint in the floodlights like a million tiny knives poised to cut convict flesh to ribbons. They survey the no-man's land between the fences—a minefield seeded with pressure-sensitive devices and scanned by electronic movement sensors. They probe the concrete footing sunk yards below ground to prevent prisoners from tunneling under the fences. In the gun towers that squat at each corner of the compound like octagonal lighthouses, guards with night-vision binoculars and high-powered rifles with infra-red telescopic sights scan the denuded fields that slope away from the prison complex. Then comes the heavy *whap whap whap* sounds of a National Guard chopper circling overhead. Beams of light play on the compound like spotlights signaling an event.

They find nothing, no sign of escape, no telltale irregularity. Still the count will not clear. It's as though one of our number has simply disappeared. We are locked in our cells and counted yet again. It's nine o'clock and we're getting hungrier and angrier.

"They gotta feed us," comes the gripe from the cellblocks. "Fuckin' jerkoffs! Give us our motherfucking food!"

Where have I heard that lament? Feed us! Shoot us! Who gives a fuck? It doesn't matter. Nothing matters. Except perseverance. Hunker down and live the interior life. Still, a man has got to eat. And some lucky bastard seems to have eluded our captors.

Evening visits and activities are cancelled, not that I expected to do anything out of the ordinary anyway. I'm enjoying this upheaval in the schedule. After now over five years in custody, going on year six, any break in the humdrum routine is at once disconcerting and welcome.

News reaches the cellblocks that the guards have torn apart the mess hall. I'm intrigued and excited to think that someone might actually have escaped. It is time for the nine o'clock count; we are still locked in our cells, unfed and disgruntled despite the hushed excitement. Again the count comes up short. Lieutenants, the captain, even the associate warden now make the rounds.

FINALLY, THE KEEPERS accept the fact that the rest of us have got to be fed. Teams of guards escort groups of prisoners from the cellblocks to the mess hall, where rumors run through the convict population like electricity. A ring of stone-faced guards stands around us as though we were persons of particular importance. Never have we felt so cherished. It is definitely a Food Service worker who has disappeared. The convicts serving the meal gloat as they pass among us while we eat and trade details of the fugitive's background and story.

I first noticed him at work in the mess hall cleaning tables. He was slender, a handsome man with skin like smooth, rich caramel, his features finely drawn and sharp as though his thin face had been lifted from a cameo. He had a wispy, adolescent beard and a shock of shiny black hair. His eyes were a murky brown like dark coffee. Some said he was East Indian from Calcutta. Others said that he came from Goa or Sri Lanka. I was told he had come to the United States by way of Guyana, land of Jim Jones and mass suicide. There are those who maintain he was not an Indian at all but was Guyanese. But it doesn't matter where he was from. He had escaped. All we needed to know was how he had done it.

A new man on the compound ordinarily arouses little interest. Each week the bus rolls in and deposits a pallid flock of convicts raw from jails and detention centers. In this age of mass incarceration and prison over-crowding, they are assimilated magically, absorbed like water in a trick glass that never overflows. Few are released. Many return. Only when the Indian began to show up on the weight pile, that hallowed ground of the confirmed convict, did I pay any attention to him.

He was skinny, evoking images of starving, Third-World children, and quiet at first, seemingly lonelier than most. The weights looked unbearably heavy when lifted by his thin arms. But because he was young—mid-twenties—his body reacted quickly to the exercise, regular meals, and rest. Soon lean knots of muscle swelled under his skin.

As his physical strength grew, so did the Indian's confidence. He showed up for his workouts in a white kitchen worker's shirt, unbuttoned and tied at the midriff like a calypso singer. He wore a strip of sheet tied around his forehead like a bandanna. Waiting his turn with the weights, he posed like a sinewy lascar.

His personality bloomed, and my interest in the mysterious Indian sharpened. I wondered what he was doing in an American prison, and I assumed he had been arrested for drug trafficking like most of the Asians in the system, mules, busted at airports with false-bottom suitcases, smuggling some drug lord's junk. He told me he was a Muslim, a soldier for Allah. I watched him pray in the rec yard, his head bowed toward Mecca. His walk became bold, nearly a swagger. When he shaved his sparse beard, I found it odd and wondered if he'd lost his faith. His smile broadened and he became more outgoing as he greeted the friends he was making among the prisoners. Gradually, his foreign look began to fade. He became almost American. As though to complete the metamorphosis, he took up running. I watched him lope around the track in the rec yard with long, gazelle-like strides.

Gathered in the mess hall, we confirm what some of us had already begun to suspect: the young Indian had rabbit fever. Escape, that obsession of the imprisoned, had invaded his dreams. We all long to escape. Our bodies and minds crave freedom like a starving man craves food. The Indian had done what each of us wishes we had the courage and ingenuity to do.

I am surprised to learn he had not been locked up for drugs. Word circulates that he was convicted of the uncommon crime of impersonating a federal officer. He was an imposter, a confidence man, a shapeshifter. The Indian had begun to implement his escape plan from the moment he hit the compound: first by building up his body and his endurance, then by cultivating an American look until, like a chameleon, he transformed himself into a full-blown federal type. Rumor has it that he somehow managed to steal a guard's uniform; he disguised himself as a staff member and then walked out the front door of the penitentiary.

It is the eve of All Saint's Day. I conjure images of the Indian at large in the free world, sprinting from house to house trick-or-treating, energizing himself with candy bars as he blends in with the rest of the ghosts and goblins. I am pleased to imagine him running free. At least one of us made it out of here.

"How much time was he doing?" I want to know.

"Six years," his coworker says. Hardly a harsh sentence in this era of lock 'em up and throw away the key.

My sources tell me the Indian's compulsion to escape was inflamed by a young wife. They claim he has three children at home who need him. I hope he'll have the good sense to stay away from family and friends while the manhunt continues. Getting free from the confines of the prison is only the beginning. Staying free requires planning and discipline.

Throughout the night the search continues. Staff is called in to canvas the prison complex once again. Because the secure perimeter appears intact, the guards suspect the missing Indian might still be hiding somewhere within the prison compound. Guards barge into my cell at all hours; they rummage through my locker and look under the bunk. I smile and toss in my sleep, comforted by their unrest. I dream of the lithe Indian, running, changing appearance, and running free.

By morning the stories have taken on a life of their own. Once again, we are ushered into the chow hall one unit at a time and made to eat breakfast surrounded by guards; we are energized by gossip. Most of us still subscribe to the theory that the Indian slipped away by posing as a staff member. It is rumored he had been spotted walking in town that morning by an off-duty officer but managed to evade capture. Many maintain he is still free, though some believe he has been recaptured and is being held in a local jail under heavy guard.

"So why are they treating us like the guy is still on the loose?" someone asks.

"Because they haven't figured out how he escaped," another answers.

Later, once we have been locked back in the units, one prisoner goes from cell to cell debunking the tale of escape by deception.

"This guy says him an' his two buddies sat out there in the rec yard and watched him climb over the fence," says the convict.

"Bullshit," someone objects. "How'd he get over the razor wire?"

"He just kind a . . . wriggled through it."

"No way, man. Nobody wriggles through concertina wire," says a voice of authority. "That stuff'll chew you up like a pool full a' piranhas."

"Besides," says someone else, "the guards in the gun tower would a' shot the motherfucker."

No one knows what to believe. The guards are mum. Even the most talkative hacks will not divulge any intelligence. Their behavior confirms the Indian is still on the loose, and his means of escape has not been detected, which means that the general population is to remain locked down until the mystery is solved.

They keep us locked up in the cellblocks all morning—except Food Service workers, who serve as the bearers of news, hearsay, and misinformation. By lunchtime we learn that a team of FBI investigators has arrived on the compound. After a cursory search of the Indian's unit and work detail, they concentrate on the huge trash compactor behind the mess hall. The smoldering cinders of rumor are rekindled.

Then, as suddenly as it began, just after noon on the second day of the lockdown, the state of emergency is lifted. We are told to "resume normal operations." Half a dozen Food Service workers are led off to the segregation cellblock—the Hole—in handcuffs. The smirks on the faces of the guards seem to say the Indian has been caught and he ratted out his accomplices. The rest of us return to the factories, the shops, and work details. Prison life resumes in the comfort of mundane routine.

Out on the weight pile, in the absence of the elusive Indian, we have his evolving oral history. I am told by those who claim to know him that his smile and easy gait hid a deeply troubled past. Soon after his arrest, his wife attempted to kill herself. She was hospitalized and their three young children became wards of the state. The Indian was not a confidence man at all but had been arrested for welfare fraud. The Feds were holding him on an immigration detainer. He was desperate to escape and save his family before being deported.

In a manner of speaking, he has escaped. But the story of his masquerading as a staff member is determined to be pure fabrication. I am told by those who know, that he hid in the trash compactor behind the mess hall—exactly where the FBI investigators concentrated their search. He burrowed his way to the end of the container farthest from the massive, hydraulic-driven steel ram that crushes the garbage into a solid block of waste. He made a nest at the end of the container, girded it with two-by-fours and pieces of wooden pallet he believed would resist the force of the piston.

Later, when the guard threw the lever and the wall of trash closed in, the wooden planks snapped like twigs under the immense pressure

from the compactor's engine. He hears the machine kick into operation, and he has a fleeting vision of freedom. But as the slow vibration
rattles his body, he struggles against the gradual shrinking of space.
Tons of garbage inch closer, squeezing in around him. His dream of
escape dies in the grip of panic. And then comes a vision of pure terror.
He understands what he'd known all along: that the wooden bulwark
couldn't possibly hold; that it never would withstand the crushing pressure of the machine. His spirit leaps. *Allahu akbar!* he cries. *God is great!*
I go to a better place.

He is mashed like a seed. Life squeezed from flesh like moisture
wrung from a rag. Teeth, hair, skin, and bone melded with two tons of
rubbish. The team of FBI investigators who went to the dump where
the prison waste is disposed found an inky black stain leaking from the
square of compacted trash as the Indian's blood seeped through the
garbage.

A few of the convicts claim the Indian was murdered in the kitchen,
dismembered, and then thrown into the compactor in trash bags. They
can't believe anyone would be stupid enough to climb into the machine
on their own, and they offer as evidence the Food Service workers still
locked up in the Hole as the investigation continues. But the Indian
had no known enemies, and in prison, even more so than in the World,
killing is rarely random.

One by one, these rumors are discredited as the suspects are released
from the Hole. They tell of having been interrogated about who might
have aided the Indian in his escape attempt. Because there is always
supposed to be a guard present when the compactor is loaded, prison
officials assume someone assisted the Indian by hurling him into the
machine concealed in trash. Others claim the escape attempt was a
disguised suicide.

We will never know the truth. All I know is that the young Indian
lived. Life animated his body. I know he had hope, but circumstance,
chance, and fate brought him to our shores where opportunity recoiled
and the doors to his future slammed shut. I know that he was lonely,

painfully lonely. He longed for those he loved and left in the World. He was bereft, as we all are in the crowd of the imprisoned. I know that he suffered, and not only in his slow time of death.

There are no other facts; there is no more history worth knowing.

Chapter Nine

COP KILLER

QUI CUSTODIET IPSOS custodes? Who shall keep the keepers themselves? A good question. Indeed, the more I come to know these Bureau of Punishment types, the more I have to believe they do harder time than us convicts. We imagine a different life, a better life. This is all they have to envision. They go home at night, yes; but we go to our dreams of freedom. They go home to the bills, the screaming kids, the nagging old lady. We retire to the solitude of the cell and the intimacy of the inner life. They have no excuse for being here, locked up with us, except the exigencies of making a living. We have the ire of the almighty federal government to blame for our absurd predicament—in custody and yet freer than our captors.

Recently I returned from a brief road trip and short stay at my favorite jail, MCC, the Metropolitan Correctional Center in New York City. One thing I'll say for the Feds, they don't give up easily. That red-headed twerp Stuart Little wasn't through with me. He and his master Rudolph Giuliani convened yet another grand jury, this one targeting my friend and mentor Norman Mailer. They subpoenaed me to testify. I was shackled and chained, put back on the punishment express and delivered to the rock 'n' roll jail, MCC-NYC, once more to dwell in my familiar haunt on Nine North.

But how the place has changed! There is no more Mafia Row. There are still wiseguys, of course, and plenty of them, what with the new Boss of Bosses, John Gotti, and the entire hierarchy of the Gambino Crime Family awaiting trial on a massive racketeering indictment. I met Gotti on the day after he was brought in. The guards treated him like royalty, and he showed them commensurate respect. The man exuded the charisma of a movie star without the vanity. Due to my previous longevity in the MCC, I had been asked to resume my position as unit clerk of Nine North. On the day Gotti arrived, the unit manager advised me that there would be some procedural changes when it came time for the orientation class afforded new inmates. Instead of the usual lecture on the rules and regulations of the institution delivered to the freshly incarcerated, Gotti, who was being held in isolation in supermax on Nine South, was given an hour alone with the other members of his crime family.

After the meeting, Gotti sought me out. "Richie," he said, "I heard good things about you from Angelo. Thanks for lookin' out." And he shook my hand. "We appreciate it."

BUT OTHER THAN the few high-caliber crime family clientele, the Criminal Hilton has been reduced to a Bowery flophouse. The place swarms with street-level crack dealers and crack heads, feral street kids caught with a few grams of rock and looking at decades in prison. A new federal holding facility has opened in Brooklyn. And FCI Otisville, seventy-five miles upstate from Manhattan, formerly a medium-security joint known as one of the mellower stops on the punishment circuit—that prison has been converted to a holdover facility for the overflow of pretrial detainees from Manhattan, Brooklyn, Queens, the Bronx, Staten Island, Long Island, the tristate region, and all over the Eastern seaboard. There is an entire unit at Otisville reserved for rats sequestered in the booming Federal Witness Protection Program, known in federalese as WITSEC. The federal prison population has more than tripled in the now nearly seven years I have been locked up. They can't build these joints fast enough to contain the glut of prisoners of the war on drugs.

Even my pal Harmless has moved on. Retired, they say. Sly Stone— he was busted. In fact, over a dozen MCC guards were arrested for a host of violations including drug dealing and prostitution and were marched out of the jail in handcuffs. I knew none of the new COs. Only the unit manager, who had been my correctional counselor, and some of the lieutenants remained from the previous regime.

During my stay at MCC, I occupied myself in the prison law library, searching for a legal loophole to slip out of having to take the Fifth before the grand jury and avoid getting hit with contempt time— "dead time," as they call it. Your sentence stops and you are doing dead time, time that does not count toward your release date. If they grant you immunity and still you refuse to testify, they can hold you in contempt for up to eighteen months, the length of the grand jury, and then they can convene a new grand jury and keep you for an additional eighteen months of dead time. You could be dead by the time they start your sentence up again.

In my hallowed tomes in the law library, I discovered a way out. My research turned up legal precedent for refusing to testify, even after being immunized, on the grounds that the US government cannot protect one who faces outstanding criminal charges in a foreign jurisdiction. *Yes!* Canada may be next door, just up the road a piece, but it is still a foreign sovereign nation. And I still have charges pending against me in that country. I wrote a brief to the court in which I averred that the government cannot immunize me against the Canadian charges and therefore I cannot be forced to testify. After a four-month stint at the MCC in the middle of my bid, Stuart Little gave up. They put me back on the BOP bus and returned me here to FCI Petersburg. The grand jury failed to return a true bill. Mailer was not indicted. I count this as a victory.

When I arrived at Petersburg, I got my single cell back due to my seniority, but I lost my sweet job in the recreation department. My name is on the list to get that gig back. Meanwhile, I work as an orderly in the housing unit. My "area of responsibility" as they call it, is the Red Section, the two-tier wing where most of the Italian organized crime guys live. It's an easy enough chore most days, takes me no more than an hour to an hour-and-a-half to sweep and mop the TV room floor, clean the two bathrooms, scrub the showers, sweep the tiers and the stairs. Then my time for the rest of the day is my own. Once a week I might spend an extra couple of hours to strip, wax, and buff the floors.

An orderly's biggest concern is which hack is assigned to the unit for the day shift. Each quarter the post assignments are rotated and we have to break in a new cop, bring him around to our way of doing things. The units are inspected weekly. So as long as we do reasonably well in inspection, most guards leave us alone. In the first week or two, a new cop may try to assert his authority, to show us who is boss— especially the rookies. But they quickly come to understand that this is our prison, we live here, we don't give a fuck about them and the "rules and regulations of the institution," and that without our cooperation they are the ones who will end up looking bad and doing hard time. The men locked up in this prison are serving sentences upwards of ten, twenty, or thirty years. Many have been down for over a decade and are winding up their time. We just want to do as comfortable a bid as possible. Most of the cops understand this and know better than to hassle us for too little.

Afternoons I'm free—as free as you can get and still be in the penitentiary. I get a pass from the unit cop and go out to the rec yard to work out or play tennis. Or I go to the law library and work on my novel or continue my legal research and post-conviction relief filings. The Second Circuit Court of Appeals upheld my New York conviction on the continuing criminal enterprise on direct appeal. They did throw out Judge Motley's six-month sentence for criminal contempt, however, which brings my time down to fifteen years with ten more years running wild. If I get credit for all my statutory and meritorious good time, and if I don't get killed or have to kill somebody, and if I don't pick up any new cases along the way, I could max this sentence out and be released after serving a little over seventeen years.

Fuck that. I have not and will not reconcile myself to their reality. I have only just begun to fight the punishment arbiters. There is still *habeas corpus,* also known as the "great writ," which translates from the Latin as "have the body," which in legal speak means have the body of the prisoner brought before a judge to determine the legality of the confinement. I prepared and filed a writ of habeas corpus alleging my imprisonment is illegal on the grounds that Judge Motley's decision to strip me of my defense midway through the trial, after she previously approved the affirmative defense theory I proposed, denied me the right to defend myself in violation of due process. It took me months to get copies of the transcripts to bolster my argument. We'll see how far I get with that. I also attacked the constitutionality of the continuing criminal enterprise kingpin statute. These causes can take years to work their way through the tortuous chambers of the federal court system, but what the fuck. What else have I got to do?

Then there is what is known as a Rule 35 Motion for Sentence Reduction, which Motley mentioned when she imposed my sentence. Rule 35 is different; it requires a district judge to reply promptly. Rule 35 motions are usually denied unless one converts and decides to become a stool pigeon. The pleading must be filed within 120 days of the final dispensation of the case. My New York judgment became final two months ago with the Second Circuit's ruling on my direct appeal, so I still have another sixty days within which to file the Rule 35.

My in-depth study of federal law has expanded yet again, gone beyond the rules of criminal procedure and appellate decisions to include sentencing procedural rulings and what is known as post-conviction relief, the ins and hopefully the outs of the myriad decisions on cases attacking specifically the sentence. I still hold to the belief that Motley was wrong and legally barred from giving me more time for my refusal to cooperate with the government. I ordered a copy of the sentencing minutes to examine the precise wording of her judgment in hopes of finding it in error. Again and always, it all comes down to words, the predominance of language in all things legal.

I continue to exist in two temporal dimensions: the here and now of day-to-day life in a confined world; and the imagined life of freedom in the greater world, a life I endeavor to rediscover through my study of the letter of the law. I can go for days and even weeks on end with only partial acceptance of where I am physically, as in my mind I wander through the complex dialectic of legal argument. I explore the lands of precedent looking to discover some solid grounds upon which to found my challenge to the mighty forces of the federal judiciary.

I rarely get visits. Mailer did come to see me once. He read the draft of my novel, which I am calling *Smack Goddess,* and pronounced it "promising." It is all in the rewrites, he told me, and he said of himself, "I'm not a good writer; I'm a good rewriter." He advised me to put the manuscript aside for a month or two, and then return to work on it with a fresh perspective. It's not easy writing in prison. There is the noise and the lack of solitude, the constant presence of other men or guards fucking with you for whatever reason. But of all the joints I've been in, here at Petersburg I have the most privacy and quiet. I have access to a typewriter in the law library and can work on my fiction or my legal case as I choose. I recently submitted a short story I wrote to the PEN Prison Writing Contest. That gives me something else to hope for.

Virginia is too far for my parents to travel to from Massachusetts. Truthfully, I prefer not to have visits, not to be tantalized with the proximity of loved ones or friends, then to go through the bittersweet moment of parting, and we are back in the prison, made to strip, have our assholes inspected, which spoils the mood of the visit.

My health is good, maybe never better. No booze. I eat a strict vegetarian diet. Plenty of exercise and rest. I love the weather. Yes, I do still traffic in the holy weed, and I inhale it whenever I can though always alert to the possibility of piss tests. Drug use is rampant in these institutions. You lock up a bunch of professional drug smugglers and confine them with an avid clientele of drug-users, people are going to figure out how to stay high. Many of the guards are in on the traffic, or they look the other way. If you are careless or unlucky enough to get caught, it's no big deal—thirty days in the Hole and loss of good-time.

I have a few good friends. There are a couple of guys here from Boston, one a famous armored-car robber from Charlestown who has become a close pal. And as always in the system, there are my Italian friends from New York and New Jersey whom I met and got to know during my long stays at the MCC. There is a Greek junk dealer with whom I play tennis, and an old-timer named Joe Stassi, who goes all the way back to the days of Luciano and Lansky. Joe has been locked up since the mid-sixties. He lives in the cell next to mine, and we have become close. He has crippling arthritis in his hands and writes with pain and difficulty. In the evenings I go to his cell and transcribe his letters and cards. He always begins with the same salutation: "Dear so-and-so, I hope this letter finds you well. As for me, I am fine. . . ." and so on. He never bitches, never asks for anything. The only comment I have ever heard Joe make about the prison staff is, "They treat us better than we would treat them."

And there are other diversions to break the monotony of prison life. Last Christmas, Val, my former lover, sent me a Christmas card. I called her, collect, from one of the pay phones in the unit a few days after I received her card, to wish her a merry Christmas.

"Did you get my card?" she asked.

"Yeah, thanks."

"How did you like it?"

"I liked it. Merry Christmas to you, too."

"No," she said, "I don't think you really liked my card. You should go back and look at it again. You might discover you like it more."

I did. Turned out the Santa in the card was made up of sixty-seven tabs of pure West Coast Brotherhood of Eternal Love Hippie Mafia approved blotter acid. For weeks after that I played tennis on LSD. The guards looked at us with curiosity and envy as we trooped in from the rec yard for the 4:00 p.m. count, tennis rackets tucked under our arms, drenched in sweat in our shorts and sneakers after yet another grueling day on the courts, and they wondered: *Why are these guys having so much fun?*

My only really tense moment here came one afternoon when a friend from Boston stopped by my cell and told me that a new prisoner had just arrived who was also from Boston. "His name is John Grillo," my friend said.

Oh, shit, no, I thought. *Of all the miserable, fucked-up federal joints in this vast Bureau of Punishment gulag, and that skanky bastard, that murderous little prick has to end up here, with me.*

I must have gone blank. "What's wrong?" my friend asked. "You know him?"

"Where is he?"

Do I know him? The cocksucker had a contract on me. He was hired by a wiseguy named Michael Capuana to kill me after I refused to allow him to shake me down. Grillo threatened to—and I'll never forget his words—he said, "I'm gonna cut your balls off and shove them up your mother's cunt. And then I'm gonna kill you." And now here he was in the same prison.

There was only one thing for me to do: I had to confront Grillo immediately. That's the thing about prison—there is nowhere to run, nowhere to hide. If I were to show even the least bit of fear, Grillo would take that as weakness and act on it. I had to go to him right away and see where we stood. If I were a real convict, I would take a weapon and kill him for the insult all those years ago. I would not let him get by. I would take a shank or a club and stab him or beat him to death on the spot.

But I am not a real convict. No, I am a man caught in this world within the World, and one who is determined to beat this sentence, to beat the system, to get out and to reclaim what is left to my life. I can't do that and murder John Grillo.

I found Grillo in the yard. He was sitting on the ground leaning against an inner fence and smoking a cigarette. He looked exactly as I remembered him: skinny, ferret-like; but utterly dangerous in that you could just read the man is a killer. Sneaky. Treacherous. Homicidal. I stood over him, looked down and said, "You recognize me?"

"Yeah," he said, "Richie Stratton. I heard you was here."

"Do we have a problem?" I asked.

Grillo laughed. He stubbed out his cigarette and said, "What problem? You mean Capuana? Fuck that guy. He fucked me. He fucked everybody. Listen, let me tell you what Capuana did."

He went on to tell me a horrendous story about Mike Capuana, rhymes with marijuana. Capuana was a budding wiseguy who would be the prince of pot. He tried to shake me down for a million bucks for protection, and he wanted half of every load of hashish I brought in through Logan Airport. I defied him, told him thanks but no thanks, and then I spirited a load of hash out of the airport without paying Capuana. Capuana was going to pay John Grillo to kill me. Whitey Bulger, the reigning boss of the Boston Irish mob, was receiving kickback payments from the freight handlers at the airport who cleared my loads. When I appealed to Whitey, he stepped in and told Capuana to back off. The contract was lifted. Mike Capuana, Grillo tells me, bought a horse farm down on the Massachusetts South Shore somewhere, and when he ran short of money he failed to pay the guy who was taking care of the animals. The horses starved. Capuana killed the guy who was looking after the place—or he had John Grillo kill him, I wasn't sure which. But Grillo claimed he hated Capuana for it.

That passed. I never felt remotely comfortable around John Grillo. I could never forget his threats, and I believe he still would have killed me if someone paid him to do it. But we made peace. He got out a year or so later. I heard through the ever-reliable prison grapevine that Grillo was shot to death while sitting in his car outside a diner in Revere, Massachusetts. Capuana too disappeared and was presumed dead.

RIP John Grillo. Adios Capuana. Good riddance to you both.

Speaking of murder, some time ago—again, I lose track of time—must be about six months ago, I got called to the lieutenant's office. The lieutenant informed me that there were two FBI agents at the prison who wanted to speak to me. I could have refused and asked to speak to a lawyer, but I was curious. What, I wondered, could they possibly want with me after all the time I had been locked up?

"What about?" I asked the lieutenant.

"A homicide," he told me.

Fred is dead. Dead Fred. Yes, my old pal Fred Barnswallow, who testified against me at trial in Maine. Fred took two slugs in the head. Or maybe it was one, I don't know. The FBI was involved because dead Fred had been a federal witness. He did a couple of years and then was released. From what I was told, he went right back to his old stomping grounds in Southern Maine. One night—or maybe it was afternoon—someone shot him and killed him. His body was found in a clump of bushes beside a parking lot. The FBI was working on the theory that I ordered the hit from prison. They are still operating under the delusion that I am some hippie mob boss who can command my minions to kill even after years in custody. I told them that they should convene a grand jury and attempt to indict me if they really believed I was capable of ordering the hit. I think they were on a fishing expedition. They wanted to know who I thought might have had Freddy killed. Of course, I have my suspicions. Then they asked if I would be willing to take a polygraph test.

I declined. For all they would have to ask is if I had any idea who might have killed Fred, or who ordered the hit to cause the needle to begin waving. It's like DEA Special Agent Bernie Wolfshein said: this isn't child's play. People go to prison. People are murdered. Some people go to prison, they get out, and then they are murdered.

Next thing I knew I was getting calls from the press in Portland, Maine. My only comment: "Karma has a way of catching up with you."

Poor Freddy. Did I order his killing? Hell, no. Why should I? I liked Fred. Using him to help me stash that huge load of Colombian pot was my mistake. I knew he was strung out on blow, and I knew he got his coke from my Colombian ex-girlfriend. I never should have been doing business with Fred in the first place. That was my mistake, going against my own rules. I felt bad when the agents killed Fred's dog. His testimony at trial in Maine didn't really hurt me. It was that other fucker, Mild Bill, that Abraham Lincoln look-alike who buried me. But I hold no grudge against any of them. Hammoud. Nasif. Biff. That rodent Herbert Humbert, the real estate agent. Fuck them all. They did what they chose to do. I chose not to become a rat and to do the time. And I'm still doing it: Time. Time . . . and more time . . . one day at a time.

Now, you see, I have figured it out. I don't need to kill people. Why? They have no power over me. I need only to pursue my study of the law and get my ass out of prison, give the Feds back this illegal and cumbersome sentence. Maybe my life here is not so bad, but it is still prison. The worst thing about prison, as I've said before, and I'll say again, is that it's lonely. It is so *fucking* lonely. Brutally lonely, especially for a man who loves the company of women. Yes, you make friends. I have made some strong friendships with people I would never have met, and probably never would have wanted to meet. And I've learned a lot about men from all strata of society. But at the end of the day, life in prison is as lonely as the tomb. You are cut off from the people you love, cut off from the real world and real life; and that is the punishment. Imprisonment is not legally meant to be a tactic used to get people to roll over and become rats—even though that is exactly what incarceration has become in the hands of the Feds.

AND SO IT goes. Shit happens. Convicts die. They climb water towers or get squashed in the trash compactor. A guy who celled near me recently died of lung cancer. He had been complaining of pain in his back for months. One morning he failed to report for work. They found him dead in his bunk. Another guy in a different unit got sliced up badly by some dude wielding a shank made by sticking a razor blade in the melted handle of a toothbrush; he nearly bled to death. Occasionally someone gets released on parole or mandatory release upon having maxed-out his sentence. Guys come back after violating parole or picking up a new case. The bus arrives with twenty or thirty fresh convicts and not enough cells to accommodate them. For a time, they set up bunks in the TV rooms and put mattresses on the floors of the single cells and doubled them up. But then they opened a couple of new federal joints somewhere and shipped a bunch of convicts out. Life, such as it is, goes on.

I think we all know, however—we sense it, we feel it, we see it, and we anticipate it—as the new day-watch hack, one Shindola Murphy, shambles onto the unit to report for work, that our lives are about to change and it will not be for the better.

That Shindola is a rookie cop is obvious. We can see he's as green as unripened fruit, having recently completed the three-week course "Introduction to Correctional Techniques" at the Punishment Staff Training Academy in Glynco, Georgia. We can tell by the way he carries himself and by how he relates to us convicts. This is his first assignment to an actual unit at a real prison, and we are his first live prisoners. He is still steeped in the philosophy of corrections—more accurately, punishment—and the "rules and regulations of the institution," which is how his superiors have instructed him to control us convicts and run a clean and orderly unit.

He's a black man, Shindola, with dark, dusty-looking, pitted skin like the surface of an old parking lot. At least sixty percent of the prisoner population in this institution is made up of black men. Because of its proximity to the District of Columbia, FCI Petersburg has a disproportionately large number of DC blacks doing time in this joint. These men do not give a fuck. Many of them are physical specimens: tall, strapping, lean and muscled, tough and fearless. They have survived some of the worst ghettos in our nation and the most dangerous jails. Not so Shindola. Shindola is a country boy, that's apparent from the way he walks and the way he talks. He's short, with abnormally long arms. He has the physique of a Hottentot, with a potbelly hanging over his belt and a big, protruding round ass. He's ugly. He has a low, sloping brow, sunken eyes in a small skull, and a sparse crop of whiskers on his lantern jaw. He's difficult to understand even for the other blacks. He doesn't so much talk as emit loud, unintelligible grunts when he wants something. The convicts have taken to calling him "Murph the Smurf."

None of this would matter to me. Shindola and I could get along just fine, except that he is obdurate, stubborn as a goat. He may even be pitifully stupid; it's hard to tell. He simply will not accept that no matter what they may have taught him at Glynco, and regardless of what his lieutenants and the captain and the associate wardens may tell him, everyone else except him understands that all that crap is theory and only written or stated procedure, whereas what he's faced with now is the practical, real-life, day-to-day application of rules and regulations designed to govern a body of men who have distinguished themselves by refusing to obey the law.

I wish I could sit the Smurf down and tell him to relax, let him know how simple it is to get along with us and how it has nothing to do with us wanting to make him look bad. It is all about mutual respect. However, if he insists on fucking with us, he will regret it. He seems to have taken exceptional resentment to me, which is too bad, really, because of all the men in this unit I probably feel more compassion for Shindola than the rest because I want to get along with him. It will make my job as unit orderly easier. But it goes deeper than that: I feel sorry for Shindola. I can see in his eyes and I can sense in his manner that he is afraid of us. He does not want to be here any more than any of us want to be here. But he simply does not have the imagination to perceive how to get along with men over whom he has authority only in as much as we allow him. Stronger men, smarter men, better looking men, more daring and more dangerous men—but men who nevertheless are prisoners and who are therefore at once powerless and powerful—powerless to change our circumstances but powerful in that we have nothing to lose.

Maybe Shindola resents me because I am white and apparently well-educated, the resident jailhouse lawyer in this unit, and I seem to have it so easy, done with my grunt work in a couple of hours each day and then free to play or busy myself writing whereas he must put in a full, demanding eight hours and often more on overtime. I understand that and, again, I would be happy to make peace with Shindola. I would tell him how lonely I am most of the time. I would confess how I miss my loved ones so much that I ache and confide how uncertain I am of my future. I would admit that I dwell on whether I will ever have another wife and a family to love and to love me, children of my own to raise, and how I worry about how warped and crazy I might be, and if my parents will still be alive and even recognize me by the time I get out of prison—if I ever get out. I could talk to him about how difficult it is to actually make it through a long sentence and get free as there is just so much that can go wrong, and how it changes your character, how you become a different person after so many years of living in these prisons. Or I could commiserate and confess how ashamed I am of how I fucked up my life, how much guilt I feel over all the hurt and wrong I did, particularly to the women with whom I became intimate. There is so much I could say to Shindola, we could embrace and laugh and weep in each other's arms.

Yeah, right. I would just as soon strangle the stupid cocksucker.

Here he comes, headed straight for my cell long after my work has been done and the Red Section passed inspection with high marks, and who gives a shit anyway? Shindola does, and that's his problem. He doesn't get it that nobody really cares. Fuck the Red Section. Okay? Fuck this prison. Fuck the Bureau of Punishment. Just leave us the fuck alone. I have work to do and it has nothing to do with anything except how to get the fuck out of doing all these years in prison.

The Smurf is dragging a garbage bag full of what is known as "nuisance contraband": extra books, extra sets of underwear, unauthorized food stolen from the kitchen, pornography, nude pictures of your girl-friend or your wife—whatever, it is all bullshit. But Shindola has taken to implementing the regulation that calls for shaking down the cells in the housing units twice weekly and confiscating any unauthorized items, as per the rules and regulations no one else follows. Shakedowns are roughly equivalent to having one's home ransacked, and being made to stand there and watch. The cops take a perverse delight in vio-lating us yet again. It's not enough that they can look up our assholes any time they please. A cell shakedown is an invasion of what little privacy we have, and it's upsetting, particularly when you always pos-sess an excess of "nuisance contraband" as well as bigger, more serious unauthorized items that are ripe for confiscation.

"Shakedown," Shindola mumbles and invites me to stand outside the cell while he goes through my possessions.

"C'mon, Murphy. Leave me alone."

"Shakedown," he repeats. "Step outside."

I get up from my desk, where I have in plain sight a serious unau-thorized item—a typewriter, and not just a typewriter, an IBM Selec-tric typewriter. I also have more than the specified number of books. I have maybe twelve or fifteen books, whereas the rules and regulations of the institution stipulate that inmates are allowed no more than nine books in their cells. I have cardboard cartons stuffed with legal papers and my manuscripts stacked at the end of my bunk—that might be a violation of some rule as well, a fire hazard. I have three or four sets of underwear over the three-set limit. Some contraband food, oranges, an apple or two. You know, whatever, it's all petty shit—except for the typewriter. That is an extraordinary piece of contraband. No one has such a machine in his cell. Be assured, the really serious contra-band—the kind that could get me a "shot," a write-up and time in the Hole, and possibly a new drug-trafficking charge—the two ounces of high-altitude Humbolt weed I have smuggled into the institution every fortnight by a corrupt lady staff member who works in UNICOR. That contraband is well stashed in one of the prison factories, and it will never be discovered by Shindola or by anyone else. And the cash money I get from selling most of the weed gets transferred street to street. A money order shows up in my commissary account, and no one is the wiser. It's business as usual. The Shindola Murphys of the Federal Punishment Bureau will never penetrate and never shut down that level of violation of their rules and regulations. We are, after all, professional criminals.

"Stratton," he calls me back into the cell.

"What's up, Murphy?"

"Where'd you get that typewriter?"

Shindola's been on the unit now for about three weeks, inspected my cell half a dozen times, seized all manner of nuisance contraband, and this is the first time he's noticed that I have a large IBM Selectric typewriter sitting on my desk.

"What typewriter?" I ask, fucking with him.

"That one right there," he points to the Selectric. The guy has no sense of humor.

"Don't worry about it," I tell him. "It's authorized."

A lie, but one I figure I can get over on with the Smurf. Actually, some convicts stole the typewriter from the safety department. They smuggled it into this unit and gave it to me in exchange for an ounce of weed. I use the machine to type up my own briefs as well as the various pleadings I have submitted to different courts on behalf of six or seven convicts for whom I am doing legal work. I use it to type up my stories after I write them out in longhand on yellow legal pads. I have had the typewriter for at least six months, through two different unit officer regimes and any number of shakedowns. The cops just figure that if I have the thing, and it's so obvious, just sitting out on my desk where anyone can see it, then it must be authorized.

"Who authorized it?"

"Who authorized what?"

He's getting frustrated. I can tell by the way his shoulders start to twitch and his head bobs. He stammers and looks around nervously.

He knows I'm fucking with him, and he's not happy about it, but not sure what to do.

"Look, Murphy, forget about it," I tell him. "The typewriter is authorized. Ask anybody. Everything's cool. We're okay here. . . . Nothing to worry about."

He grunts and moves on hauling his bag of nuisance contraband, which is even heavier with the things he seized from my cell. Whatever he's taken, it's okay; I'll get it all back, and more. As long as he's accepted my lie about the typewriter, everything is as it should be.

Shindola writes me a pass to the recreation yard, and I'm outside for the afternoon. But when I return to the unit for the four o'clock count, the typewriter is gone. *Son-of-a-bitch! That fucking Shindola!*

As if that were not enough, now Murphy has begun to enforce the ridiculous rule that during the day while the unit is supposed to be undergoing the daily sanitation routine, convicts will be permitted to watch TV *only* in the Blue Section TV room. It is another of those rules most of the hacks ignore. The Iran-Contra hearings are going on, and a few of the prisoners who live in the Blue Section are following the hearings closely on CNN, while others insist on watching their soap operas or music videos. This has created unwanted strife among the prisoners. Every so often Shindola gets up from his desk and goes around to the different sections and shuts off the TVs. By the time he returns to his desk and sits down, they are all back on. Shindola starts to holler to shut off the TVs. The convicts respond by turning up the volume. The noise level escalates.

Murphy doesn't seem to understand that he's not a good cop. A good cop keeps the peace and maintains security. Shindola creates havoc and imperils our lives by pissing everybody off. Nor does it seem to have dawned on him that even at the highest levels of government, from the president of the United States—a former movie star—and his crony, the director of Central Intelligence, and a lieutenant colonel named Oliver North with the National Security Council staff, from the top on down, as proven by the Iran-Contra affair, these guys don't play by their own rules and regulations. So why should we? And why should he?

The homeboys from DC are most affected by the implementation of the new TV rules and have taken to fucking with Shindola relentlessly. But he's like a pit bull. The more they—or we, for I have joined the ranks of those who wish to drive him from our midst—the more we resist Murphy's rule, the more he digs in and creates more grief and turmoil with the dogged insistence that he is only enforcing the rules and regulations of the institution. He just cannot seem to grasp that life in prison, much like life in the World, falls far below the ideal.

Today we are subjected to a double dose of the Smurf as the evening-watch hack banged in sick, and Shindola is stuck pulling sixteen hours straight. You'd think he'd be tired and just sit at his desk and leave us alone. But not Murphy, no, he can't help himself. There's an Italian guy in the unit we call Alley Oop, who, two or three times a week, cooks up a big pot full of spaghetti in his cell using an elaborate heating element known as a "stinger" he made in the UNICOR factory, and with some obvious nuisance contraband and unauthorized food. The odor of pasta and sauce permeates the unit. It smells good. Alley Oop will often share a bowl of the "macaronis," as he calls it, with the evening-watch hack. Nobody gives a shit. Except Shindola. He busts Alley Oop, seizes the stinger, the pot, the pasta, the sauce, garlic cloves, everything, and writes Alley Oop a shot that could result in some Hole time. A good convict, Alley Oop doesn't even object.

But later, after the 9:00 p.m. count, Shindola is at his desk when suddenly the lights go out. Someone has hit the main circuit breaker and cut the electricity in the unit. Then, as Shindola panics and stands from his desk looking about in the dim glow from the emergency security lamps, he is pelted with a hail of pool balls coming from the Yellow Section, where most of the DC blacks live. Shindola is hit and he goes down. He's on the floor with his hands and arms cradling his head as he crawls under his desk for cover. One of the pool balls hits the clock above Shindola's chair and smashes it. Convicts stand on the tiers and cheer as the pool balls rain down on Murphy, who cowers under his desk. Finally, he hits the panic button on his body alarm, and minutes later the goon squad marches into the unit.

We spend the rest of the night and the next morning locked in our cells. Nine convicts, all blacks living in the Yellow Section, and Alley Oop are locked up in the Hole. But apparently no one rats, as they are all released a few days later. Shindola reports for work after a few days' sick leave with a golf ball–size goose egg on his head. But he's undeterred. In fact, he's coming down on us even harder, shutting off all the TVs, insisting the unit orderlies put in a full, eight-hour day, shaking down the cells every day. He's enraged, flabbergasted when he sees that I have the IBM Selectric typewriter back in my cell. Once again, he confiscates it, has it locked up in the unit officer's closet. He doesn't understand that even the other cops and the lieutenants are all pissed at him as well because his strict adherence to the rules and regulations of the institution that most of them ignore makes them look bad and gives them all more work.

Shindola's on the prowl, and he's more determined than ever to show us who's in control. He doesn't seem to have noticed that no one is in the TV rooms watching TV. The orderlies, the prisoners who are off work, the genuinely sick, and the malingerers are all hanging out on the tiers or in the common area milling around, drinking coffee and smoking cigarettes. A truly perceptive hack would sense that something is up. But Shindola is too busy hunting for nuisance contraband and muttering to himself to pick up on the conspiratorial vibe and sense that some plan is afoot.

The unit officer's phone rings. Shindola is down on the bottom tier in the Green Section shaking down cells. He's got to get back up and over to his desk to answer the phone mounted on the wall. He seems unsure what to do with his bag of nuisance contraband, as he knows that if he leaves it on the tier while he goes for the phone, the prisoners will take all their stuff back. So he drags the bag with him and does not even notice that nearly everyone in the unit, at least ten men, are hanging out watching him.

This is a nasty old convict trick, and any seasoned hack would have picked up on it right away. Not Shindola. He grabs the phone receiver and sticks it to his ear. Someone—I'll never know who, but I suspect whoever it was lives in the Yellow Section—someone has taken a gob of fresh human shit and smeared it all over the earpiece of the cop's phone. Shindola gets an earful of shit and is obviously having a hard time hearing whatever is being said to him through the clogged receiver and his shit-filled ear.

"Shit on the phone! Shit on the phone!" Shindola screams and drops the receiver. He looks around wild-eyed and lopes off to the second tier of the Blue Section, where there is another officer's phone. You would think he'd at least check the phone before he grabs the receiver and sticks it to his other ear. But in his haste to answer the call, he does not. This one also has been pasted with shit. Shindola gets a double dose, shit in both ears. He drops the receiver, screams, and falls to his knees. The convicts all laugh at him. Shindola may even be weeping. For a moment he does not seem to know what to do. He's rubbing both ears as he tries to clear them of the shit. Then he hits the panic button on his body alarm.

"Shit on the phone! Shit on the phone!" Shindola bellows and sobs. Moments later the goon squad enters the unit for the second time in as many weeks. They find no riot, no convict dangerously out of control, just Shindola on his knees weeping, trying to clear his ears, and both phone receivers still smeared with shit dangling from their wall mounts.

It's hard to say who really wins this round. I get my typewriter back even before it leaves the unit. The evening-shift hack is an old timer who wants only to put in his eight hours and go home. I convince him he should open the closet and give me the typewriter. "It's authorized," I tell him. He knows I'm lying, but he does not care. When Shindola returns to work after a few days off, he's oddly subdued. He appears broken, resigned to a bullshit job. He ignores us now, and we treat him like he does not exist except when we have to go to him for something: a roll of toilet paper, a pass to the gym or the law library. He sees I've got the typewriter back and pays it no mind. Rumor has it he's been seeing the institution shrink complaining of depression.

The post rotation at last removes Shindola from our confines, and we get an experienced cop who lets us do our time and keep up appearances with a minimum of hassle and turmoil. My days ease back into the dull comfort of routine. Then, only a week after the post rotation, early one morning I am in my cell at work on the contraband typewriter when, through the narrow rectangular window above my desk, I see first one, then two, then several cops run past. Keys jangle as they react to an obvious state of emergency.

"Oh, God! Jesus!" I hear someone shout, a rare display of panic. There is more shouting I can't make out. One of the guards hits a body alarm, and soon every hack within running distance is heading toward the southeast corner of the compound, where one of the manned gun towers stands fixed against the southern sky like a lighthouse warning of lives shipwrecked here.

Then . . . all is quiet, until perhaps thirty minutes later when the unit phone rings. Several cops enter; we are locked down for the morning with no breakfast and no explanation. There is never an explanation for a lockdown or anything else our keepers decide to subject us to; it's as though they figure we are not mature or intelligent enough to handle the information. The Bureau of Punishment rulers reason that any body of adult men subject to having their assholes inspected at will has no right to know what is going on.

When at last we are released from our cells but kept locked in the unit to await the call to the chow hall for lunch, the rumormongers maintain that there was a fight between two guards in the gun tower, and one of the guards shot and killed the other. *Who?* No one seems to know. This hardly seems credible. Guards fighting and shooting each other—it's too good to be true. The day-shift unit hack will not give up a word of what happened or who was involved.

When, finally, we are released for the noon meal, as I make the short walk to chow, I see where someone has scrawled on the outside wall of the mess hall: *Convicts 1—Guards 0.*

THE OLD CON, that font of prison intelligence, has the real story—of course.

"There wasn't no fight," he says and curls his thin lips in a sneer. "That's bullshit. You think these cops are gonna start killin' each other? Hell, now that would be a real cause for celebration."

My thoughts exactly. He has all our attention as he strokes the stubble of gray whiskers on his chin and gazes at us with his bleary, milky gray eyes. "No way. But I'll tell ya' what really happened."

He pauses, betrays the glimmer of a smile. "Some hack blew his brains out." And he nods pensively. "Yep, an' it weren't no accident, neither. He reported for work in the gun tower this mornin', took out his service revolver and"—the Old Con points his trigger finger into his mouth and cocks his thumb—"kaboom! Splattered what little brains he had all over the inside of the gun tower."

"Damn, ain't that some shit," Red says. "Who was it?"

The Old Con shrugs. He doesn't need to say it; I already know.

"New guy," he says and takes a sip of coffee. "Can't say as I knew him myself. Name a' Murphy." He looks over at me. "Just come from your unit, didn't he?"

THAT EVENING THE story is all over the local TV news. In our unit cheers and boisterous laughter comes from the TV rooms. Turns out there is a Mrs. Shindola Murphy, who seems stunned as much by the presence of the news cameras and reporters as by her husband's suicide.

"He hadn't been himself," she tells the reporters, "since startin' that new job over at the prison."

And there are little Shindolas, a babe in arms and a three-year-old boy who looks just like his departed dad.

At first, I'm not sure how to take this turn of events or how I feel in my heart of hearts about the fact that this rookie cop, Shindola a.k.a. Murph the Smurf killed himself with, no doubt, more than a little help from me and the convicts in this unit. Actually, I am having trouble connecting with my heart of hearts—that part of me that has remained untouched by these years of imprisonment and the necessary annealing of the emotions and cloistering of the soul that comes with having to survive many years of internment in these places.

You can't be a man who is subject to tender feelings and expect to make it in prison. Witness Shindola. He let it get to him. I should say: *Fuck Shindola*. Good, I'm glad he killed himself. He was a dick. I have got to understand and come to terms with what goes on in these prisons. All the worst aspects of masculinity—selfish aggression, imposing physical domination, psychological control over those perceived to be less confident, preying on those who are weaker and gentler or not as clever—those vicious aspects of primitive survival are heightened and intensified when you take a bunch of highly testosterone-charged males who do not give a fuck about the law and care less for each other and lock them all up together under the command of keepers, who also must survive in this loveless world and who are equally if not more susceptible to being changed by living here. These places, separated from the family of man and woman, are breeding grounds for uncaring, brutal human beings—guards, staff, and convicts alike.

But, alone in my cell late at night when all is quiet, I can still reach out into the cosmos beyond the fences and gun towers, and I can still try to connect with that man I used to know, touch my heart. Yes, that man was arrogant, a fool trying to be somebody he was not, self-centered and crippled by hubris—but he had a heart. He believed, and I still believe, that there is more to me than the criminal, the prisoner, the callous convict I have become. There is a man who cares for and loves his fellow man. The man I used to know is buried but living and breathing, locked up. And that inner man is sorry, sorry we fucked with Shindola Murphy to the point where he saw no way out except to kill himself.

That man suspects God created and loves Shindola, even as he created and loves me.

Chapter Ten

JAILHOUSE LAWYER

EUREKA! THIS IS it, the eureka moment: I found it! The appellate court decision that will set me free. My knees go weak. My balls vibrate. *Can this really be true? Am I reading these words, or am I hallucinating? Have I won the lottery, or am I dreaming?*

I am standing in the law library at FCI Petersburg, a place where I have spent many hours in my now nearly seven-year-long study of the law, and I have just read the words that must by law nullify my twenty-five-year sentence. *Words!* Language. That which separates us from the other beasts of creation. Words imprisoned me. And words shall set me free. Listen to these words: *coercive* rather than *punitive*. Isn't that beautiful? Isn't the English language wonderful? Yes, it is. Especially when it will set you free.

Dear Judge Motley, bless your rotund black ass. There are those who will say that you did this on purpose, that you knew when you imposed my sentence—the ten years on the CCE, the kingpin, non-paroleable sentence, to run consecutively to the fifteen years I had already received in the District of Maine, for a total of twenty-five years—that when you uttered these words, "for the reason that it might convince you that cooperation with the government is in your best interest;" that when you enhanced your sentence *not* because of the seriousness of the crime, *not* to punish me for the massive amounts of illegal vegetable matter I possessed, imported, and distributed, no, but rather to convince me "that cooperation with the government is in your best interest;" that you knew what you were doing. And they might argue that, when you went on the record, which I now have and have read over and over again, that you deliberately said it again even more clearly: "Now, Mr. Stratton, if you decide to cooperate with the government in this matter, you have 120 days to apply to the court for reduction of your sentence, and the court will consider reducing your sentence based upon the nature and the extent of your cooperation with the government. So that in addition to the fifteen-year sentence you now have a sentence of ten years to follow that." I heard you say those words, and some would believe, dear Judge, that you understood your sentence was illegal and that you did it knowingly, purposefully.

No, I don't believe so. God bless Judge Motley. I love her dearly. But she is hardly an enlightened jurist. She is a wonderful woman, and I have come to revere her rulings—not for her wisdom, but for her ignorance of the finer points of the law. Or maybe it is not ignorance at all but contempt. As a black woman in America, having tried and succeeded as she has against the odds, she still knows somewhere deep in her soul that the law is a rough tool that can be used to hammer and hector the weak into submission as much as it is a fine scalpel that can cut to the quick and excise the malady. Perhaps after many years on the bench she has grown blasé, bored with the sheer volume of so many words spoken or written in so many court proceedings, so many defendants, lawyers, prosecutors, issues, and arguments. Crime! Overwhelmed by the persistence of crime and criminals. Perhaps she is simply tired. I did notice her dozing on the bench several times during my trial.

Whatever the case may be, the six months Judge Motley gave me for contempt of court was thrown out on my direct appeal. My attack on the conviction is based on the grounds that when Motley stripped me of my defense after she had given me permission to proceed with an affirmative defense theory, she made reversible error. I have a habeas corpus on that issue still pending in the lower courts. But with my direct appeal of the New York conviction having been denied, now at last it is time for me to file my Rule 35 Motion for Sentence Reduction, and to put Motley Crew on notice that she fucked up royally. Her sentence is illegal! It is coercive rather than punitive, enhanced to try to force me to cooperate, and courts have ruled that is not allowed.

Indeed, my particular sentencing aberration is even more clearly prohibited. It says it right here in the *Federal Reporter*, ruled in a case out of the Second Circuit Court of Appeals, the circuit with jurisdiction over appeals of rulings in Judge Motley's court: "It is one thing to extend leniency to a defendant who is willing to cooperate with the government; it is quite another thing to administer additional punishment to a defendant who by his silence has committed no additional offense." *United States v. Bradford*, 645 F.2d 115, 117 (2d Cir. 1981) (quoting *United States v. Ramos*, 572 F.2d 360, 363 n.2 (2d Cir. 1978))."

Fuck, yeah! Bloody wonderful! Right on, baby! . . . *by his silence has committed no additional offense* . . . The guy kept his mouth shut. How is that a crime? In what country? Not in America. Since when does silence merit additional punishment? It all seems so clear to me, and I knew it even as dear Motley uttered the words. It just took me years of working through the convoluted dialectic of legal lingo to find my way to this understanding: my sentence is illegal because it was enhanced to try to force me to cooperate with the government, and therefore it cannot stand.

I compose and promptly file my Rule 35 Motion for Sentence Reduction in Judge Motley's court, and point out that her sentence is illegal on its face. Weeks go by with no response. Then, in her magisterial wisdom her Motleyness denies my motion with no written ruling, just a simple *No*. Fuck you, Stratton. Do the twenty-five years and shut the fuck up. (See, obviously she didn't do it on purpose.) Okay, good. See ya', Motley. You blundered yet again, and there is recourse. Now, thank you very much, I will take it higher. I will proceed to the upper reaches of jurisprudence, where the rulers supposedly know and even make the law.

Energized with unequivocal legal precedent, I sit down to draft the brief and appeal Judge Motley's decision to the Second Circuit Court of Appeals. In my brief, I argue Judge Motley's denial of my Rule 35 is in error on the grounds that her sentence is illegal because it was *coercive* rather than *punitive,* ah yes, and I state that I have a Fifth Amendment right not to implicate myself or anyone else. More weeks go by and I hear nothing. Then I get notice in the legal mail. I have been granted oral argument before the Second Circuit Court of Appeals.

Holy shit! Me, Dickhead Stratton, some lowly convict, hophead, unregenerate doper, I am going to be permitted to stand before a panel of esteemed jurists in the hallowed halls of the Court of Appeals for the Second Circuit in New York City, one of the most prestigious courts in the country, and argue my appeal?

Oh, no. This does not strike me as a good idea. As much as my inflated legal ego might enjoy the experience, I doubt it would be a wise move. I am not a member of their club. I am a confirmed and convicted outlaw. The judges might resent me playing in their sandbox. This is not about my career as a jailhouse lawyer; this is about winning. So instead I call Ivan Fisher, my co-counsel at trial, Mailer's good friend, and ask him if he will enter an appearance and argue the appeal for me.

When I reach Ivan and ask him to argue the appeal, he's amazed to hear that I got as far as having been granted oral argument. "What's your issue?" he wants to know.

I explain it to him. "Never did sit right with me," I say, "that Motley could give me more time for refusing to rat. She proved my defense. As I tried to argue to the jury before she shut me up, the whole New York prosecution really was all about trying to force me to cooperate with the government and implicate Norman. Motley's sentence is clearly *coercive* rather than *punitive.*"

"That's your issue? Hmmm . . ." Fisher reflects. "And you found case law to back it up?"

"I did, yes. Ample case law directly on point. Second Circuit case law."

"Really? Richard, this is intriguing. Send me copies of your brief and the government's response."

I do, and Fisher agrees to argue the case. Time slows down as the date of the oral argument draws closer.

"WE WON!" FISHER yells over the phone when I reach him in his office on the evening of the day of oral argument.

"*What?* How do you know?" I ask. "Did they rule from the bench?" Highly unlikely. I'm dumbfounded. What's he talking about? How could he know this?

"No . . . no, they didn't rule—yet. But I'm absolutely sure," Fisher assures me. "There is no doubt in my mind. Listen, the judges didn't even ask the government any questions. It was clear to them, given Motley's statements on the record at sentencing, that the sentence is illegal. Their only question to me was: What is the remedy? Believe me, Richard. Go to sleep on it. Bet on it. We won. *You* won. *You're going home, boobie!*"

Now I have become excruciatingly aware of the passage of time. My days are solid masses of waiting punctuated by mail call, visits to the unit counselor's office to see if I have any legal mail, and evening telephone calls to Fisher.

"We won, what the fuck, Ivan: *where is the ruling?*"

And then I have it.

It takes the appellate court eight weeks to issue their ruling. A piece of paper with words on it. Here are the words that will set me free:

UNITED STATES of America, Appellee v. Richard Lowell STRATTON, a/k/a "Richard Lowell," Appellant. No. 937, Docket 86-1504. Cite as 820 F.2d 562 (2d Cir. 1987). United States Court of Appeals, Second Circuit. Argued April 8, 1987. Decided June 5, 1987. "Following defendant's conviction on drug-related charges and imposition of a ten-year sentence to run consecutively with the sentence previously entered on another conviction, defendant moved for a reduction of sentence. The United States District Court for the Southern District of New York, Constance Baker Motley, J., denied the motion, and defendant appealed. The Court of Appeals, Oakes, Circuit Judge, held that defendant's sentence was impermissibly enhanced due to his failure to cooperate with the government.

"Sentence vacated, case remanded for resentencing in front of a different judge."

Hallelujah! Praise God. Praise the law. Praise language: *impermissibly enhanced due to his failure to cooperate with the government!* Keeping my mouth shut shall set me free! How beautiful is that? How righteous. Talk about language—how about the beauty of silence? And the appellate court slapped good Motley down by taking the case away from her and ordering that I be sentenced by a new judge who will hopefully know what the fuck he or she is doing. Yeah, baby! Pink Rats rule: we're pink because we don't fink.

BACK ON THE Bureau of Punishment bus, headed for New York City: MCC, once the Criminal Hilton, now just another federal shithole. I've spent more time in this jail in the years I've been locked up than anywhere else. While still at Petersburg, as part of my ongoing efforts to beat this sentence down, I went before the parole board. The fifteen-year sentence I received in Maine was paroleable, so I petitioned the board to parole me from the fifteen-year sentence into the ten-year, non-paroleable sentence upon completion of the minimum five years, one-third of the fifteen-year term. And they did. They figured, why not? This convict isn't going anywhere; he's still got to do another ten years with no parole. That happened even as I attacked the illegality of the New York sentence. So, truth be told—and I am certainly not offering up this information to the new sentencing judge—I am already on parole from the Maine fifteen-year sentence and serving the New York non-paroleable ten-year sentence that has been declared illegal and vacated by the court of appeals.

This gets complicated. We have entered the arcane world of federal sentencing law. What's the best that could happen? I could go in front of the new judge charged with the responsibility of resentencing me, he or she could rule in my favor, and I could walk out of the courtroom a free man. Fisher believes release is a distinct possibility. Much, he says, will depend on how the prosecutor, Stuart Little, responds. If the government still has a hard-on for me and Norman Mailer, and if the prosecutor still clings to some notion that I will give in and roll over, they could look for new ways to fuck me.

My mother comes down for the hearing; the old man stays at home. Mary tells me that Emery is proud of the fact that his son chose not to become a stool pigeon and spend the next however many years being shunted around the country from courtroom to courtroom to testify against friends and enemies. Ah, the shame of it! I'd rather do the time. But what if Judge Motley had said twenty, thirty, forty years? How do you measure your integrity in years? How many years is my soul worth? My mental state? Stand me up in front of a firing squad. Fry my ass in the electric chair. Gas me. Slip me some lethal drug cocktail. Who cares? Emery? I miss the old man, but I wonder: Does he really give a shit about his son? The son he virtually ignored until I got into trouble? And me, will I now have children of my own, now that I may actually get out of prison while my dick still gets hard? And, if so, if I get out and have sons and daughters of my own, will I be a better father than Emery? Jesus Christ, help me, I hope so. Fathers and sons, it's all such a mystery to me. I'm closer to Norman Mailer than I am to my own father. But I do love the old man, and I believe that in his own Yankee WASP way he loves me.

These are the kinds of ruminations that will keep a convict awake in his cell at night.

Interesting that the appellate court took the case away from Judge Motley. The circuit court judges assumed her Honor would not be unbiased in resentencing as my efforts, and their decision, make her appear ignorant. The new judge's name is Thomas Griesa, pronounced *gree-say*. I, as is my habit, have renamed him Greasy. He's a tough one to read. A graduate of Harvard University and Stanford Law School appointed to the federal bench by President Richard Nixon in 1972. The little research I did on Greasy tells me he's considered to be a fair if not particularly diligent jurist.

He enters the courtroom in his robes and takes his place on the bench. He looks tired. No nonsense. Straight to business. He has no investment in this case.

"Mr. Fisher," the judge says after a quick review of the paperwork, "I see where the Court of Appeals vacated Mr. Stratton's sentence, and we are in my court to have a new sentence imposed."

"That's correct, your Honor."

"It would appear," the judge continues, "the original sentence was declared illegal and vacated because it was based on a failure by this defendant to cooperate with the government. Courts have determined it is impermissible to enhance a sentence based solely upon failure to cooperate."

"Right again, Judge."

Griesa nods. Nods again. So far so good. He looks at Stuart Little. "Is that the government's position as well?"

"Yes, your Honor, but—"

"Wait," the judge interrupts, "let me finish. Now, my question to you both—and to this defendant, since I see where the filings in this case were submitted pro se—my question to you all is this: What is to prevent me from imposing the same sentence, that is, the ten-year term to run consecutively to the fifteen-year term; or, alternately, what is to prevent me from imposing a twenty-five year sentence—or an even longer sentence—and basing it not on Mr. Stratton's failure to cooperate but instead on the large volume of illegal drugs Mr. Stratton was convicted of having imported and distributed? Do you see what I'm saying? Because in my review of the case, I see where Mr. Stratton was convicted under the continuing criminal enterprise statute—a very serious offense—of having been the organizer and manager of a sophisticated and lucrative longstanding criminal organization that imported massive amounts of drugs into the United States."

What? No, no, no, I'm thinking in a panic, this is all wrong. Not me! A bunch of hippies. Freaks. Hippie mafia outlaws. Kids fucking around with some weed and a little hash . . . Please, Judge . . . More time! No, God, no. This is *not supposed to happen.* This is not why we are here. That would be a major fuck-up. If I were to go back to prison with a twenty-five-year, non-paroleable sentence or even more time, that would be the exact opposite outcome of what I set out to accomplish. We are here to have my sentence corrected, not to have it enhanced.

Even Ivan Fisher seems momentarily jarred from his grasp of the proceedings. "Ah, no, Judge. With all due respect," he says, "I do not think that is the intent of the appellate court decision. That would call for a finding other than what the district court determined at the original sentencing, after hearing all of the evidence and imposing a minimum ten-year sentence."

"Hmmm . . . What is the government's position?" Griesa inquires.

Stuart Little says, "Under the circumstances, Judge we would need to research the issue."

"Yes, I think you're right. I'm not sure myself that what I have suggested would be permissible. I am going to adjourn and ask you both to brief me on your findings. And then we will set a new date for the resentencing."

My mother and I hug as deputy marshals escort me from the courtroom. "I'll come visit," she says.

"This is not at all what I expected," I say to her and to Ivan Fisher.

"No, it's not," Fisher agrees. "And I don't think . . . well, I don't know. You better get your butt to the law library and research the issue.

By the way, the assistant US attorney told me that he is aware that you have been paroled from the fifteen-year sentence into the ten-year sentence, and he intends to notice the Court of this. So you better be prepared to answer that issue as well. You've got to do the work on this, Richard. You brought us this far."

Damn . . . That did not go at all as planned. More time? Shit! Where did Griesa come up with that idea? I win an appeal and get more time. No, that's not right. It can't be. I must not come out of this worse than I was going in. And that is precisely the rationale that will protect me. Fisher brought it up: Judge Motley, after hearing all of the evidence and after listening to my allocution, set her sentence at the minimum of ten years on the CCE. This new judge is not being asked by the appellate court to resentence me based on the evidence presented at trial. He wasn't the trial judge. No, he is only being asked to address the illegality of running the two sentences consecutively "for the reason" that I refused to cooperate. Nothing else. He is not charged with, nor given the responsibility of, redetermining how much time I should get. He is empowered only to address the illegality of the sentencing based on an impermissible finding.

In the law library—my retreat and intelligence domain—I find case law that says in precise legalese exactly that. The lower court is not permitted to punish a successful appellant more severely upon his having overturned a case on appeal, as to do that would have a dampening effect on a defendant's right to appeal. Of course, makes perfect sense. Who would want to appeal a judgment if they thought they could get in even deeper shit if they won? Very good reasoning. This is why I have come to love the law. It really does make sense—sometimes. It is the lawmakers who are full of shit. Politicians. Scumbags. *Life with no parole for smuggling pot.* They are out of their fucking minds. They must be smoking crack.

Scribbling away on yellow legal pads, I make my notes and draft the brief, then turn it over to Fisher's associate counsel for review. Finally, we submit the brief to the court. Judge Griesa sets a new date for resentencing. Days and nights at the former rock 'n' roll jail as I await my day in court are lived in a state of focused anticipation. I believe in the weight and veracity of my argument.

NORMAN MAILER COMES to visit. He has startling news. Biff, my co-defendant and failed rat, after doing a little over four years in prison, was paroled. He came home, and then he killed himself.

"I knew he was depressed," Mailer says. "He was living out in Amagansett. Alone. He looked great. Never better. He worked out in the gym every day. He actually went to the gym on the morning he decided to end it, said good-bye to everyone there, and went home and . . . checked out."

I don't know what to say. Mailer and Biff were close. "How—?"

"Well, you know Biff. Nothing messy. He wanted to leave a good-looking corpse. He put a vacuum cleaner hose on the exhaust of his car and asphyxiated himself."

Some people go to prison, do the time. And then they kill themselves.

WHEN WE ARRIVE in the courtroom on the day, Judge Griesa's clerk tells us his Honor wishes to confer with the parties in chambers before we appear.

"I've read the briefs . . . from both sides," Judge Griesa begins. He's in an easy chair beside his desk. Fisher, Stuart Little, the judge's clerk, and I sit around like so many members in an exclusive men's club chatting about the state of the union. "And I see where Mr. Stratton, you have appeared before the parole board, and that you were granted parole on the original sentence imposed in the district of Maine."

"Yes, that's right, your Honor."

"My reading of the law and of the facts in this case would lead me to believe that the remedy here is to run the two sentences concurrently instead of consecutively. Is that correct?"

Fisher answers. "Yes, judge. That is our belief as well."

"And you have been incarcerated how long, Mr. Stratton?"

"Not quite seven years, your Honor."

"I see," Griesa says and nods judiciously. "And if the two sentences are run concurrently, the ten-year sentence will become the controlling term. Is that your understanding?" he asks of us all.

Stuart Little answers. "It would be, yes, not only because Mr. Stratton has already been paroled on the fifteen-year sentence but also since the sentence in this court, as it is non-paroleable, takes precedence. Further, it will have been imposed well after the original sentence."

This sounds a silent alarm in my head. They had better not be thinking that the term imposed here would begin upon imposition and not be retroactive back to the very day I was arrested. No, no, don't even go there.

"Well, what I am trying to determine is how much more time Mr. Stratton will be required to serve if I run these two sentences concurrently. Ten years without parole. You've served over six years. I suppose that is something the bureau will determine. But I want to make certain that the sentence and the term of incarceration are commensurate with the seriousness of the offence."

He looks at Stuart Little. "What is the government's position?"

Stuart Little speaks. "Your Honor, the government would not oppose your combining Mr. Stratton's two sentences. Quite frankly, I am tired of litigating this case. Mr. Stratton has several other pleadings pending. If Mr. Stratton will agree to withdraw the other petitions he has filed, the government will consent to your suggestion of running the two sentences together. My guess is that Mr. Stratton will still have some time left to serve."

"Mr. Fisher?" Griesa inquires. "What are your thoughts on this?"

"Judge, I think you need to ask Mr. Stratton."

Peace! Raise the white flag! Surrender. I quit. I will go back to jail and keep my legal filings to myself, or aid other convicts in their cases, but file no more on my own behalf—if you will just let me go. That means withdrawing my attack on the New York conviction on the grounds that Judge Motley stripped me of my defense—an issue the lawyer who wrote my direct appeal neglected to raise. I believe I have a strong argument. But what might I win? Overturn the conviction and go back for a new trial. Then run the risk of getting convicted a second time and having a long, legal sentence imposed. No, that is not a gamble I am willing to take. Take your winnings and leave the table, Dick. Quit the game while you are still ahead. Stuart Little is in no mood to have to try this case all over again, and I'm not either. He is ready to throw in the towel if I agree to stand down and cease and desist my attacks upon the conviction.

"That's fine with me, your Honor," I agree. "I'll withdraw my other pleadings."

"Good," says the judge. "Let's go make it official."

So it is done. And as we leave the courtroom, Fisher shakes my hand.

"You did it," he says. "Good work, Richard. Brilliant. Come see me when you get out. I may have a job for you."

Chapter Eleven

CONFESSIONS OF A RELUCTANT ONANIST—OR, SEX IN JAIL

FCI Otisville, New York, September 1987

THIS MORNING I had the most ridiculous and oddly degrading run-in I've had yet with Bureau of Punishment staff. I've grown accustomed to having my asshole inspected in the many years I have been locked up, told to lift my balls and had my scrotum examined, and I am used to being referred to by number: 02070-036. As well, I am inured to being shunted from prison to prison, jail to jail, cage to cage in shackles and chains like a zoo specimen, I am familiar with sleeping on concrete floors, pissing and shitting in plastic buckets, whiling away hours and days in crowded bullpens. I'm not bitching. It doesn't bother me. It comes with the experience. It's jail, and I admit I deserve all this and more because I refuse to obey their asinine laws prohibiting cannabis. But I must endeavor to make sense of this experience in order to understand what goes on in this confined world for my own need to discover meaning in my life and to give me hope to go on living. And to leave a record. Therefore, I tell this story.

It was six o'clock on a cool, fresh spring day. Dew still glistened on the grass, and the smell of damp concrete was in the air. I felt good to be alive.

If only I could let my mind go free and forget where I was. On my way from the housing unit to the gym and recreation yard during the special, ten-minute controlled movement to allow motivated convicts early morning access to the exercise facilities, I must walk past the mess hall where all the cops and staff hang out drinking their morning coffee. I was walking along, minding my own business, feeling fit and frisky for a middle-aged prisoner who worked hard and played harder before coming to jail. After so many months of being confined 24/7 at the MCC, I was enjoying the new day sunshine, the clean morning air, and my refreshed, solitary headspace.

As I started up the walkway toward the gym, a lieutenant came running out of the mess hall and called out to me—that's right, a lieutenant, not some lowly hack, a brass, officer type—and he was running like this was some kind of emergency. "Hey, you!" he shouted.

Ordinarily, I ignore a motherfucker who addresses me like this. Hey, you! *Fuck you.* Speak to me as a man. Show some respect. But this guy took me by surprise. And the way he was running, looking all flustered, I was startled and taken aback. "Who, me?" I responded. I was like Robert De Niro in *Taxi Driver:* "You talkin' to me?"

It had to be me; there was no one else around. He came up behind me—a tall, lumbering white man going to fat. He looked concerned. I won't say he was sweating, but he was flushed and a bit winded. I held no contraband and was still too surprised to be annoyed. This is the question he asked me: "Are you wearing underpants?"

I was baffled and taken aback. "What?"

What exactly do you say to a cop who stops you at six in the morning and asks if you are wearing underpants? I had no ready reply. I had on a pair of loose, white nylon athletic shorts, a T-shirt, and sneakers, and at first I thought he meant was I wearing *only* underpants, as from a distance the shorts I had on could have been mistaken for boxer shorts. So I answered, "No. These are regular shorts. Look," I said and turned around. "They have a pocket."

He shook his head and leaned in closer. "You've got to go back to your unit and put on some underpants," he told me.

"Oh, I get it," I said. "You mean am I wearing underpants *under* these shorts? Right? Is that where we're going with this?"

Now I was getting angry with myself for allowing this cop to assail my dignity. I thought I had him figured out; he was fucking with me, and I was looking to fuck with his head as much as I could without getting locked up in the Hole. But I knew I had to be careful, as I am newly on record with the Bureau of Punishment as a sex offender. While still housed at MCC after my resentencing, I was caught in a basement classroom in the education department getting a blowjob from a young Indian sociology professor. Nora is her name. Petite, long black hair. Horny and without inhibitions—the ideal woman, my kind of girl, a female who likes sex as much as I do. I had signed up for as many college classes as they would allow me to take during my recent holdover at the rock 'n' roll jail. There was some consideration that the Bureau of Punishment designation gods might not return me to FCI Petersburg but instead keep me at MCC until the BOP number crunchers could recalculate my sentence. The thinking was that if I had only a few more months to do, I might even finish my bid in New York City.

Nora the sociology professor from Empire State College and I took an immediate fancy to each other and a hankering for each other's bodies. It was lust at first sight. One day as class was dismissed, she asked me to hold on a moment. There were only ten convicts in the class, and as soon as they had left the room, Nora asked me in as plain-speaking a manner as one could ever hope for, "How would you like it if I gave you a blowjob?"

Though surprised, I had the presence of mind to reply almost in kind. It seemed like a great idea and I wanted only to encourage her, so I said, "I would like that very much."

"Sit on my desk," she told me, taking command of the situation. I did, and she unsnapped my blaze-orange jumpsuit. My dick was already stiff as a pool cue. She kneeled before me and quickly, expertly took me in her mouth. All was going swimmingly. I was about to ejaculate when

Mr. Wall, the tall, white-haired, and clubfooted head of the education department, opened the classroom door, lumbered in, and caught us. Nora was expelled from the jail. I was put on the next punishment bus out of Manhattan and shipped here to FCI Otisville. But Nora and I have remained in contact. We are in touch by letter and by telephone. I have even managed to have her name added to my visitors list.

Still, I was and am hyperalert to any kind of police activity in and around my genitals. "Of course, I've got on underpants," I said. I recalled there had been some notice from staff about proper convict dress on the compound since there are several women working here at FCI Otisville. One would suppose the Punishment thinking is they don't want to see a lot of free-hanging johnsons and risk getting the ladies all lathered up. I can understand that. Sex in jail is oddly omnipresent in its apparent absence. It's as if everybody is charged up by what they can't have. The Punishment bureaucrats have been forced by Equal Rights legislation to allow women to work in these joints. There have long been female guards at MCC, and we know where that went. They set up a prostitution ring. Human beings will find a way to fuck. It's what we do.

In a lot of the state joints they have conjugal visits. Just outside the prison walls they have trailers nicknamed the "fuck trucks." A convict's wife and kids can come visit for the weekend. Seems reasonable and even enlightened. But in the federal punishment system they do not acknowledge the baser human drives or offer any effort toward healing such as trying to help keep families together. It is all about control and subjugation. Degradation and dehumanization. Right down to your asshole and your underpants. It's as though they want to send you back out onto the streets more damaged and perverse than you were when you entered the Bureau of Punishment.

"Let me see 'em," the lieutenant said.

"You want to see my underpants?" I asked. I wasn't going to let him off easy.

He nodded.

"Take my word for it," I said. "I'm wearing underpants."

He shook his head. "No. I have to see them."

They believe nothing we say. I felt like asking, "You want to see my cock, too?" But I knew that would move me over the line, and probably get me a write-up for disobeying a direct order or some such horseshit. So I shrugged, pulled my shorts down to my knees, and revealed a clean pair of white jockey briefs.

"Okay . . . okay. Pull your shorts up," said the lieutenant, looking embarrassed.

"This wasn't my idea," he went on as though he hoped to redeem himself in my eyes. "The associate warden told me to come out here and check to see if you're wearing underpants."

I smiled at him. "Really?" I said and pulled up my shorts. "The associate warden. I'm flattered. Does he want a date?"

The lieutenant stammered, "Go on, you're dismissed." And he turned and walked away.

THIS SEEMINGLY MILD invasion of my dignity has lodged in my gullet like a bone and upset me more so than it should. For this is a world where one must surrender any vestige of privacy and pride. Still, it rankles deep inside that I have allowed myself to be reduced to the point where I will readily submit to a random underpants check. Is this what it has come to? Who I have become? Of course it is. I have been brought to face my conceit: that I could take on these *federales* and expect to win. Stratton versus the United States government indeed. I have been forced to recognize my hubris for what it is—a fatal flaw and my downfall.

So I look for the lesson and recognize that in submission there is power. In the close and personal land of diapers and underpants there also lives the seed of creation. And if, like Onan, I must spill my seed upon barren ground, then let me find my inspiration and my pleasure in pissing on their rules and regulations.

THE FORMER WARDEN at this prison, FCI Otisville, was recently named director of the entire Federal Bureau of Punishment. *Whoopy-do*. I had angled to get redesignated here; Otisville is close to New York City and to my parents' home in Massachusetts. It's a fairly new facility with large, two-man cells and a big recreation yard. But that was before they turned Otisville into a holdover stop. Now, because there is a witness protection WITSEC unit here—one whole, closely-guarded unit filled with important rats—security is unusually tight, much like at a maximum-security penitentiary. I'm ready to go back to the relative comfort of FCI Petersburg to complete my sentence. But the BOP bureaucrats can't seem to figure out what to do with me. So I sit here in limbo, like in that Jimmy Cliff song from *The Harder They Come*.

THE OTHER DAY a guy on my tier died of heart attack. We were all locked down because of heavy fog. They are afraid to let us out on the compound when there is fog in the air for fear we might disappear like spirits in the mist. We heard the guy's death go down— raucous, impossibly drawn out, and bitterly painful for all. His cellmate banged on the door and yelled for the unit cop, who ignored him. There was no question the guy was freaking out; his cellie was in cardiac arrest. No one came to his aid, and when they finally opened the cells and let us out, the guy was dead. His cellmate was shipped out immediately to try to avoid any repercussions to Punishment staff.

They will spot-check to make sure you are wearing underpants but pay you no mind if you're dying.

I GOT A letter from Nora last week to say she's coming to visit. Can you imagine how stupid these Punishment people are? They caught me with a civilian contract employee in flagrante delicto, in blazing offense—I, in my blaze-orange jumpsuit, Nora on her knees before me with my stiff cock in her mouth. I did manage to cover the offending member, and Nora jumped to her feet, but there was no question what we were up to when Wall walked in and busted us. They fired Nora immediately. But now, lo and behold, no one catches it when I ask to have her name put on my visiting list! And they consent. When I got to the line on the visitor's application form where I was supposed to tell how I knew Nora, of course I lied. I wrote that she had been a friend on the street from before I became a prisoner. I could hardly admit that we became intimate during forced coitus interruptus as part of my ongoing prison sex education.

Today is the day. In anticipation of Nora's visit, I cut out the pockets of my jumpsuit. Naturally, I wear underwear; I don't want to go through that again. But I choose a pair of loose-fitting boxer shorts with an open fly. This setup is what seasoned cons refer to as "the mouse in the pocket" trick for reasons that will become clear. I may be jumping the gun here, but I have faith in this woman, good Nora from Bombay. I know from experience she's one of those rare and prized females who enjoy to provoke and to partake in sexual desire under dangerous circumstances. Her letters seethe with eroticism. She's not driving all the way up here from New York City to gaze in my eyes and hold my hand. This is as much of a sex adventure for her as it is for me.

I am called and march dutifully to the visiting room ready to risk it all for the treasured touch of a woman. Nora is dressed in a traditional Indian gown, a gossamer violet-hued sari, and with a scarf wrapped over her head. With her eyes painted and a round vermilion mark in the middle of her forehead, she looks exotic, a vision from another world, which indeed she is, and nothing like the hip young New Yorker who was my teacher at MCC and showed up in jeans and demure blouses.

"I'm so sorry I got you in trouble," she says after I give her a brief squeeze and kiss on the mouth—the only contact allowed as per the rules and regulations of the institution.

We sit and I say, "That kind of trouble is no trouble at all."

She gives me a sly smile. "How is it here?"

The visiting room is crowded: lots of kids, whole families up from the city to visit dad or son. We sit side-by-side in molded plastic chairs. There is a hack at the front desk where convicts and visitors sign in, and two other cops are up and circulating around the room to keep an eye on things. There is also a mirrored globe hanging from the middle of the ceiling that I know contains video cameras to record events in the room.

"It's okay," I say. "At least I get to go outside."

"I can tell," she says. "You look fantastic. Much healthier than when you were at MCC."

"Thanks. You look pretty good yourself," I say. "I love the outfit."

"I'm not wearing any underwear."

My cock perks up. "You had to tell me that."

"My pussy is getting wet just looking at you." Nora smiles and stands. "Would you like something . . . from the vending machines?"

"Yes, sure. How about a bag of popcorn? I've been craving popcorn."

We go over to the bank of food vending machines, she buys the bag of popcorn, and I pop it in the microwave. Back in our seats, with the bag of popcorn resting strategically in my lap, I say, "Put your hand in my pocket."

She does and quickly understands there is no pocket but rather easy access to my unfettered dong. Her small, moist hand slithers in and takes me tentatively at first, probing deftly, as though gauging my measure.

"Unnnnnhhhhh," Nora moans. "You feel so heavy."

Back when I was her student at the MCC, Nora at first gave no hint of her wanton side. She seemed studious, interested in me because I was not what she expected. She was intrigued to know how and why an educated middle-class white boy had chosen a life of crime. I may never have articulated it to her, but I think we bonded in our mutual attraction to danger. I'm certain part of why she volunteered to teach classes at MCC was because she thought to come in contact with *the other*—big, bad men, so accustomed is she to small, docile men. She told me in one of her letters that as a girl growing up in Bombay, she and her family lived in a large block of flats. From the window of her room she could look into the bedroom of a couple living in the building beside hers. The man of the apartment would often stand or sit while his wife knelt before him and took him in her mouth. This impressed Nora. The image stayed with her as she could see how the man and the woman seemed to enjoy the ritual bonding. As an adult, Nora too was attracted to fellatio as a means of giving and receiving pleasure.

People come and go around us. Couples embrace, hold hands. Kids eat junk food from the vending machines, and they run about chasing each other. Nora's hand slides up and down beneath my jumpsuit. There is enough activity in the room so that no one seems to take any notice of us. She squirms in her seat and commences humping my hand.

"The cameras," I groan. "They've got cameras in here."

This seems to excite her all the more. "Put your hand under my dress," she implores me. "Stick your fingers in my pussy. . . . I'm so wet."

One of the cops circulating through the room makes a beeline in our direction.

"Whoa, hold it," I say. "Here comes the cop."

She's oblivious. "You get to play with it all the time," she says and keeps stroking me.

Thankfully, the roving cop veers off and continues down the line of seats and away from us.

I announce, "I'm going to come."

"Good. Come. Let me make you come."

The bag of popcorn in my lap moves up and down. I keep eating faster and faster. Then the room goes out of focus. The earth continues to turn on its axis. Life goes on. There is no stopping us now. The undertone of babbling voices dies away. I leave my body, leave the room, but not in my mind, for my mind is blank. My whole being is caught up in a dimension of pure sensation. This may be the apocalyptic orgasm from which there is no return. I might just expire here in the visiting room at FCI Otisville. Cause of death: acute orgasmic ecstasy. Nora's hand on my cock is holding me by the very root of my carnal existence and taking me outside of my body, outside of this prison, outside of my confined life to . . .

The floodgates are open. There will be no holding back the flow. I quiver, my whole body goes into spasms, my member throbs and ejaculates, and then my muscles go slack. I float in and out of the here-and-now in post-orgasmic bliss and only gradually come back to the reality of where I am. In my lap, clearly an unauthorized event has taken place.

"Nora," I pant, resting my head on her shoulder, "that was like a religious experience."

She smiles and looks at me wet-eyed. We kiss and her mouth feels sticky. Only then do I notice she has her hand out and is licking the semen from her fingers like a bear licking honey from its paw. "Mmmmmm, you taste so good," she coos.

In my lap, all over the top of my thigh, a big stain has formed where my seed soaked through the jumpsuit. My face is flushed. I'm still breathing heavily, sweating.

"Put your hand up my dress," Nora urges me.

Fuck these people, I'm thinking, and I reach for her snatch. One good turn deserves another. The cop on the desk receives a phone call. I glance over at him and our eyes meet. He replaces the receiver and gets up, strides toward us. I've still got my hand up under Nora's sari and she is slithering her wet cunt back and forth on my fingers.

Nora gets off. She moans, shakes, cries out—but it could be an exclamation of joy or surprise. I remove my hand even as the desk cop arrives in front of us. Now I'm the one licking my fingers.

"You," the cop demands, "come with me."

"Where are we going? My visit's not over."

"Yes, it is. Up, let's go." And to Nora. "You. Out!"

"Hey, don't talk to her like that," I chastise him. "Get some manners."

He's taken aback. "Me? After what you just did!"

"What? What did I do?"

It's the only way to handle these people—play stupid. Deny everything. Act like you don't know what they are talking about.

"Come with me," he says and puts one hand on his body alarm, set to hit the panic button.

"Relax," I tell him. "I'm coming." I should say: I came. It is done. You're too late.

I stand. The stain on the front of my jumpsuit looks like a pattern in a Rorschach test.

"Good-bye," I say to Nora and go to kiss her. The cop steps between us.

"OUT! Now!" he barks. "This visit is terminated!"

"Get a life," I tell him. And to Nora, "Thank you," I say and give her hand a squeeze. "That was a really nice visit."

"I enjoyed it, too," she says and smiles. "Good-bye."

The cop escorts me into the shakedown room. I stand facing the wall.

"Turn around," he orders me. He's tall, Germanic-looking, probably in his early thirties, wearing wire-rimmed glasses and the Bureau of Punishment baseball cap. The tag pinned to his shirt says his name is Swick.

"We had the camera on you all the time," he declares menacingly. "You had your zipper down and were exposing yourself."

"Bullshit, Officer Swick," I say, defiant. "I never had my zipper down. This jumpsuit doesn't even have a zipper."

"What's that stain on the front of your jumpsuit?" he demands.

Another guard enters, a young, pimply kid. They are both excited, carrying on as though this were the bust of the day. He nods, says to Swick. "We got it. It's all on tape."

I look down at the gooey stain. "This? Oh, I spilled a soda in my lap."

"No, no!" the younger cop practically shouts. "We got it all on film. You had your penis out!"

As usual, they got it wrong. They knew an unauthorized event had taken place, but because they couldn't catch me right, they invent an offense—indecent exposure—that never happened. A phone mounted on the wall rings. The desk cop answers it and says, "Yes, we've got him right here."

"Strip," the young hack tells me.

I take off the jumpsuit and my shorts—also wet with semen—and drop them on the floor.

"Bend over and spread 'em."

I assume the position. The young hack picks up my jumpsuit, touches the guilty stain. He rubs his fingertips and thumb together and pronounces, "That's not soda! That's cum."

"Mountain Dew," I say. "Or was it Seven Up?"

It's all I can do to keep from laughing in this guy's face. Except I'm standing there bare-ass and feeling vulnerable. The cop looks up my ass, inspects up under my scrotum. My cock is so content it's indolent, doesn't even care.

"He denies everything," the desk hack says into the phone. "Okay." And he hangs up. "Get dressed," he instructs me. "Go back to your unit. The lieutenant is going to review the tape and decide what to do with you."

Whatever they do to me, it was worth it. Like I give a shit. That was one of the most amazing orgasms I've ever had—incredible the difference a woman's gentle touch can make. But with my resentencing and impending release, if these fools can ever figure out how much time I've got left to serve, I really don't want an incident report and the loss of good-time. Oh, well . . . I ask myself, Stratton, *will you ever learn to behave? Will you ever fully submit to their rules and regulations? Or will you always be this recalcitrant outlaw in search of punishment?*"

BACK IN MY cell, I rummage through my belongings, find the print-out of the rules and regulations of the institution, and I look up the sanctions under which this alleged misconduct might fall. There are actually several possible violations I could be guilty of. They are, in order of severity: Code 205: Engaging in sexual acts; Code 300: Indecent exposure; Code 327: Unauthorized contact with the public; Code 407: Conduct with a visitor in violation of Bureau regulations; and Code 409: Unauthorized physical contact (e.g. kissing, embracing). All of these offenses are punishable with Hole time, possible forfeiture of earned good-time, and other punishment such as loss of visiting privileges for a specified period.

Love! These federal fuckers have outlawed love. Just who the fuck do they think they are? Of course I will dispute all their charges; that is my standard MO. Yes, I slipped up when I agreed to submit to the underpants check—a momentary lapse. My attitude at this point is *fuck it*. The orgasm has emboldened me. No more will I admit to their indignities. Let them prove it. I'll take it all the way to the Supreme Court. And then, even if I am convicted, I'll tell them to blow it out their asses! No Bureau of Punishment bureaucrat is going to tell me I can't be loved.

There comes the call over the PA: "Inmate Stratton report to the lieutenant's office."

Off I go.

"STRATTON," SAYS THE investigating lieutenant, "you got a jack job out there in the visiting room."

His name is Metzger. They all have names like that—bunch of fucking Nazis. But Metzger and I half-ass get along. I ran into him at the penitentiary in Lewisburg, and again here. He loves to pull me up for political discussions, calls me a lily-livered liberal, which I'm certainly not, more like a flaming radical freethinking American. He's a Vietnam vet, and though I applaud his service, I tell him I believe the reason for the war was a horrendous lie and that I refused to serve. I complain the war on drugs is an even bigger and ultimately costlier farce or fraud, the American people are the victims, and he should find himself a real job. He laughs and tells me I'm the one wearing the jumpsuit. True that.

Curious terminology—jack job. I prefer to think of it not as a job at all, more as a calling. The woman was called to make me feel human, even if only for a fleeting moment. And I was able to reciprocate.

"I don't know what you're talking about," I respond.

Metzger sneers. "You can't deny it. We've got the whole show on video. I saw it myself. . . . And then she licked her hand!" he exclaims in disgust. "Jesus, I couldn't believe it when I saw that."

"C'mon, you're just jealous," I tell him. "You probably never had an old lady who swallowed."

Now Metzger takes offence. "I should lock you up."

"Go ahead," I say and offer my wrists. "I don't give a fuck."

"That's your problem, Stratton. You're a sick bastard," he says, shaking his head. But I see that now he is smiling, enjoying this unique contretemps.

"Me? I'm sick? What about you guys? Bunch of voyeurs sitting around watching people trying to act like humans."

He grins. "You know what? I don't think you're being rehabilitated, Stratton. I think you're getting worse."

"Wrong again, Lieutenant. What happened out there this afternoon—and I'm not saying anything did happen—but if it did, that was what I call rehabilitation. I haven't felt this alive in years."

METZGER THROWS ME out of his office. He knows, as I know, there will be no sanctions. A bag of popcorn moving up and down in a prisoner's lap. His head turns red, he seems to go into convulsions—maybe he's having some kind of seizure. A petit mal and not *la petite mort*. Who can say? The evidence is inconclusive. The telltale stain on the jump-suit—the hordes of offspring I will never father—of course, they know what happened. I know what happened. But the alleged guilty member never appeared on camera.

There was no flesh. They cannot outlaw the spirit of love. The essence of the orgasm is, after all, invisible.

Chapter Twelve

THE OLD DON

BACK IN THE penitentiary at last! How pathetic that I have reached the point where I rejoice at being returned to a real prison. But those transit facilities—MCC, Otisville, K Dorm at Lewisburg; and the county jails along the way; and the intermittent doses of diesel therapy—they make it impossible for a convict to settle into a healthy routine. It becomes a stunted and buffeted version of the cloistered life. There is no access to my beloved volumes in the law library. No mail. No phone calls. No bed of one's own upon which to rest one's weary bones. It's like living in a series of bus depots—traveling, traveling on, but never arriving at a destination.

The only advantage to diesel therapy is that one gets to see the outside World as it blurs by, glimpsed through the barred and meshed Bureau of Punishment bus windows. The trip up from Manhattan to Otisville was not unlike taking a freeworld weekend trip from the City to Westchester and beyond, Orange County, to enjoy nature in the rolling hills and verdant vales of the country in springtime. Life is out there, so close: trees, fields, streams, and rivers, all God's miraculous creation. Separated from the World, I have come to appreciate it so much more. Seeing the World through the bus windows, I am flush with excitement at the thought that I will one day in the not-so-distant future be free to walk again unfettered by chains and shackles, and to get down on my hands and knees and thank God for life, for this opportunity to experience freedom.

And journeying on from Upstate New York to Virginia, with multiple stops along the way, one gets to meet fellow travelers, convicts from all over the vast American prison system, and to hear good and bad news from joints far and near: Who got out. Who got jammed up with a new case and may never get out. Who got out and got rearrested and is looking at a whole shitload of time. Who got shanked and bled to death just months prior to his release. What new prisons have been added to the ever-expanding federal gulag. News. Some news one would rather not hear. Here's the rub: the closer one gets to realizing freedom, the harder the concept of freedom is to grasp and hold on to—like the World streaming too quickly past my eyes through the bus window—for the fear mounts that something, anything, could go wrong. The bus might crash. A riot might jump off in one of the institutions along the way. One could be forced into an untenable situation, be forced to defend oneself, or simply fuck up, and the free world would remain out there, fleeting, forever beyond reach.

UPON MY RETURN to Petersburg, I find that I have become a minor celebrity, hailed as the jailhouse lawyer du jour. How many prisoners litigating pro se win an appeal in the Second Circuit Court of Appeals? Precious few. And to have one's sentence vacated and then reduced for *refusing* to rat? Unheard of. In fact, there are those know-it-alls who doubt me and would hint that I must have rolled over and cooperated, until I make available the published appellate court decision.

I could be making big bucks fleecing these unschooled and desperate cons on a promise of reprieve, but I work for commissary— ice cream, cigarettes to be used as currency, sneakers, or a tennis racket for a big case—and I won't take a case unless I believe it has merit.

Joe Stassi, the octogenarian *mafioso* who dwells in the cell beside mine, beckons me into his presence. He too has recently returned from a road trip. They shipped him to the federal prison hospital facility in Springfield, Missouri, a kind of retirement home for geriatric gangsters. He says he is fully recovered after a hernia operation and has had some melanoma spots removed from his pendulous, Buddha-like ears, his cheeks, and his forehead. At the time, due to his age and longevity in the system, Joe is one of twenty or thirty prisoners at Petersburg still living in a single cell; I am another, largely due to the status I have achieved as a writ writer. After the Shindola incident, the cops don't fuck with my typewriter; some have even come to me asking for legal advice.

The old man's cell is spotless. It has the look and feel of a monastic chamber. More than once I have passed by and seen him down on his hands and knees with a rag polishing his tile floor so it shines like it has been varnished. Everything he owns, all his personal property, is put away. His three pairs of shoes are lined up beneath the tightly made bunk. On his desk there is only a calendar, fetish of the imprisoned, and a framed photograph of his grandchildren. I expect Joe has a letter or some cards he wants me to write for him. His arthritis is even worse than it was when I left for New York. Now, he says, when he tries to write, his hand seizes up and becomes a claw. His handwriting has been reduced to a childlike scrawl.

But no, the old man says he only wants to ask me a question. Joe invites me to sit down at his desk while he perches on the edge of the bunk. He leans in close and tells me sotto voce, with sibilant echoes of Marlon Brando in *The Godfather*, that he appeared before the parole board the last time they came to the institution, and the panel of examiners who reviewed his petition for parole had recommended that he be released.

"That's great, Joe," I tell him.

"No." He shakes his head. "The national board . . . they denied me," he whispers. "Told me to bring it all. Here, look at this." And he hands me an official document.

It is a notice from the National Parole Commission. I read where, indeed, the local examiners who interviewed Joe recommended that he be paroled "for humanitarian reasons" and noted his "advanced age, strong family ties and exemplary institutional record." But the national commissioners overruled the local board and denied his parole on the grounds that it would "depreciate the severity" of his offense. Joe goes on to say this was his third time appearing before the board. "I been locked up twenty-three years," he continues, "never had a shot, nothin'. But they don't wanna lemme go. My brother died in prison. They want that I should die here, too."

I'm not surprised. Joseph Stassi, also known as Joe Rodgers and Hoboken Joe, though not as well-known as some of his more famous peers, is an organized crime figure of major international and historic significance. Now in his early eighties, he's also the oldest convict in this prison, perhaps in the entire federal system. Joe keeps to himself. He doesn't associate with the other Italian Mafia goodfellas. He doesn't talk to most of the other prisoners. He's respectful but aloof with staff. He never discusses his case with anyone. He's a solitary figure in this land of diminished individuality as he goes about refining his daily routine, striving to live long enough to get free and die in the world of the living.

He's up early every morning and sits in the TV room to watch the news on CNN before the rest of the convicts arise. I see him already dressed in his immaculate, creased khakis, his powder-blue fly fisherman's cap, and black, soft leather shoes. As soon as the compound opens for breakfast, Joe makes his way to the chow hall, where he eats some bran cereal, then he goes out and walks around the compound until work call to help move his sluggish bowels. I've studied him over the years of close cohabitation. He doesn't smoke; he's lean and healthy except for the arthritis in his hands and beginning scoliosis in his spine. Stassi has the raspy voice of a crime boss who has ravaged his vocal chords yelling orders and curses at his underlings. Because of his age and the arthritis, he's been given a medical exemption from work and spends his days mostly in his cell. With my new unit orderly job and our side-by-side cells, I now spend much more time in the old man's company.

We became close in the way one makes friends in the penitentiary—guardedly at first, through forced communal existence and what amounts to a kind of intensified familiarity. In prison, one lives in closer contact with strangers than one abided with members of one's own family. There they are, the other convicts, for months and years on end, the same men every time you turn around: in the toilets, in the showers, in the lines and at tables in the mess hall; in the lines for commissary or at the laundry; in the TV rooms; on the weight pile or out walking in the yard; in lines or signed up on lists to use the telephone. We are all trapped together in here. It's like living in a hall of mirrors; we even begin to resemble one another. Day in and day out, Joe and I see more of each other than do most married couples.

Before now, what little I knew about Joe Stassi's status in the ranks of organized crime I learned from observing the other wiseguys, even those who were said to be capos or bosses, as they afforded Joe the utmost in penitentiary currency: respect. An associate with the Gambino Family confided that Joe was a don, a boss, and more—a kind of mafia ambassador at large who was there when it all began and was the go-between with the Jews and the Italians. Joe's letters home to his wife and to his son, Joseph Junior, who lives in the Dominican Republic, and the cards and letters he dictates and I transcribe to his other correspondents, are void of personal information. I heard from the prison grapevine that he is doing time for heroin trafficking, and that his case may have had something to do with the infamous French Connection heroin importation conspiracy.

Some time ago another convict loaned me a book entitled *Gangster #2: Longy Zwillman, the Man Who Invented Organized Crime*. The Zwillman book contains several photographs of some of the most powerful gangsters of the early twentieth century, among them the founding fathers of the American La Cosa Nostra, Charles "Lucky" Luciano and Frank Costello. There is also a photo of Zwillman with a group of well-dressed, tough-looking men seated at a table laden with glasses and bottles in a nightclub, and in the company of some glamorous women, including Abner Zwillman's girlfriend, the actress Jean Harlow. Sitting next to Zwillman is a man identified as Joe Rogers. In a caption under the picture—the only reference in the book to the mysterious Mr. Rogers—the author notes Rogers ran Zwillman's numbers racket in Union County, New Jersey. There is another stunning blond seated next to Rogers—who, I later learn, is Joe's wife, and a former Miss America.

The Zwillman book intrigued me not only for the photo of Joe, but also for its history of the bootlegging industry in New Jersey during Prohibition. It chronicles Abe Zwillman's rise from a pushcart vender selling fruits and vegetables in the streets of Newark to becoming one of the most respected and influential organized crime figures of the era. Zwillman stole Jean Harlow away from Howard Hughes. He got Harlow a two-picture deal and himself half interest in Columbia Pictures by giving his old gambling associate, Harry Cohn, five hundred thousand dollars in cash to buy out Cohn's brother, thus establishing the mob as a major player in Hollywood. Zwillman and other mobsters corrupted public officials high and low. They swung the 1960 Presidential election for Jack Kennedy by buying votes in Illinois and West Virginia. When called to testify before the McClellan Senate Committee hearings on organized crime, Zwillman supposedly opted out and ended his remarkable career and his life by committing suicide, allegedly hanging himself in the basement of his West Orange, New Jersey, mansion.

When I ask Joe if that is he in the photo, fifty years younger and seated at the table with the beautiful blonde and the Syndicate royalty, he allows that it is; he goes on to confide that he loved and looked up to Abe Zwillman like an older brother. Joe says Zwillman was always impeccably dressed and groomed; he prided himself on his dignified outward deportment. "Abe was a perfect gentleman," Stassi remembers.

"And charitable, he ran soup kitchens for the poor during the Depression. He had a million friends, from the highest to the lowest. He would have Catholic bishops and Jewish rabbis in his home for dinner."

"Do you believe he killed himself?" I ask him.

Joe shrugs; he's noncommittal. "I was in Havana at the time. Knowing Abe, it's hard for me to understand." And he shakes his head, pulls on one of his wrinkled earlobes as though trying to hear some faint voice from his past. As an afternote, he adds, "The Jews made the Mafia. Without the Jews, the Italians couldn't wipe their ass. The Jews were the ones that done the real work."

Joe's Italian, of Sicilian ancestry, but he claims his closest underworld allies were all Jews: Meyer Lansky, Zwillman, Ben Siegel—known to those who didn't know him as Bugsy—and a New Jersey bootlegger named Max Hassel who took the young Stassi under his wing and made him his protector. By "the work" Joe says, he means the series of hits carried out in the early thirties by the mostly Jewish killers of Murder, Inc. Those killings, of the Mustache Petes who controlled the Black Hand (as the early Mafia extortion rackets were known), opened the way for the modern mob to take control of bootlegging during Prohibition under the planning and leadership of the affiliated East Coast bosses known as the Big Six: Lansky, Zwillman, Siegel, Costello, Joe Adonis, and the Boss of Bosses, Charlie "Lucky" Luciano. Joe says he knew them all.

Given my elevated status as the jailhouse lawyer par excellence in the joint, Joe has decided to invite me to look into his case to see if I might be able to cast a ray of hope upon his bleak future. "Bring it all" for a man of Joe's age could easily mean dying in prison.

"I'm not gonna say nothing," he tells me. "I'll just let you look at my papers, an' then you tell me if you think there's anything you can do. I want you to be honest, Richie. I know you will be, that's why I'm askin' you."

Joe's papers consist of copies of documents from his Bureau of Punishment central file—his "jacket" in convict-speak. I learn Joe was arrested on a fugitive warrant in Florida, indicted in Corpus Christi, Texas, for conspiracy to import heroin from Sicily, allegedly smuggled to Mexico and then into the US across the border at Laredo. He was tried, convicted, and sentenced to eighteen years. Seven years later, while serving time at the penitentiary in Atlanta, Joe caught a new case. He was charged in a conspiracy to import heroin from Sicily through France to Montreal and into New York with a French national—who was also doing time in Atlanta—a conspiracy facilitated on the street by Joe's younger brother, Jake, as part of several major heroin cases that grew out of the French Connection investigation. Joe was taken back to New York, held at the MCC, tried again, convicted, and given an additional thirty years to be served consecutively to the eighteen he was already serving, for a total of forty-eight years. All his direct appeals on both convictions and sentences were denied. His Rule 35 motions were also denied. After doing sixteen years, the mandatory minimum one-third on the forty-eight, he became eligible for parole. He waited until he had twenty years in on the sentence before first going in front of the parole board. He was denied "due to the serious nature of the underlying offense."

Now the National Commission has once again refused him, citing the nature of his crime, which strikes me as significant since major organized crime heroin cases are not uncommon. I feel certain there has to be more to the Parole Commission's decision not to let Joe go.

The old man's convictions and sentences go back to the days before the Bureau implemented SENTRY, the computerized data management program the Punishment number crunchers use to compute sentences. I take pen to paper and start to do the math on Joe's accrued good-time earnings to see exactly how much time he would be required to serve in order to "bring it all" and max out his sentence. Under the old sentencing laws in effect for those charged with crimes committed before 1987, there are two types of good-time a prisoner can earn: statutory good-time given by law at a rate of ten days per month and amounting to one-third of the total sentence if there are no infractions and losses of good-time, and meritorious good-time that can be earned at a rate of five days per month through one's work assignment if recommended by the convict's work supervisor and approved by his case manager. So it is conceivable, if one earns all of one's statutory and meritorious good-time and does not have any taken away, that one could max-out a sentence in a little over half the time imposed. In Joe's case, he should have been able to max-out in twenty-four years and change—if he got all his good-time. And with twenty-three-plus years already served, he should have been short only a few months of a release date, perhaps even eligible for release to a halfway house immediately.

Here I find an anomaly. From the MCC after his conviction in the New York prosecution, Joe was shipped to the super-maximum–security penitentiary in Marion, Illinois. Once he arrived in Marion, it appears from the sentence computation sheets I review in his file, Joe was put in the Hole, and both his statutory and meritorious good-time were stopped and not resumed until years later when he was transferred to the federal prison in Talladega, Alabama. At Talladega, Joe served another half a dozen years, receiving all his good-time, before being transferred here to Petersburg.

But the stint in Marion is out of the ordinary, and there is no explanation in the files as to why Stassi was sent to the super-max—the Alcatraz of its day—locked in the Hole, or why his good-time was suspended. Though he may not wish to speak about his case, to understand what took place, I have to inquire of the old man.

"First of all, I never had nothin' to do with narcotics," Joe insists.

Of course not, I think. Everybody in here is innocent, even if we are all guilty. I know it's a lie, but let him profess it if he must. These wiseguys will never admit they are in the junk business. Kill a dozen men, yes; deal dope, no, never! Pure horseshit; but it's not my business to point this out to the old man.

"It's that fuckin' rat Bobby Kennedy who done this to me," Joe claims.

"Bobby Kennedy?" I say. "What does he have to do with your case?"

"He was attorney general at the time. Kennedy made his special prosecutor, man name a' Arnold Stone, come after me when I left out a' Cuba after Castro took over. The father, Joe Kennedy, he hated me. We hated each other. I still hate the son-of-a-bitch. Bobby was convinced I knew something about who killed his brother Jack in Dallas. So they framed me."

I don't believe him; this sounds far-fetched, and I can tell by the familiarity in the way he pronounces the word *narcotics* that Joe Stassi was in the junk business—at least for a time and probably not directly, through associates, perhaps using his younger brother, Jake, as his front man. After the heyday of Prohibition and once the mob was forced out of Cuba, as mafiosi went about looking for a new means of extraordinary illicit income, of course they were importing and distributing large quantities of heroin. They set up opium refining labs in Sicily. They established a worldwide network to smuggle and distribute processed heroin. Luciano was a junk dealer. As was Vito Genovese, godfather of the Genovese organized crime family with whom Joe was affiliated. The list goes on and on. Nearly all the major heroin dealers I met over the years were either American wiseguys or Sicilians, or they were closely associated with the Italian Mafia. But I'm not about to argue with the old man. It doesn't matter; what I am looking into has nothing to do with his original convictions, only his time served. I need to know why he was sent to Marion and why they stopped his good-time.

"Well, here's what happened," Joe begins. "While I'm in New York, at the MCC after I get convicted in front of Judge Knapp . . ." And he goes off on a tangent about Judge Knapp and the Knapp Commission's corruption investigation of New York City's police department until I bring him back to the subject at hand. "Anyway, one night these men try to escape . . . Italians. So they come to me first, of course. They were lookin' for my permission. I tell 'em, 'Look, you do what you gotta do. Just don't involve me.' You understand? I'm not lookin' to escape climbing out through some hole they knocked in the side of the jail.

Now they're goin' to climb down nine or ten floors to the street on a bunch of sheets tied together. It seemed crazy to me. But that's their business, not mine. So they go out at night after lockdown. Turns out, right across the alley from the jail there's an assistant DA workin' late in his office in the courthouse. He looks out the window, sees these individuals climbin' out, slidin' down the sheets. He has a gun, a pistol, in his desk. He takes it out and yells out the window at these individuals, and when they run, he shoots them. So they all get caught. Now remember, I got nothing to do with this. But because the parties are all Italians, and because they were seen comin' to me to show respect by askin' my permission—and maybe one of these rat bastards in there mentions my name, I don't know—but they question me, the lieutenant and the warden, and I tell them I don't know nothin', so they send me to Marion and lock me in the Hole for ninety days under investigation for the escape attempt."

Joe pauses. He licks his flinty lips and then imbues himself with hatred.

"Rats!" Joe snarls and grimaces. "That's the only way they make these cases. But you can't believe these fuckin' stool pigeons. They're only saying what the agents an' the prosecutors want them to say. What I'm saying is the truth! I had nothin' to do with this. I'll take a lie detector test, I'll swear an affidavit; I don't care. What I'm telling you is the way it really happened."

At the mention of rats, Joe looks at me with a fierce glint in his eye, and I see the throttled rage and intense criminal passion that earned Stassi an underworld reputation as the most dangerous man in La Cosa Nostra.

Interesting, I'm thinking, and not just the story of the escape attempt, which is pure MCC insanity, the kind of event that could only happen at the rock 'n' roll jail. But mainly for the fact that they locked Joe up under suspicion, they never actually charged him with the escape attempt, and then failed to resume his good-time after he was let out of the Hole and while he was still being held at Marion after the investigation had cleared him of involvement in the thwarted escape. This was clearly wrong. They still had not credited his statutory or meritorious good-time. I can see we have a valid issue, a possibility to get Joe his good-time credited.

"After they let you out of the Hole in Marion, did you work?" I ask him.

"Yes, of course. They make you work. I had a job as a baker in the kitchen."

"And did you ask if you were being given good-time?"

Joe shrugs, sneers. "I never ask these fuckin' people for nothing," he says. "But they told me I was put in for all my good-time. Here."

He shows me a wrinkled document clipped to the back of his file. It's what is known as a cop-out, a request to a staff member that some-one wrote out on Joe's behalf while he was at Marion. The scribbled response at the bottom of the page asserts Joe was receiving all his good-time—though, from my calculations, clearly he was not.

I tell him, "Well, just from looking at these records, I'd say we're talking about at least three-and-a-half, maybe as much as four years, of statutory and meritorious good-time that you were denied—or never credited—once you were cleared on the escape charge. Plus, the three months you did in the Hole. If you could get all that good-time back— that's what, close to two years you could have taken off your sentence? Which would mean you could max this thing out in"—I make some additional calculations—"you could possibly be released. Joe, if you got all this time back, you could go home in a few months."

Joe nods, but he doesn't allow so much as a glimmer of enthusiasm. Apparently, he had done some calculating of his own and figured he must be getting short. But he's been locked up long enough to under-stand how difficult it is to get these Bureau of Punishment bureaucrats to admit that they made a mistake and even harder to get them to cor-rect it, particularly if it means doing anything to help a convict.

Still, we decide it's worth a try. I agree to write up the necessary paperwork and file it on Joe's behalf.

First we must appeal to the warden in what is known as a BP-9, which is routinely denied even when there is obvious merit. We would then appeal the warden's decision to the Regional Punishment Bureau higher-ups in a BP-10. Once that is denied, therefore exhausting all administrative remedies, we would file a writ of habeas corpus and try to get a federal judge to rule. This could take years. Joe might well be called and judged by the Creator and condemned to serve an eternal sentence in hell before he gets any relief in this world. But our efforts are not about reprieve necessarily; this is about hope. Keeping hope alive just might sustain the old man, and keep him alive long enough to outlive his sentence.

As I come to know Stassi better over the few weeks I'm at work on his case, he begins to open up, cryptically at first, with shrugs and nods and grunts, a *yes* or a bitter, hissed *no,* and then he lets go. He is completely devoid of braggadocio, a quality as rare in a convict as remorse, of which he apparently has none. Yet during our evening meetings in his cell, as I become the old man's confessor, with his Catholic need to unburden his soul, Joe tells me of things he did in his life that, he claims, he has never told anyone, including his wife—who is still alive and has been waiting for him these many years at the home he owns in Brooklyn.

JOE STASSI IS the oldest of nine children born to a man who earned his living as a street sweeper. He grew up on Stanton Street in New York's Lower East Side. It was the early 1900s, when hordes of tough immigrant Jewish and Italian kids took over the streets from the Irish gangs.

"My ambition was always to be a gangster, a gunman, whatever you want to call it," Joe tells me. "What started me was school. When I went into the first grade, I stuttered. The teacher got disgusted with me. She put me in a corner and put a dunce cap on me. The kids in the class all start callin' me dummy and stupid and laughin' at me. With the result that I started to hate school. I hated that teacher for what she done to me. I started being a truant, playing hooky."

He licks his dry lips a few times, a kind of silent stammer.

"I had a little girlfriend who was also a truant," Joe says and at the memory his face softens to a faint smile. "She liked ribbons from a certain pushcart. The only way I could get it for her, I had to go and grab it and run and get chased. One day I got chased, the man grabbed me by the shirt. He tore the shirt off my back! I had no shirt to go home, for stealing!" He laughs, childlike. "Finally, I was arrested for robbing a bakery shop—for bread, to eat. I was livin' on the street. Hungry all a' the time. After letting me off a few times, the judge had enough of me. He sentenced me to two months in the Catholic protectory for juveniles."

It was Joe's first stint in a penal institution, he says, those two months in the Catholic reformatory that became the foundation of his education as a professional criminal. "From young kids like me you had youth up to sixteen or eighteen years old. And we were all put into different yards according to our age. I was in the small yard with the youngest group. In those days, kids didn't wear long pants. In the bigger yards where they had the older kids, they used to have what they called 'droppies.' They got to wear pants that were below the knees. I used to look over and see the older kids and all I could think was that I wanted to be just like them, so I could get over there in that yard and wear pants that came down below my knees."

Once he was released from juvenile detention, Joe says he went back to the streets. "I was livin' in the alleys and abandoned buildings with the other runaways. One day, I come around a corner and run right into my father. He was so surprised; I think he thought I was dead. He hugs me and says, 'Joey, Joey, please come home.' He was practically cryin'. But I pulled away from him. Then he went to chase after me. He tried to kick me in the ass. It was cold, ice on the sidewalks. He slipped on the ice and fell on the sidewalk. I stopped and looked back at him lyin' there on the pavement, and I knew he was hurt, and I didn't know what to do. Do I go back and help him up? Go home and go back to school?"

Joe pauses, looks at me, and smiles ever so slightly, wistfully nodding his head. "No, I didn't. I turned and run, left my father lyin' there on the sidewalk. Years later, I owned a newspaper and a printing plant in Jersey, and I put my father in charge of the whole business. I bought him and my mother a home, the only home they ever owned."

When he was fourteen, an older boy he met in jail gave Joe his gun to carry. "He had a problem with some people that was lookin' to kill him. They came around the neighborhood every night around midnight. They used to come down Stanton Street and on Chrystie Street turn left and we were waitin' for them. We shot at them, and believe me, windows were cracking upstairs. Who the hell knew about a gun? We were kids. You just pointed and pulled the trigger. And to make it even worse, the ones that we shot happened to be good friends of mine."

Arrested for robbery, possession of a weapon, and other petty charges while still a kid, he says it was the connections he made with older criminals in jail that gave him entrée to the New Jersey beer barons and bootleggers of Prohibition. The most influential of these men was the undisputed boss of the New Jersey rackets, Abner "Longy" Zwillman. Just two years older than Joe when they met in the early twenties, Zwillman was already well established as the smartest, if not the wealthiest and toughest of the brash Jersey gangsters. Abe was born and raised in Newark's predominantly Jewish Third Ward. His father died when he was just fourteen, and Abe took it upon himself to become the breadwinner. He quit school and went to work selling fruits and vegetables from a pushcart. When the Irish kids would roam into the Third Ward to harass and bully the peddlers, the cry would go out in Yiddish, "*Reef der Langer!*" Go get the Tall One, the Defender. Longy came running and chased off the outsiders.

With Prohibition, Zwillman went to work for Joseph Reinfeld, owner of Reinfeld's Tavern, a local hangout for up-and-coming racketeers. Reinfeld bought whiskey from the Bronfman brothers' Seagram's Distillery in Montreal and began shipping directly to the Jersey shore, where Zwillman would oversee the off-load and distribution to speakeasies all over the East Coast. By 1922, Newark had become the bootleg capital of the country, and Zwillman, though just nineteen, presented Reinfeld with an offer he couldn't refuse: a fifty-fifty partnership or Longy would go out on his own. Reinfeld knew that to spurn Zwillman would mean war, and Longy had the muscle. By this time, he also had all Reinfeld's contacts and plenty of cash. Reinfeld swallowed his pride; they shook hands. Before Prohibition ended, the Zwillman-Reinfeld partnership made them both millions in tax-free cash dollars.

"Right around this time, there was a war going on," Joe says. "There was always wars, but this one I remember was the war between the Jews and the Italians to control Newark. Newark was where most of the liquor for the whole East Coast came into the country and was distributed. And Newark, Elizabeth, Union City was where we had all the big breweries. Tugboats would bring barges up the river with tens of thousands of gallons of molasses and pump it into the stills. We owned everybody: judges, police, politicians. Nobody bothered us. Except other mobs."

Joe says that it was through Zwillman and his partner Jerry Catena that he became friendly with the men who conceived and ran the national crime syndicate. Both a loyal soldier and long-range thinker, Stassi learned early on to follow Meyer Lansky's first law: retreat to the background, turn over the high-visibility street activities to others. Joe became a master of the low profile. He never used his real name. He moved from place to place. "All the mobs knew I was connected," he explains, "but no one knew exactly how or why. I was the only one who was free to go wherever I wanted, meet whoever I wanted without having to report. I never had to report because I was with Abe and Meyer."

Joe remembers that around this time Lansky and Ben Siegel had their headquarters in a building on the Lower East Side. They were at war with the four Fabrizio brothers from Brooklyn. One of the brothers, a killer known as "Tough Tony" climbed onto the roof of the building where Ben and Meyer had their office and dropped a bomb down the chimney. One man was killed and Siegel was injured. Tough Tony was seen fleeing over the rooftops. A few weeks later, as Tough Tony was having dinner at his parents' home, a couple of Ben and Meyer's men showed up dressed as cops and demanded to talk to Tony. When he got up from the table and went to the door, the men barged in and shot him to death right in front of his parents.

"Ben was honorable, a good guy with plenty of guts," Joe says of Siegel. "When there was trouble, Ben was always the first to go in. He'd help you. I remember Abe had an apartment at the Riviera Hotel in Newark. There were steel bars across the windows; it was impossible to get in unless Abe let you in. That's where a lot of the meetings were held. One day we get a tip there's a group of men in an apartment across the street and maybe they're planning to hit us. Ben takes out a gun, runs over and starts shooting up the place. He got shot in the arm but just kept shooting and ran them all off."

Siegel was the most outspoken man Joe ever met. "Fun to be around," he remembers. "No bullshit. People would say to Ben, 'If you ever need anything, just let me know.' Ben would say, 'Well, as a matter of fact, I do need . . .' whatever, five grand, just to call the guy's bluff. Then, when the guy starts making excuses, Ben would say, 'You no-good son-of-a-bitch. Who the fuck do you think you are, asking me if I need anything?'"

In the forties, Stassi was one of the first men invited to invest when Siegel began to explore the possibilities of founding a gambling empire in the deserts of Nevada. Siegel and a guy named Little Moe Sedway were partners in a small hotel in what was to become the mob's richest jackpot. "Moe was buying up property, and they tried to get me interested. I had a place in Lake Tahoe with Lou Walters—that broad, Barbara Walters' father. I was looking at Cuba and the Dominican Republic. Ben come down and visited me in Havana a couple of times," Joe says. Then he adds, almost as an afterthought, "When Ben was killed, everyone was shocked. They thought it might have been Little Moe that had it done."

"Who thought that?" I ask.

"Meyer and Abe," Joe answers.

"Wait a minute, you're saying Meyer Lansky never okayed the hit on Siegel?"

"Please. That's all nonsense. Meyer loved Ben. I was the one who looked into it. I went out to California, I investigated it for Meyer and Abe."

"So who did—"

"Excuse me. Listen to me, I'll tell you."

Joe says he hired an ex-detective, Barney Wozinski, a PI in LA, to investigate the Siegel killing. "There was a cigarette girl Ben was always talking to. Ben's girlfriend, Virginia Hill, was jealous of this girl. One day Virginia Hill got that cigarette girl and beat the bejesus out of her. When Ben heard about it, he went out and got Virginia Hill and beat the hell out of her. Virginia Hill left for Switzerland.

"The night Ben was killed, there was Al Smiley and Swifty Morgan with Ben when they drove in from Vegas. They stopped for dinner at Jack's, the fish place on the pier in Long Beach. They dropped Swifty off at the hotel, and Al and Ben drove to Virginia Hill's house. I talked to Al, he said they only just sat down, Ben on the couch, him on the side chair, when the shot came through the window. Al says, 'Believe me, Joe, I was afraid I was gonna get killed.'"

Joe insists the stories that have been written in any number of books and portrayed in movies like *Bugsy* and *Lansky*—which portray the Siegel killing as a mob hit okayed by Meyer Lansky at a sit-down in Havana with the exiled Luciano—are fictional, gangland lore gleaned almost entirely from second- and third-hand information, some of it no more than rumors and gossip.

"We were as close to it as you could get," Joe goes on. "I spoke to everyone. Whoever did it had to be a marksman that shot through the window from outside, someone that knew how to handle a rifle. The police found casings from a military-type rifle. What we found was the one that killed Ben Siegel was Virginia Hill's brother. He hated Ben, and Ben hated him."

Joe learned Hill's brother was a sharpshooter in the Marines. He had a rifle he kept in the gas station down the street. "The day after the killing, Barney Wozinski went to the gas station looking for the rifle. They called Virginia Hill's brother. He disappeared and the rifle disappeared."

"So the story that Ben owed all the bosses a lot of money in cost overruns for construction of the Flamingo is not true?" I ask.

"That's bullshit. Ben owed nobody money, and if he did, he was honorable, he would pay it. As far as the Flamingo, every partner in there knew they were going to make their money back many times over. Nobody was worried. We knew Vegas was going to be big."

Joe shakes his head, sighs. So many wars, so many killings, so many hits—who can keep them all straight? But the Siegel killing, that one he remembers. "It came from me. I told Abe and Meyer it was the brother, and everybody accepted it. Ben was killed by a sniper with a rifle. If it was a hit, that's not how it would have been done."

Joe says he laughed when he heard Joe Valachi claim he turned rat because Vito Genovese gave him the kiss of death. "There's no such thing as the kiss of death. You think they're going to give you a warning? Please. You're all right when they curse you. You need to worry when they're nice to you, invite you for dinner."

He imparts the methodology of a mob hit. To kill a man like Ben Siegel, Joe says, they would send a friend, someone he would never suspect, who could get in close and shoot him in the head with a revolver. "Never walk away from a body without making sure you put one or more in the head and the party is dead." The way Sam Giancana was killed. Or in a public place, usually an Italian restaurant, send in a couple of torpedoes and blast away. Like the Carmine Galante still life, blood and pasta. Or Joey Gallo staggering out of Umberto's Clam House and dying on the sidewalk on Mulberry Street. Or the recent killing of Big Paul Castellano gunned down in front of Sparks Steak House in Midtown Manhattan. Classic mob hits befitting a boss. But snipers? Too risky. "If you're going to kill a tough guy like Ben Siegel, you are going to make sure he's dead," Joe says.

"Always empty a gun before you toss it. Someone finds an empty gun, they're likely to keep it or sell it. If they find a partially empty gun, they'll turn it into the cops for fear of being connected with whoever got shot," Joe advises, warming to his subject—the fine art of murder. And I see the other Joe Stassi, the wily professional hitman lurking behind the old man's kind, artistic visage.

"How many people have you killed, Joe?"

He waves his hands, closes his eyes. "So many . . . I can't remember."

Yes, he is a murderer, he confesses. This slight, hunched, and reserved old man is an accomplished killer of more "individuals" or "parties" than he cares to remember. When I ask if he is burdened by the memory of the men he killed, he goes silent, retreats within. And then he nods and admits that he is haunted by two killings in particular. "I killed my best friend," he says.

"Max Hassel?"

"No," he sighs. "I killed Max, too. But I'm speaking of another party."

"Who?"

"I'll tell you . . ." But he can't quite bring himself to say the man's name. It was his best friend, that's all I need to know. Joe says the order for the hit had come to Zwillman and Lansky from Jimmy Alo, who took over as the boss in New Jersey after Joe Adonis was deported to Italy.

"I hated Alo," Joe says. "He was a piece of shit. I hated him almost as much as I hated Adonis. This fuckin' Adonis," Stassi practically spits his name. "Don't get me started talkin' about that son-of-a-bitch."

But now that the bile is flowing, Joe can't contain himself. Adonis, whose real name was Joe Doto, had assumed the alias out of conceit that he was the handsomest of criminals. Joe says Adonis epitomizes the power-crazed boss who orders his soldiers to kill on a whim. Adonis had once called a sit-down that, had it not gone Stassi's way, would have ended in his death sentence. Adonis resented Stassi ever after. There was also an issue over a girlfriend. Joe believes the order to kill his best friend had come from Adonis, through Alo, to Meyer and Abe merely to place Stassi in conflict with the men to whom he answered.

Joe goes on to describe a meeting where the bosses gathered to decide some important piece of business. Luciano was presiding, Stassi says; it may even have been the meeting the bosses called when Dutch Schultz lobbied for permission to clip Manhattan special prosecutor Thomas E. Dewey, who had made it his mission to lock up Schultz and the other syndicate mobsters.

"I can't remember exactly what it was about," Joe says. "We knew the Dutchman was out of control." He closes his eyes, smiles at the memory. "The meeting was going against Dutch. He was sick as a dog with a bad case of the flu. He was coughing and sneezing, sittin' off in the corner so as he won't infect the rest of us. Everyone voices their opinion except Adonis, who's standin' at the mirror combing his hair. Now we're all wai- tin' for this arrogant cocksucker to weigh in, even though it don't make no difference, Dutch was out-voted. We all knew it was crazy to think about hitting someone like Dewey. The Heat that woulda brought down would be unbearable. But Adonis, this asshole, he finally turns away from the mirror an' makes an announcement. 'The star says *yes*,' he says. When Dutch hears this, he jumps up an' goes over to Adonis. He hugs him in a headlock an' slobbers spit an' mucus all over Adonis' face!" Joe cracks up, his frail body quaking with laughter. "Can you imagine? 'The star says *yes*.' Dutch says, 'Now, you fuckin' star, you have my goimes!' Adonis was sick for a week with the Dutchman's flu."

When Jimmy Alo took over, he inherited Joe's hatred for Adonis and went on to provoke plenty of his own. Joe's ready to kill at the mention of Alo's name. He knew why Alo ordered the killing of his friend, but he didn't agree with the death sentence. Joe says he protested, he went to Zwillman and argued against the hit. "Abe said he agreed with me, but it didn't matter. We were out-voted by the others, who claimed my friend was in the wrong." Joe believes the hit was part of a power play by a gangster named Nick Delmore who wanted to take over running the Jersey operations for the Syndicate.

Again, Joe stresses it wasn't an isolated killing. Hits were not ordered unless they were sanctioned by the bosses. This killing too was part of the larger power struggle between the Jews and the Italians. "I don't believe in killing for money," he says. "There was always another reason—cheating or talking to the law, disobeying orders. They always had a reason, even if the reason wasn't always right."

Joe, being the independent operator he was, had friends on both sides of the conflict. It was the ultimate test of Stassi's loyalty and his treachery.

"This friend of mine, he loved diamonds," Joe says, remembering the night he killed his best friend. "I told him I had some stones I wanted to show him. So we agree to meet in the parking lot at this train station out in the country."

Nick Delmore was supposed to provide the getaway car. When Joe called Delmore once the plan was in motion, his wife answered and said Delmore had hurt his leg and couldn't come to the phone. Joe was enraged. "'What? You tell that son-of-a-bitch . . .'" But Delmore ducked him, left him hanging. Fortunately for Joe, unfortunately for his friend, the man drove to the station instead of coming by train. Joe killed him in his own car, sat beside him and shot him in the head as he examined the diamonds, then Joe used his friend's car to dispose of the body.

"I'll say it to the whole world, Nick Delmore was no fucking good," Joe hisses, full of venom. "Later, they made this no-good rat bastard a boss. One regret I got in life, I should have killed Nick Delmore."

"So you're saying, what you really regret is that you didn't kill Delmore, not that you killed your best friend."

Joe glares at me. I want to make him say it. I want him to confront all his demons. Why? I'm not sure, except that I feel there is some truth for me to be found in the old man's story, exorcising his demons as a way of dispelling my own naive fantasies of gangster glory.

"I did it on orders," he says. "Maybe you don't understand. Who I was, at that time, if I didn't follow orders, I would be killed. That's all. There was no other way. That's how they come to have such trust in me."

"Abe and Meyer. Because you killed your best friend."

He nods. "Yes. If you ask me, ninety percent of killings take place between close friends."

This confession elicits another. Joe tells me how he killed his other close friend and benefactor Max Hassel, again on orders from the bosses. "They knew I was the only one who could get close enough to Max to do the job. I didn't wanna do it. There was a sit-down. I protested, but the decision went against me. If I didn't do it, they woulda killed me."

Joe grimaces, his mouth trembles, he closes his rheumy eyes and shakes his head.

"The bosses," he laments, "they lie around in their pajamas, they pick up the phone and say, 'Go here, go there, do this, do that . . .' I had to do it. It was the life I chose. What do you want me to say, I'm sorry?" he asks. "I'm not looking to be forgiven. I'm just trying to tell you what I done, and what I learned."

Joe reasons some men join the military or the police and kill in the line of duty. Or they become politicians or businessmen and kill with the pen. Joe was a soldier in a different army, fought a different war. The way he sees it, they're all mobs: the government, the police, Wall Street, big corporations, just in different rackets. What Joe did was part of the struggle to get out of the ghetto, an assault on the culture that shunned him, an attempt to be assimilated and respected.

"You ask me a question: What do I believe in, religion or money? I'll tell anyone who says religion, they're a fucking fool. I don't believe them. Money is the most important thing in the world. Without money, you can't do nothing."

"What about family? Love?" I ask him. "Don't they mean anything to you?"

"Well, money fits in. Love, when there's no money, love falls out. You get married to a girl that had everything. A good life. Or when she needed a dress, she had a few dollars to buy it. She's married now, she's got a house to clean, she's got kids, a husband. Love, what's love? You get laid, it falls out. You go home and you ain't got the money to pay your electric bill, your food bill, where's love then? And family . . . listen to me, you need money to provide for your family."

After proving his fealty, Stassi was entrusted with bigger hits. He was given responsibility for the planning and implementation of some of the most notorious gangland executions in mob history. Joe was like a producer and director of high-level contract killings. He tells me how he got the contract to kill his old pal Dutch Schultz, whose real name was Arthur Flegenheimer, one of the most notorious gangsters of his day. Shultz was Public Enemy No.1 when the mob decided it was time to take him out. Joe arranged to meet the Dutchman at the Palace Chophouse and Tavern in Newark. Because Joe was so well known in the neighborhood, he sub-contracted the hit to two of Murder Inc.'s most accomplished triggermen: Charlie "The Bug" Workman and Emanuel "Mendy" Weiss. Joe acquired the weapons, including a rifle; he planned the killing; he provided the getaway car and mapped out the escape route. Dutch was hit with a hail of bullets as he sat in the chophouse waiting for his meeting with Joe Stassi.

Joe remembers he was just twenty-two in 1928 when he took his first trip to Havana. He loved the place. "It was wide open. Beautiful young whores everywhere, every street corner, every bar. In one club, there were twenty-five girls. You picked the ones you wanted to be in a live sex show. There was a guy in the show who was famous for his huge donkey dick. I was shocked to see these young girls take that giant cock. Men would go in there with their wives or their girlfriends. Then the women would come back by themselves later on to get fucked by these giants."

He remembers there was no crime, no robberies. Maybe an occasional knife fight. Stassi made it his business to become well acquainted with all the top Cuban officials.

After the gold rush of Prohibition, Zwillman urged Joe to go into that other enduring vice, gambling. Stassi took over the numbers for Zwillman and began opening dog and horse racing tracks in Jersey and Florida. During the Depression, when everyone else went bust, Joe continued to rake in millions in cash, socking it away in half a dozen safe deposit boxes in the vaults of the Manhattan Trust and other banks. "I just kept stuffing it in there," he says. "I never even had time to count it."

Stassi lived in the best hotels under assumed names, and he married the lovely Frances Paxton of Charlotte, North Carolina. Frances had once been crowned Miss America, but she had to forfeit the title when it was learned she had been married and divorced. Joe says he and Frances were out every night in the most popular restaurants and clubs—El Morocco, Copacabana, the Stork Club. In the late thirties and early forties, he took over the Hollywood Restaurant and Nightclub on Broadway between 48th and 49th, which became one of the hottest spots in town. He went to every major heavyweight fight; he hobnobbed with movie stars and celebrities: Frank Dempsey was a close friend; Jean Harlow, whose affair with Longy was long and torrid; Joe DiMaggio, who took to hanging out in Newark with the local mafiosi; Frank Sinatra, whom Stassi first met at Willie Morretti's club in Jersey; Toots Shor, and any number of other savvy denizens of New York nightlife. But it was Havana that kept drawing him back.

"I used to go there practically every New Year's Eve," he says. "People would come from all over the world to celebrate at Sloppy Joe's in Havana." Joe remembers drinking with Ernest Hemingway, whoring with Ben Siegel and other gangsters who came to the island to visit him. When Lansky decided to expand the mob's gambling interests in Cuba, because of the trust he had in Stassi, Meyer asked Joe to act as his man on the ground in Havana overseeing operations. By the fifties, Stassi was in partnership with Tampa, Florida, Mafia boss Santo Trafficante Jr. in the Sans Souci casino and with Philadelphia godfather Angelo Bruno in the Plaza Hotel and Casino. "Meyer told me Santo was looking to open up the Sans Souci. Meyer was waiting on the license to open the Nacional, and he asked if I'd be interested in going in on the Sans Souci with Trafficante. I said, 'Yes, lemme meet him.'"

It was around this time that the FBI began keeping close track of Stassi's movements. Stassi's son, Joseph Junior, married the daughter of a Cuban senator, Miguel Suárez Fernández, who was a close friend of Fulgencio Batista. Stassi, Lansky, and the other mobsters underestimated Fidel Castro. They lost millions when Castro's men came down from the mountains and drove the gangsters off the island. "The Plaza was one of the first places they wrecked," Joe says and shakes his head ruefully. Castro's men arrested Jake Lansky, Meyer's brother, Santo Trafficante, and a few others. And they were looking for Stassi. "I called the Capri and they told me, 'Joe, don't come here. They just pinched everybody.'" Before that, Joe says, he got arrested every week, but they never held him. From the fact that they had arrested Jake Lansky and Trafficante, Joe knew this time it was serious. He lay low for a while, then he fled the island. "There had been revolutions before," he says. "I thought Castro would only last a year or two. My son stayed on another year. But in the end, I lost everything I had invested there. I had bought a lot of real estate for little money. I had bought a copper mine. I heard the mine became very productive—for the Russians."

In 1960, Jack and Bobby Kennedy moved into the White House. Prior to the Kennedy regime, FBI director J. Edgar Hoover adamantly refused to acknowledge the existence of an organized crime cartel. Ignoring Thomas Dewey's racketeering prosecution of Luciano in 1936, the Murder, Inc. trials in the forties when Abe "Kid Twist" Reles first revealed the existence of the national crime syndicate, and the revelations of the Kefauver Committee Hearings in the 1950s, Hoover dismissed the notion of the Mafia. Only after the Apalachin, New York debacle when dozens of gangsters from all over the country were caught meeting in upstate New York, would Hoover reluctantly admit the possibility that there were criminal groups operating in concert to control nationwide illegal enterprises. The G-Men went from pursuing Reds and bank robbers to stalking racketeers. From then on, FBI would stand for Forever Bothering Italians.

Nothing had prepared Stassi and the other mobsters for the zeal of young Bobby Kennedy. His drive on organized crime and labor racketeering had the tenor of a vendetta with Irish Catholic overtones. Joe believes the beef goes all the way back to the days of the patriarch, Joseph Kennedy Sr., who made his stake as a rumrunner and held on to the distribution rights for Scotch whiskey from England after repeal. Joe Kennedy would later be named ambassador to Great Britain. Joe Stassi tells me of his early brush with the man whose beloved son would be elected president, and then be murdered in Dallas.

Stassi was living at the Warwick Hotel at 54th and Madison, where Joe Kennedy also happened to reside. Joe says he never did business with Kennedy back in the bootlegging days, though he is aware that Abe Zwillman and his partner Joseph Reinfeld—whose combined efforts, the government would later allege, accounted for at least forty percent of the illegal beer and liquor distributed on the East Coast— often moved Joe Kennedy's shipments of Scotch. There was a cocktail lounge at the Warwick where Joe says he would sometimes meet a woman whose last name was Rogers, coincidentally the same name as Joe's alias. Joe Kennedy also knew Miss Rogers; in fact, he was dating her. One time Kennedy came into the cocktail lounge and found Joe Rogers sitting tête-à-tête with Miss Rogers. "Are you two related?" Kennedy asked with a wry smile.

Joe smiles faintly at the memory. "After that, a fella I knew well tells me, 'I was speaking to the law and was told to advise you to move out of the hotel. The management doesn't want you. You're gonna get put out, maybe arrested to get you out.'" Joe heard later that Kennedy might have had something to do with Stassi's wearing out his welcome at the Warwick. "Joe Kennedy was law in the Warwick Hotel. If he made a suggestion . . ." Joe gestures, cocks his head. "I moved out. Later I'm told Kennedy said I was one of two people in his life he hated."

"Because of Miss Rogers? Seems kind of extreme," I say.

Joe admits he doesn't know if it's true any more than he knows why Bobby's office saw fit to frame him on narcotics charges. "I think they just hated Italians. It goes back to the way the Irish were treated in Boston. You know how it is, it all starts when you're kids, scrappy neighborhood kids in the streets, you're with this gang or you're with the other gang. It's the same thing when you grow up."

The nexus between organized crime and the Kennedys was long-standing and Byzantine, and it morphed into an unholy covenant. It was at Joe Sr.'s behest that Zwillman and the mob helped get Jack elected in 1960. The CIA and at least two high-ranking mafiosi—Joe's partner Santo Trafficante and John "Handsome Johnny" Roselli—with the connivance of the Kennedy White House, were plotting to assassinate Fidel Castro. And to make it personal, Jack Kennedy, Chicago Mafia boss Sam Giancana, and Frank Sinatra were all fucking the same woman, Judith Campbell Exner. The relationship between the mob and government spooks goes back at least to the days when Luciano was released from prison and allowed to return to Italy for his help to the Allied forces during World War II. The clandestine alliance is thick and rife with treachery and denial.

Joe says that when Bobby took the helm at the Justice Department, he made Stassi one of the first to be targeted and to take a fall. After Joe decamped Havana, he was approached by the FBI. He agreed to speak to them with the proviso that he would not discuss anything to do with his personal business or that of his friends; he said he would talk only about what he knew of the political situation in post-revolutionary Cuba. "They asked me, 'Are you a good American?' I said, 'Yes, I'm a good American.' But Stassi gave them very little information. He said he was returning to Cuba to visit his son and would talk to them again on his return.

In November 1962, almost a year to the day before the Kennedy assassination, Joe says he met in New York with Santo Trafficante and Carlos Marcello, the New Orleans Mafia boss who was hounded out of the country by Bobby Kennedy. That meeting, Joe believes, was surveilled by the FBI and led them to believe Joe was privy to information about the planning of the hit on Jack Kennedy. "They kept asking me about that meeting. What did I discuss with Santo and Carlos? That's all they wanted to know."

I also want to know. "What did you and Marcello and Trafficante talk about at that meeting?"

"Nothing. We had breakfast."

"C'mon, Joe. You expect me to believe that? I'm sure you never met with anyone without discussing something."

He holds up his hand. "I don't remember."

"The Kennedys?"

"We might have talked about all the Heat we was gettin' from that little prick, Bobby."

"Do you believe Trafficante was involved in the assassination?"

"Please. Santo wouldn't have the balls," Joe obfuscates.

"I'm not saying him personally," I probe, sure the old man knows much more than he is saying.

He shrugs. "Santo was a piece of shit."

Joe has nothing good to say about Santo. Cheapest man he ever met. Whenever there was money owed, Trafficante was nowhere to be found. His own people told Joe that Santo fucked them out of money all the time. The FBI was aware of the rancor between the partners, and they hoped to exploit it.

"I never talked to them after that," Joe says. "So they come after me."

In 1963, Stassi was named by Joe Valachi during testimony before a Senate committee as a member of La Cosa Nostra. By then, the FBI had already classified and targeted him as a Top Hoodlum. Under Justice Department supervision, they opened an extensive investigation.

Soon after, Joe was indicted on the heroin importation case in Texas. He went on the lam and lived for three years as a fugitive sought around the world in one of the most extensive manhunts of the time. Finally brought to ground at the Canada Club in Pompano, Florida, Joe says he was framed on the narcotics case in an effort to make him talk about the mob and about the Kennedy killings.

"What about Carlos Marcello? Do you believe he was involved in killing Jack or Bobby?"

"Knowing Carlos . . . it could be. Carlos was a dangerous man. And smart. And he hated Bobby—we all hated Bobby. Bobby run Carlos out of the country. But him and Santo—no . . . unless they had some fool to do it for them."

"Or some patsy."

"Anything is possible," Joe allows. He believes money would have been all the motive they needed. "And for a hit like that, they would've needed inside help."

"Like who?"

Joe shrugs. "How should I know?"

"And you believe, all these years later, you still think this is why the government refuses to let you out?"

"Excuse me," Joe barks at me. "You of all people should know how these people are—they never forget! They want me *to die* in here."

He's got a point. Given my own experience with the Feds, Joe's story no longer seems far-fetched. I want to go deeper, looking for insight into the most notorious crimes of the century, the Kennedy killings. "You say Marcello—all of you—hated Bobby. You hated Joe Kennedy—"

Joe interrupts. "I still hate the cocksucker! I hate him in his grave—Irish bastard. He brought all that curse on his own family."

"That's what I'm saying, the way the Kennedys turned on you after what Zwillman and the others did to get Jack elected—you certainly had every reason to want to clip them, right? Why wouldn't you have wanted to make a move on the Kennedys? That was what you did, Joe, that was how you handled these kinds of situations."

"How would I know?" Joe stonewalls me again.

"*You* would know. It's exactly the kind of thing they would have entrusted you with."

But Joe refuses to give me any more than he gave the FBI.

"I don't know nothin'," he says and waves me out of his cell. "Now go. Leave me alone. I'm tired."

I WRITE UP and file Joe's BP-9. A couple of weeks go by with no response. Then the old mobster and his jailhouse lawyer catch a break. There is a new warden here at Petersburg, a young, recently appointed administrator named J. J. Clark, who, Joe tells me, was his case manager when he was at the supermax in Marion. I approach Clark one morning while the warden is out making his rounds, and I ask him if he remembers Joe Stassi.

"Of course, I remember Joe Stassi," he says. "Why do you ask?"

"You know Joe is here?"

"I'm aware of that, yes."

I tell him of the discrepancy in the accumulation of good-time in Joe's case, and that a BP-9 should be on the warden's desk seeking credit for good-time Joe was denied.

"I'll look into it," Clark tells me.

This might mean nothing, of course. These people will look you in the eye and tell you what they think you want to hear, and then do nothing. But I have done all I can. And Warden Clark, as Joe's former case manager, should be conversant with the facts. So this has more promise than the expected routine rejection. Joe is pleased with my efforts on his part.

There is hope. And nothing to do now but wait.

Chapter Thirteen

BANISHED

FCI Ray Brook, New York

I AM ALSO in a holding pattern as I wait for a new release date based on my now concurrent sentences.

It's been over five months since my court appearance and still no word from the Punishment Bureau number crunchers in Washington. Doing time is so much more arduous when one is made to wait, and with no set release date it becomes a real-world version of purgatory. Time is even more abstract and daunting. I am forced to ponder the nature of time and consider that there really is no such thing, there is only our perception of time passing when in fact it is always now, every day is today, every moment is the moment we are living in, and when one is in prison and made to wait, the moment seems to drag on like a week on Neptune.

Waiting is hell.

MY WAIT TAKES a turn for the worse when I receive official correspondence from the Bureau's central office in Washington, DC, regarding my request for a new sentence computation. Based on Judge Griesa's ruling at my resentencing, I figure I have to be getting way short, no more than six months to a year to serve before release. But these Bureau of

Punishment fuckers are not happy with the outcome in Griesa's court. They don't give a rat's ass what the judge said. As I feared they might, the faceless drones at the computer terminals in Washington are trying to act like my ten-year sentence did not commence until the day it was imposed at my re-sentencing in New York fully six years after my arrest! They want me to do another eight-plus years on top of the seven I have already served. In their new computation, I get a projected release date in 2005.

No, no way. This cannot be. They are out of their fucking Punishment Bureau minds. I will not submit to this. My agreement with Stuart Little and Judge Griesa's court not to file any more motions does not include beefing over this latest injustice.

Back in the law library, I do the research, then I write a letter to Judge Griesa, cite the relevant case law and BOP administrative rules, and request that he instruct the Bureau to interpret his sentence as retroactive, *nunc pro tunc* in legalese, meaning *now for then*, beginning back on the very day I was arrested in Los Angeles. Several weeks pass, and then I get a letter from the court. Judge Griesa concurs. He writes an order directing that his sentence is indeed *nunc pro tunc* and should be so construed. The Bureau of Punishment reluctantly concedes to the judge's order, and they back down on that one. But they still fail to recompute my sentence.

Instead, they come banging on my cell door one morning well before dawn.

"Stratton! Pack your shit! You're moving out," a hack informs me, and he slides a cardboard box under the door.

"Where am I going?" I ask.

Dumb question.

"You'll find out when you get there."

These Punishment bureaucrats are vindictive sons of bitches. They hate it when they feel like a convict might beat them out of some time. In their perverse wisdom, they decide to prescribe another dose of diesel therapy. Word has it that they are pissed with me for the work I've done on Joe Stassi's case. They want me out of Petersburg, away from the old man, and back on the punishment highway where I won't be able to file any more legal paperwork on behalf of senior citizen Mafia hitmen.

"What did I tell you?" Joe says when I tell him they are shipping me out. "These people don't quit."

THERE IS TURMOIL in the Bureau of Punishment. Riots erupt in Atlanta Penitentiary when Cuban *Marielito* prisoners go off to protest their continued imprisonment in the land of the free after being kicked out of Castro's jails. I join a group of convicts shipped out of FCI Petersburg. The BOP puts three busloads of us back on the road in the torture chamber on wheels to make room for prisoners shipped out of Atlanta. They keep me in transit for weeks, with no access to the courts and no way to reach out to anyone to object.

While in holdover back in K Dorm at Lewisburg, I experience a harsh reminder of the world I live in. On the way to chow one morning, I see a young Latino stabbed to death on the red-top outside the mess hall. It happens so fast, with a kind of choreographed grace, that it takes a moment for me to understand what I am seeing. The shank disappears into the man's gut once, twice, three times, then is ripped around semi-circle, disemboweling him. The weapon is handed off, and a crowd of convicts shuffles past before the guards can identify who did the work and who has the piece. I look away, absorb the violence and keep walking. Remembering my jailhouse lawyer friend Marcus's advice, I saw nothing. I don't want to be identified as a witness and get jammed up here with all I have going on in my case. *Do your own time.* Such is the self-centered world I live in.

But then I can't resist. I turn at the door to the mess hall and glance back to see the gutted convict lying and bleeding red blood on red tile. Curious, I think, as I sit down to eat, and hear the alarm sound, and see the gang of cops fan into the mess hall to shake us all down and search for the weapon they will never find; interesting how the convicts choose to kill on the red-top, the open area covered with red tile directly in front of the manned control center and with guards everywhere. They do it, I conclude, as if to say: *See, we will cut them open and spill their guts before your eyes, and you still won't see who did it.*

Maybe that's why they do it on the red-top—for the aesthetics, the pure art of the kill.

Idling in K Dorm, questioned about the killing, I deport myself according to the Joe Stassi school of interrogation etiquette. *What did you see?* Nothing. *What do you know?* Nothing. *What have you heard?* Nothing. I am just another number in a jumpsuit and pair of Peter Pans and subject to having my asshole inspected with no claim on my life and what goes on around me other than what happens inside my head. Name and number: *Stratton, 02070-036.* Sentence: indeterminate. Designation: unknown. Release date: unknown. Living in an indefinite state with no explanation for this continued delay in recalculating my sentence except that, in holdover status, I have no access to anyone with the authority to find out and tell me how much more time I will have to do before I am to be set free.

It seems like the plan is to keep me in suspense until I snap and strangle some motherfucker. Ivan Fisher, my mother, congressmen from Massachusetts—no one can get any straight answers from the Punishment bureaucrats. I'm told I must contact my case manager when I get to wherever they are sending me and request the new sentence computation. So shut up and do the time. Every day is one less day I will have to serve.

AT LAST I am trussed up in shackles and chains, outfitted with the black box, and once again made to board the Punishment Express. I settle into the notion of another mystery transfer with no idea where they will deposit me at day's end. Again, I cherish the one good thing to be said for all this bus travel: that I get to see some of the World. After so many years being deprived of nature, dwelling in blocks of steel and concrete cells, trapped in herds of men, just to see God's living creation, even through barred and metal-mesh-covered windows, and to breathe free air, and feel a sense of moving through space is like being unearthed from a tomb. I long for freedom now that it's so close—or is it? I do not know. But I feel the absence of liberty ever more keenly, as though my soul were being held in suspension between the living and the living dead. Surely depriving one of one's freedom, and with no idea how long the captivity will last, this is the cruelest punishment of all.

We are heading east and north, leaving the rolling farmlands of eastern Pennsylvania and traveling up into the wooded, mountainous territories of northern New York. Some convicts we pick up along the way at FCI Danbury in Connecticut claim that we are destined for a federal prison in Ray Brook, near Lake Placid, New York, at the upper reaches of Gulag America's Siberia, close by the Canadian border.

Night descends as we enter the Adirondacks. I get to see little of the surrounding countryside. Dense stands of tall cathedral pines make the last leg of the journey feel like a long ride through a tunnel. I am reminded of the Maine woods and of my days and nights working the Canadian border in that other, long-past life. When we arrive at the prison, I trundle down from the bus in my restraints, look up, and see a glittering of stars so bright they appear to rain down like hail on my head. A shooting star streaks across the sky. I take a deep breath of air that smells of pine and feels like medicine. For a minute, it feels good to be alive.

Over the next ten hours we are processed into the institution, never a pleasant experience. Our bodily cavities are probed for contraband. We are made to sit or stand for hours in the bullpen while the Receiving and Discharge staff tries to figure out where to put us.

Night becomes day. The cops at Receiving and Discharge don't seem to know what to do with us. Ray Brook, we are told, is full to over

150 percent capacity. The entire Bureau of Punishment infrastructure is quaking under the pressure of too many convicts in too few prisons and cells. In this joint, convicts are made to sleep on cots in the units' common areas; single cells have been doubled and even tripled with prisoners sleeping on mattresses on the floor. For administrative purposes, I present a particular problem because of my previously long sentence, high security level, and no set release date.

The shift lieutenant is called in to review my paperwork. I recognize him as the officer on the BOP bus who wrapped the loudmouth convict's head in duct tape, suffocating him to death. This lieutenant, who mummified a man, was given a promotion and removed from the transportation detail. Makes perfect sense in federal law enforcement logic: fuck up and get promoted. I know not to object when it is deemed prudent to put me in administrative segregation—also known as the Hole—until I can be reclassified and released to general population.

MY FIRST TWO weeks at FCI Ray Brook I live in a dark, narrow, stripped cell with graffiti-scarred walls. My meals are delivered on a tray shoved through the trap in the cell door. It is mercifully quiet. I see no one, speak to no one, have no idea what is going on outside the cell, and dwell within my overwrought consciousness. It all seems so bizarre. Win an appeal, get my sentence reduced, and then end up in solitary confinement with no set release date. My dream life takes over. It is the same recurring dream. I am in some abstract prison, locked in by immaterial walls and invisible fences, a kind of thought penitentiary, living with the knowledge that I am not free to leave, not even free to think as I please, and no one can tell me why. There are no answers, only more questions, and more rebuffs from stolid bureaucrats who appear to withhold the answers.

I awake to find dream and reality have merged.

THEN ONE DAY in early May, just as arbitrarily and with no explanation, I am released to general population, given a bedroll, and told to make my way to my assigned housing unit. This might be interpreted as a positive development. At the least, I expect it will give me an opportunity to discuss my situation with an actual case manager and get some indication of how much longer I am expected to serve. But I might also see it as a sign that the authorities have concluded my stay is to be lengthy, when in my mind I am due and ready to be released.

Spring is in evidence as I walk out onto the compound. I look around. Glory be to God! There are no gun towers. No high walls. And there are—what is this?—flowers! Yes, flowers. Turns out, the warden is a freak for flowers. The convicts on the campus-like compound wear civilian clothes, jeans and warm-up suits instead of army-issue hand-me-down khakis. Originally built to house athletes for the 1980 Winter Olympic Games in Lake Placid, the physical facility seems more like a junior college than a medium-security penitentiary. The housing units are named for Native American tribes and set high on a hill with a view of the mess hall, administration buildings, the gym, recreation yard, and prison factories below, and in the distance above the razor wire and chain-link fence it is possible to make out pine-covered ridges and the sheer rock crag of Scarface Mountain.

A prison with a view: there is something majestic about this setting. As prisons go, Ray Brook strikes me as strangely beautiful and peaceful. The housing units are spacious, with sweeping walls and arced tiers, and they are remarkably quiet for prison. Floors in the common area are carpeted, and there are no clanging steel-barred doors. The cells are like mini-hotel rooms that would be comfortable for one man, but are tight for two. Before I got here, I'm told, before the riots in Atlanta and the massive over-crowding of the entire punishment gulag, there were no controlled movements; prisoners were given keys to their cells and could come and go within the compound as they pleased. Now all that has changed with the influx of higher security prisoners. Still, compared to Lewisburg and even Petersburg, this joint feels more like an overcrowded sanatorium.

The crisp, clear air and the extreme weather are perhaps the most remarkable features of this mellow spell in my penal experience. Spring seems to come and go in a matter of a fortnight. Summer is brief, hot and humid, and thick with insects. Fall is a memory. Then winter arrives overnight with a blizzard in mid-October. The housing units are overheated, and the windows are sealed. In the morning, when I step out into the fresh air, it's so cold the mucus in my nose immediately freezes. I slide down the hill on sheets of ice. For someone who never felt comfortable in the cold, and after my southern sojourn in Virginia, this North Country seclusion seems contrived to punish me for my successes in the courts. Maybe it is just that I imagine retaliation on the part of the faceless punishment administrators, but the fact that they seem unwilling or unable to recalculate my sentence strikes me as a conscious dereliction of their duties. I try not to let it bother me, but it does. Frustration mounts. *What the fuck!* Just tell me how much more time I will have to do so I can settle in and do it without this constant uncertainty.

My case manager is useless. She's a buxom young Punishment Bureau novitiate who has been elevated to her position from a lowly guard for the reason that she has one or two years of secondary education. She seems at once thrilled and terrified by her position of power over so many apparently dangerous men. When I finally meet with her in early fall, she instructs me to write a cop-out to the records department asking for a new sentence computation—something I have already done several times—and tells me to back it up with whatever legal documents I have to verify my claim that my original sentence has been vacated and a new sentence imposed.

The problem with this is that my property—the cardboard cartons of my legal papers, the typed and hand-written manuscripts of my novel and short stories, and such personal possessions as I was allowed to keep—has still not arrived from Petersburg. My case manager tells me that some of the boxes were sent home to my mother, who as of the last time I spoke with her had not received them. While others, those containing my writings, are being held while I am investigated for "operating a business while in the custody of the attorney general."

"What business?" I ask her.

"Writing," she says.

"It's not my business," I protest. "It's . . . It's a craft, a discipline. Something I do to keep from losing my mind."

She quotes the title of one of my short stories and tells me that, if and when it is determined that I have not been paid for my work, and if the stories are not found to be a threat to institutional security, my manuscripts will also be sent home to my mother.

Fuck! All that work! I was almost finished with my rewrite of the novel. Joe Stassi was right: these people never quit.

"What about the new sentence computation?" I ask, near exhausted with frustration.

"You will need to resubmit the court documents to prove your case," she says.

I HAVE TO write to the courts and seek additional copies of the necessary documents. Weeks go by. Nothing happens. Then months pass. Seasons change. I make friends with a fellow named Drago, an astrophysicist and former Princeton professor originally from Eastern Europe. He's been imprisoned, sentenced to five years, for allegedly attempting to poison his department chairman, a well-known physicist who, my friend claims, was awarded the Nobel Prize in physics based on work that he stole from his young assistant and published without giving Drago due credit. Drago tampered with a bottle of generic aspirin, supposedly substituting arsenic he made into tablets to resemble the real pills. The crime became a federal offense when Drago replaced bottles of aspirin with the poison and placed them on the shelves of a pharmacy. He then purchased them to give to the professor so that he would poison himself. The plan failed when the sales clerk in the pharmacy noticed the aspirin bottles had been tampered with. Drago claims his case resulted in the implementation of tamper-proof bottle caps.

Drago is engaged and intense when discussing the origin and future of the cosmos. Other times he seems dejected and isolated. We walk in the yard, and he tries to explain his mathematical projects, his endless calculations of the expanding universe, then returns to the housing unit to work on his equations, where, he claims, he has developed a mathematical formula that proves the existence of God.

I don't doubt him, God may well be found in the numbers, but I don't understand the math. I don't know what to believe. Nothing seems real to me anymore. When at last I get a meeting with the Bureau of Punishment staff person in charge of the records department, she tells me that they are unable to recalculate my sentence "at this time" because of the chaos in the system created by all the transfers due to the riots and overcrowding. I can't see how any of that has bearing on my situation, but I know better than to argue or to even question these people. She says that I will be notified when the new release date has been determined. But she says that could take several more weeks. I file more administrative remedies, BP-9s, BP-10s. I write letters to Judge Griesa and to the director of the Bureau of Punishment. Nothing produces any results.

It is hard for me to settle into any kind of a routine and get back into my writing. I'm reeferless, the synapses in my brain call for THC, but I haven't cozied to the cannabis underworld in this joint, and I don't have the inclination to seek out and turn a guard to have stash smuggled into the institution. There are a lot of wiseguys from Boston and New York doing time here, some of whom I know, but there doesn't seem to be much action in the way of contraband save garlic and olive oil, which is just as well. The last thing I need at this juncture is to get jammed up for violating the rules and regulations of the institution. For perhaps the first time in my now seven-plus years in the system, I do not fear a urine test.

My PARENTS VISIT once, making the long drive from eastern Massachusetts. My father, Emery, doesn't say much. Both mother and father profess to be proud of the fact that I chose not to rat, and, given my relief in the courts, it appears to have been a wise decision. The old man looks at me as though I were someone he's been associated with for a long time but never really knew, never really understood. I feel like I know him better than he knows me. He's a man who would avoid confrontation at almost any cost. Even during World War II, he was stationed far from the front lines, in Australia, where he was put in charge of providing entertainment for the troops on R & R from the war in the Pacific. I hesitate to call him a coward. He has an above-average intelligence and is a near prodigy at playing cards. Cribbage is his game of choice. He may have character strengths I am unable to discern. His choosing not to be a tough guy may be an act of bravery. But a man who feels fear and overcomes it in the crucible of physical danger gains insights the man who shuns confrontation will never have.

Mary is the fighter in the family. No one disrespects her or insults her or any member of her clan and gets away with it. She's a passionate ally. She tells me she has been corresponding with Massachusetts congressman Barney Frank in hopes of getting him to compel the Bureau to act. It's hard to say what, if anything, anyone can do. The Bureau of Punishment is a jurisdiction unto itself. The bureaucrats validate their singular powers with the rationalization that they are burdened with responsibility for the isolation, upkeep, and control of the most dangerous men in the world, and therefore they can only be held accountable to themselves. Of all federal bureaucracies, the Punishment Bureau may be the most impregnable and autonomous. Still, Mary is not one to give up. She's now reaching out to Senator Ted Kennedy's office.

Mary also tells me that she did indeed receive the carton containing my manuscripts. We make a plan for her to mail the draft of the novel to me one chapter at a time. I will do my revisions, then return the manuscript to her for safekeeping.

SUDDENLY, IT'S SPRING again. Mud season in the Adirondacks. Busses arrive with more prisoners and no place to put them. When one of the busses disgorges another batch of convicts from FCI Petersburg, I get news of the old don, Joe Stassi.

"Joe got out," a convict I recognize from Petersburg tells me when I see him in the mess hall. "The warden made them give him back all his good-time, and he went straight to the street—no halfway house or nothing. He was so happy—though, you know Joe; he never let them see it. He told me, if I run into you, 'If you see Richie,'" and he imitates Joe's raspy whisper, "'let him know how much I appreciate what he done for me.'"

Imagine that—a victory! I helped to free one of the most sophisticated gangsters and talented killers of the golden age of the Mafia! Wonderful. I think of his reunion with his wife, Frances, who waited for him all these years. Would there still be love between them? Or rancor after too long a separation? And his children—Joe Junior, with whom he remained in close contact while he was locked up, and a daughter from whom he was estranged—would there be reconciliation? Joy? Forgiveness? Or bitterness, alienation, and regret? Might Joe have been better off dying in prison than returning to a changed world that holds no place for him? And would there be any hope for redemption? Or is his next designation hell?

Ah, so many unanswered questions. I can meditate upon such mysteries all day, even as my new friend Drago contemplates the genesis of the cosmos. I can feel glad I was instrumental in getting this highly skilled killer back out on the streets and pray he's too old to kill again. And wonder that I helped free a Mafia don who was a prime mover in the formation of organized crime, suspected of having inside knowledge of the Kennedy killings, yet can't get my own ass out of stir, can't even find out how much more punishment this transporter and distributor of herbaceous smokeable plant matter is obliged to endure.

But perhaps I protest too much. For the next thing I know, as I feel near to having coerced the bureaucrats into an indefensible position where they must act or withstand the wrath of Senator Ted Kennedy, instead of a new release date they prescribe yet another major dose of diesel therapy.

I leave the mountain and go down once more into the valley.

DAYS ON THE bus, nights in county jails. Again separated from my property, at last I am deposited at the federal prison in Talladega, Alabama, where once again I am placed in administrative segregation—the Hole. I bunk with a bank burglar who delights in recounting long, detailed stories about the many complex, successful heists he and his partners pulled off before they were all arrested, when one of their girlfriends ratted them out. "Never trust a bitch," he says.

In going from the dry, overheated air of the prison in the mountains and the stuffy air of the bus to the air-conditioned frigidity of the Alabama plains, I come down with a cold that rapidly worsens to what feels like pneumonia. I can't eat. I'm so weak I can barely move. It's all I can do to roll over on the bunk, sit up, and struggle to a sitting position, then stand to aim my limp dick at the urinal next to the bunk and pee urine so dark it looks like weak coffee.

Nobody gives a shit. I'm too weak to care. They ship my cellie out. Days pass and I don't seem to get any better. I'm sweating and shivering at the same time. I hunker down in the air-conditioned nightmare and ask the Lord to forgive me and deliver me. I don't want to give the authorities the satisfaction of croaking here in Alabama where nobody knows my name, only my number, and my people have no idea what has become of me. Yet death feels near. It seems to hover in the morgue-like refrigerated air. My hands tremble when I reach for my face to feel I'm still here.

One morning, they take us out of our cells, stand us in a basement hallway, and order us to strip. I have to lean against the wall to keep from falling over.

"You all right, convict?" one of the hacks asks and prods me with his rib-spreader.

I muster every bit of strength from deep down in my shriveled-up scrotum and answer, "Yeah."

"Lift your ball sack. Turn around and spread your ass cheeks."

This guy seems to take pleasure in describing our private parts in graphic terms as though to remind us that even these most personal regions are now government property. We are ordered to dress, tricked out in shackles, handcuffs, and belly chains, and marched out to board the BOP bus.

It's a little over twelve hours on the Punishment Express up through Tennessee and into eastern Kentucky. I'm too sick even to enjoy my view of the World passing by through the bus windows. Early the next day, we arrive in Ashland, just west of West Virginia and barely south of Ohio. I somehow manage to get off the bus, have my restraints removed, and make it through Receiving and Discharge.

MIRACLE OF MIRACLES, when I recover enough strength to meet with my case manager, I learn my new release date has been calculated and awaits me.

What's this? I hold the piece of paper and stare at the new release date.

Something's not right. These numbers do not compute.

Chapter Fourteen

THE TAO OF PUNISHMENT

Disciplinary Hearing
FCI Ashland, Kentucky, June 1990

You have no rights. This is a kangaroo court. Whatever they say you did, you did.

"So why am I here?"

"We want to hear your side of the story."

"There is nothing to tell. Nothing happened."

"Was this a racial incident?"

"No, fuck no."

"Watch your language, convict."

"What happened?"

"Nothing."

"Why were you and inmate Rector fighting?"

"We weren't fighting."

There are three inquisitors. One is my case manager. I call him Axelrod, not a bad guy as far as these Bureau of Punishment stiffs go. And a lieutenant, a man I hardly know. And the captain, who has my central file before him. They take turns asking the questions. I have been at this prison for barely half a year. This is the first time I have appeared before a disciplinary committee in the eight years I've been locked up; not the first time I have been under investigation, but the first time they actually caught me violating "the rules and regulations of the institution," as they like to say, as if I give a shit about their rules and regulations.

The captain looks perplexed. He's trying decipher my new sentence computation sheet.

"How much time has this inmate got left?" he asks the unit manager, Axelrod, who shrugs in response.

"That's a good question. We're waiting on a final sentence computation from the central office," Axelrod explains. "This convict was sentenced to fifteen years in his first case in the District of Maine. He picked up another ten years in New York running consecutive to the fifteen, for a total of twenty-five years. And he got six months added on for criminal contempt of court, which was overturned on appeal. Is that right, Stratton?"

"So far, yes."

"Then he got some time cut," Axelrod continues. "Stratton, do you want to explain what's going on with your sentence?"

"I don't really know myself. It's still unclear. The two sentences were made to run concurrent instead of consecutive. But there's been a dispute regarding my earned and statutory good-time."

"Never mind," the captain says. "I'll wait on the new computation."

"He could possibly be released soon," says Axelrod, who has actually been trying to help me recover the good-time the Bureau of Punishment sentence number crunchers want to withhold.

"So why are you getting in fights? If you could be going home soon?" asks the captain. "That doesn't make sense."

I have no answer. Certainly, it makes no sense. I don't understand it myself.

"You got a problem with blacks, Stratton?"

"No."

"You a member of a prison gang?"

"No."

"Any tattoos?"

"No."

"Roll up your sleeves. Open your shirt."

They believe nothing we say.

No tattoos.

"Drugs? Gambling? Homosexuality?"

The unit manager shakes his head, says, "He's a convict, keeps to himself."

I would say: *I do good time.*

"According to the incident report, you and inmate Rector were fighting in the TV room. Do you deny this?" the captain asks.

"Yes."

"So you're saying the officer filed a false report?"

"No. I'm saying he was mistaken. I fell down. Rector was trying to help me up. He fell on top of me."

Axelrod smiles. The captain and lieutenant laugh.

"This guy would deny the sun is shining," Axelrod says. "Hey Stratton, is the sun shining?"

"I can't tell. I haven't been outside in a while."

Now all three of them laugh.

"Go on, get out of here," the captain tells me.

The guard standing by the door cuffs me behind my back. "Where to, Captain?" he asks.

"Take this convict back to seg."

HELLO, HOLE. How does that song go? *Hello wall . . . How'd things go for you today?*

Another deferred decision, that's how. It's as if these people can't figure out how much more punishment I deserve. I have been in the Hole a little over two weeks. Unlike cartoon convicts, I choose not to mark the days with hash marks etched on the cell wall. I keep track of the passage of time in my head. It's not about time, really, in the literal sense, not about the tick-tock of the clock. I learned some years ago how to do a long bid: winter-summer, winter-summer. Skip spring and fall. Seasons pass. Time means nothing until the possibility of release becomes real.

Never mind all that, I tell myself. *Pay attention to the here and now. Live in the moment. Bend reality with your imagination.*

I am not impatient to be released back into general population, back into the relative freedom of the compound, the noise and tension of penitentiary life. I enjoy the enforced solitude. If one is to be lonely, better to be truly alone. If only I had something to do. There are just so many push-ups and crunches a convict can squeeze out in any given twenty-four-hour period. Then to start all over again. My kingdom for a book . . . a pencil and paper . . . anything to occupy my restless mind besides the endless fretting over time. Still trying to convince myself time does not exist. Nothing is real but the steel walls of the cell, the beating of my heart. I have no memory, no life before I came to prison. I do not know anyone or who I am or why I am here. And furthermore, I don't care to. Nothing matters. Nothing lasts. Nothing makes sense. I can't count on anything but myself in this time and place.

It's the not knowing how much more punishment I will be forced to endure that plagues my mind, like not knowing how bad I really am. Drug smuggler. The worst of the worst. Fucking scum of the earth. Poisoning the youth of America. Ruining the minds of our children with that shit. That wacky weed. The Supreme Court held, in *Solem v. Helm 463 U.S., 77L. Ed 2d 645*: "The principle that a punishment should be proportionate to the crime is deeply rooted and frequently repeated in common-law jurisprudence." So give me fucking life. Or take me out to the village square and hang me. Flog me to death. Draw and quarter me. Tie my limbless torso to a four-wheel-drive truck and drag me through the streets. Let the good citizens see how we deal with these druggies. There is only one thing worse than a drug smuggler, and that's a communist drug smuggler. Or a terrorist drug smuggler. Fuck 'em. Let 'em all rot in prison. Who cares?

Or . . . not. Let him go. He's already served eight years. It was only weed. Cannabis. Hashish. Been around for centuries. God made it. Millions and millions of people all over the world enjoy it. It's legal in Holland, and the Dutch have not lost their minds. Maybe reefer has been given a bad rap. *Hello? Is there anybody out there?* Some people maintain it is medicine, beneficial for a number of maladies including nausea and weight loss due to chemotherapy. Depression and anxiety. Always worked for me. Whereas booze is what got me in trouble. Fights and aberrant behavior. Automobile accidents. Saying things and doing things I regretted in the morning. Hangovers. The worst thing I can say about pot is . . . well, this: it got me locked up. Though, not really. *I* got me locked up. I went against my own beliefs, violated my code of ethics and worked with a known coke addict, my now dead friend Fearless Fred, and that commenced a shit-storm of one fuck-up after another.

I should consider myself lucky that I'm still alive. So many have died.

Prison rescued me. Punishment saved me from my own selfish behavior. Prison forced me to confront my unbridled megalomania. Prison humbled me. I learned that I am not really in control of the outward aspects of my life. God rules, we humans submit or go astray. Throughout these prison years, I have consoled myself with the notion that the authorities may have my body, but they will never have my mind. They can never control my attitude or even my opinions. In my head I will continue to say: *Go fuck yourself. You will not break my outlaw American spirit.*

But how to occupy these days in solitary? How to fill this void of time in the Hole? Hour upon hour with nothing to do but cogitate. Or masturbate. I could play with my prick. Some guys in the joint jerk off two, three times a day. They take their porno magazines, "fuck books" they call them, or "fiend," and go into a stall in the communal bathroom and beat their meat. That gets old fast. No, I'll leave it alone. I want to see how far I can go on pure mental energy.

Of course, there is always sleep, and the strange alter-life of dreams. Great dreams in the Hole. It's so quiet I can actually get a solid night's rest and dream vividly. It used to amaze me how much bank robbers sleep once they get locked up. They must have rich dream lives. They are usually tall and thin. I see a tall, skinny guy who sleeps twelve, fourteen, sixteen hours a day, chances are he's a bank robber. He'll get up to eat, then go back to sleep. They must need a lot of rest to replenish all the adrenaline they burn up robbing banks and partying with the proceeds.

My meals, delivered on trays slid through the slot in the cell door, punctuate my wakeful hours. The food is standard prison fare. I don't eat red meat or pork, haven't eaten it since my early twenties—some sort of hippie vegetarian pothead. Not that they serve much meat in the joint. Occasionally they serve fried chicken, which usually results in a run on the mess hall. I was in the mess hall one evening when they served fried chicken, and a rat of the four-legged variety ran out from the kitchen. All these hardcore convicts freaked out. Except this one big old Southern boy who sat idly munching on a chicken leg when the rat ran by his table, and without so much as looking up from his drumstick, stomped on the rat with his heavy steel-toed boot and broke the creature's back. The rat writhed and twitched for a few moments, then expired. A small puddle of dark blood spewed from its pointy snout.

No great loss in being kept from joining the throng of cons in the mess hall. Standing in long lines to receive your issue of sustenance. Prison is all about standing in lines. Fuck that. Awful shit. Soul killing. Being in the Hole, having my meals served to the cell, hell, this could be compared to my former self—Dr. Lowell, ensconced in a suite at the Plaza Hotel ordering from room service. Though not quite.

RECENTLY SOMETHING EXTRAORDINARY took place at this prison, an event so remarkable I will never forget it. I will go so far as to say it was life-changing. One of my real-life heroes came to visit and spoke to us convicts as though we were men of substance, his brothers. A convict doing time here, an optometrist who got pinched on a medical fraud case, claimed to be a friend of the great world heavyweight champion Muhammad Ali. Nobody believed him. I have always loved Ali. I admire him not just as a fighter, though he was The Greatest, but also as a man. He stood up for what he believes. No Viet Cong ever called him nigger. It took real courage to stick to his convictions and refuse to be drafted and fight a war so many believed was wrong, and to give up his heavyweight title as a result of holding fast to his beliefs. It is one thing to profess certain values, quite another to stick to those ideals when threatened with great personal sacrifice or years in prison. I was hopeful the optometrist was on the level when he told us Ali had agreed to come to the prison and speak to the population.

At last the day arrived. Ali was due to show up any time. The optometrist kept assuring everyone the champ was coming. "He'll be here," the guy said. "Believe me, Ali doesn't say he's going to do something and then not follow through."

But it wasn't Ali we doubted; it was the optometrist. When it came time for the four o'clock count and still there was no Ali, we figured the optometrist was full of shit. Nothing interferes with the four o'clock count; these Punishment people take it very seriously. They will write you a shot and lock your ass up in the Hole for interfering with the count. So when four o'clock rolled around and we heard that mournful whistle blow to announce the end of the workday and a return to units for count, everybody was ragging the optometrist, calling him another full-of-shit con telling stories to make himself appear important.

Imagine all our surprise when there came an announcement over the PA system that anyone who wished to see a special visitor to the penal institution should assemble in the recreation yard. Could it be Ali? Who else? I was optimistic for the veracity of the optometrist. Only a man of Ali's stature could cause these bureaucrats to delay the four o'clock count.

Prisoners of all color and stripe streamed out to the yard to see the great Muhammad Ali. And there he was. Parkinson's had already begun to take its toll, but Ali was still whimsical and sharp-witted as ever, and light on his feet. The warden stood before the assembly and began some banal introductory remarks. Ali stood up, danced out beside him, and threw a few mock jabs and hooks. Did the Ali shuffle.

"Sit down, man," Ali told the warden. "These are my people!" Indicating us, the throng of prisoners. "They didn't come out here to listen to you!"

And in that brief time and place—killers, dope dealers, fraudsters, punks, genuine tough guys, Asians, black and white Americans, Aryan Brotherhood and Black Panthers, Colombians and Cubans, bank robbers, pederasts, criminals, and blood suckers, prisoners of the war on drugs—we were all of one accord. Ali told us not to define ourselves by our past. We are not the sum of our previous mistakes, Ali said. We are ever becoming who we are, redefining ourselves in the moment, even now as we sat listening—not to some "nigger," not to Cassius Clay, not to some draft dodger—but to Muhammad Ali—The Greatest. A man who stood up for his beliefs.

"You all made one mistake or you wouldn't be here," Ali said. "You got caught! There're a lot of big crooks out there that never get caught. They steal more money with a pen and a briefcase than you did with your pistol."

There is a way through this, Ali was saying, there is a sacred path that goes both inside and out. His life spoke of it. Deeper in is the way out.

ALI'S WORDS AND the example he set in his own life sustains me and gives me hope during my sojourn in the Hole. I too have been called names. Criminal, inmate, convict, prisoner, kingpin, drug smuggler: these are the words the authorities use to describe me. But there is something to be said for having taken responsibility for my actions and having served the time. Whatever else they may call me, they can never say *rat;* that's a name I would have had to take to the grave. Here, in the solitude of the prison cell with Ali's words sounding in my head, I am forced to go deep within, compelled to confront who I really am, to question who I hope to become, and to ask what I will do with the rest of my life.

This time, these eight years, the experience of being locked up for trafficking in a plant, has tested me and strengthened me in ways I might never have known had I not been caught, or had I chosen to become a government informer. Yes, there is a way out, and I found it here. It's the way of learning and embracing who you really are and what you believe about yourself. So perhaps we can make a truce, my evil twin and me. We can say I stood for something.

Chapter Fifteen

UNCERTAINTY PRINCIPLE

THEY LET ME outside today. For forty-five minutes I was allowed to exercise in a narrow cage like a dog run attached to the rear of the cell house. I paced, did some push-ups—same old same old. But being that it was outside, it felt different. And there were a few cons out walking the compound who called to me.

"Hey, brother, how you doin'?"

One guy folded his hands and put them beside his head like a pillow, some kind of sign language. I didn't get the meaning until I was returned to my cell in the Hole and saw a pillow on my bunk. Nice. Imagine my surprise when I felt under the pillow and found a skinny joint—a "pinner" as we call a joint so thin you can suck the whole thing down in one long deep drag. Only one problem: no matches.

While I was contemplating how to address this issue, unit manager Axelrod appears in front of my cell.

"Open F-3," he calls.

A hard clank of steel on steel. A whirring and grinding sound of gears, the cell door slowly sliding open. I'm thinking, *Shit, someone ratted me out. He's here to shake me down and bust me for possessing the pinner. I've been set up. Haven't even had time to stash the joint. It is tucked in the breast pocket of my jumpsuit.*

"Move over, Stratton," Axelrod says and sits down on the bunk beside me.

This is highly unusual. Staff members don't just cozy up to convicts. Something is wrong.

Axelrod is wearing a Bureau of Punishment baseball cap, gray slacks, white shirt, and blue blazer with the Punishment Bureau seal on the pocket. He's not from around here but transferred in from some other region. The Punishment bureaucrats move staff around almost as much as they transfer convicts. The idea is not to let anyone get too comfortable in any particular joint. That's when corruption seeps in.

Axelrod is from Oregon. He's tall, slim, in his forties, my age or a few years younger, though he relates to me as though I were a child or a precocious teenager, and a juvenile delinquent. We bonded, somewhat, as much as one can with these BOP types when you are a prisoner; we found a common interest in the writings of Ken Kesey, another Oregonian and a wrestler. Axelrod saw me reading a copy of Kesey's novel, *Sometimes a Great Notion*. We talked about wrestling. Axelrod wrestled in high school, as did I, and we discussed Kesey's other book, the more celebrated *One Flew Over the Cuckoo's Nest*.

This led to a discussion of a prisoner called Rojas, who bunks in my unit and has taken a liking to me. Rojas is a street-level crack dealer, a Dominican from Washington Heights caught up in the angry mood of the times. He can't be much more than twenty-two, and he has an eighteen-year sentence for possession of a handful of rock cocaine. Rojas sometimes sits up in his bed in the middle of the day or at night and wails loudly, or makes inhuman, birdlike chirping sounds that cut through the daytime clamor or echo in the quiet of the night like the call of a mating loon. Scared the hell out of me first time I heard him go off. I came to marvel at the volume and timbre of sounds issuing from such a small man, and I applauded him for having the courage to make himself heard. I clapped and cheered him on. The other convicts used to scream at him to *shut the fuck up*. But then they began to clap, too, and Rojas beamed with pride. He became known as the Bird-man of Ashland. Axelrod and I talked about how this place bears some resemblance to the nut ward described in Kesey's novel. He asked me if I thought Rojas was a danger to himself or to others. I said I thought he was harmless, just acting out.

Now Axelrod looks at me and says, "You know, you're as crazy as any of them, Stratton." He tips the brim of his cap back, exposing the whiter flesh of his upper brow and his receding hairline. "Have you considered psychological counseling?"

I shrug. I'm preoccupied, worried about being caught with the joint and getting another shot, loss of more good-time, and blowing my still unknown release date.

"Seriously," he goes on, "you're going to be required to go through some pre-release counseling. But it's pretty basic: how to balance a checkbook, stuff like that. But I would recommend you talk to the shrink. These places, you know, after you've done as much time as you have, they can mess with your head. You don't want to get out there and put a beating on the first sucker who steps on your toe."

He's got a point. I'm not the man I once was. Though who is to say if I am crazier or saner? Gentler or more violent? Wiser or still a fool? The reefer in my pocket would argue for the latter.

"It was just one of those things," I say, referring to the fight with Rector. "I'll be okay. I'm not really angry."

He nods. "As long as you're aware that . . . well, eight years in the joint can have some lasting effects on how you deal with—"

"Frustration," I finish his sentence, then admit, "I try not to think about it. I thought I might have learned something about patience, but all this hassle they're giving me over the good-time, and not knowing what the fuck is happening with my release date, it has me wrapped pretty tight. So . . . I snapped."

"Short-timer's syndrome," Axelrod says. "Rector's going home in a few months, too."

"It was really nothing," I say. "Stupid shit. I have nothing against Rector."

I'm thinking: *a few months? Fuck that. I want out of here in days, weeks at the most.*

Axelrod nods. "You know," he says, "I gotta tell you, in all the time I've been with the Bureau, almost twenty years now, I've never seen anything like this happen before."

He pauses, gives me time to wonder what he's talking about.

"I must've had ten, fifteen inmates come to my office in the last couple of weeks," he goes on. "Blacks. Whites. Latinos—your little pal there, Rojas. Inmates don't usually step up for each other. But every one of 'em said the same thing: 'Stratton's a good man. Cut him some slack. Rector, too. These guys aren't troublemakers.'"

This surprises me. Like Axelrod says, it goes against the convict code, which decrees: Don't stick your nose in anyone else's business. See nothing. Hear nothing. Say nothing. *Feel* nothing. I'm amazed to hear Axelrod tell me that convicts actually put in a good word for Rector and me.

"You've got a lot of friends on the compound," Axelrod says. He's so close to me I'm afraid if he looks down he'll spot the reefer nestled in my jumpsuit pocket.

It's true, I do have a lot of friends, mostly because I do legal work and don't charge. I've become the jailhouse lawyer in demand since I had my twenty-five-year sentence vacated and was resentenced to ten years. Now if I could just get these fuckers to set my ass free.

"Open F-3," Axelrod calls out, and the cell door cranks open.

Axelrod stands. "Let's go," he tells me.

"Where're we going?"

"I'm going home. You're going back to your unit."

"What about Rector?" I ask. "I'm not leaving if he's still locked up."

Axelrod says, "I cut Rector loose while you were in the yard. I'm giving you both a pass. No shot."

Relief. "Thanks."

Good move. Let the black guy out of the Hole first so it doesn't look like the white man's getting preferential treatment.

Now if I can just get out of here without getting busted with the pinner.

Axelrod is on me like grease. He and the seg cop take me into the shakedown room to strip-search me. What the fuck would I be smuggling *out* of the Hole? The irony is not lost on me that in fact I am smuggling a joint out of the Hole. I'm trying to slip the pinner from the pocket of the jumpsuit without them noticing. It's either that or roll it up in the jumpsuit and toss it on the pile of soiled laundry on the floor.

Forget it, I can't do that. I want to smoke it. I snag the reefer with two fingers, wrap it in the palm of my hand. It's the old smuggler's axiom: the bold way is the best way. If Axelrod sees what I'm up to, he chooses not to question me. The seg cop tells me to drop my drawers, bend over and spread 'em. As he peeks up my ass, I slip the joint in my mouth, tuck it under my upper lip like I know what I'm doing.

"Open your mouth," the seg cop orders me.

I do. The joint is stuck in the groove above my gums. This is all perfunctory anyway. This cop has probably strip-searched thousands upon thousands of convicts, looked up any number of Hershey Highways. He hands me my khakis.

Axelrod wishes me luck. We shake hands.

"When do you think we'll hear something from the Bureau on my release date?" I ask.

"Should be any day now," he says.

The seg cop speaks into his radio. An electronic door release sounds. The sally port door pops open, and I walk from the Hole, the segregation unit, out into the relative freedom of the compound.

Back in the unit, I find a letter on my bunk. It has been opened and inspected for contraband, read for evidence of illegal contact with the World. They open and review all our mail except legal correspondence.

This letter is from PEN America, signed by a man named Fielding Dawson who writes to congratulate me on my short story having won First Prize in the PEN Prison Writing Contest. He wants to know where he should send the $200 prize money.

This is great news. I am thrilled. But I contain my joy; there is no one I want to share it with.

It's springtime in the Ohio River Valley. They say this area has one of the highest lung cancer tolls in the country due to air pollution from the coke ovens used to form and melt steel and iron. On cold damp mornings over the winter, I felt the trapped coke oven residue in the air settling into the alveoli of my lungs like a thin toxic patina. I grew heavy with the air. People who live here all their life croak at an alarming rate once they hit forty. So why would you stay? Where would you go if your only job prospects were working in the coke ovens or the prison? The local 7-Eleven?

I'm out walking in the yard. This is an extended version of freedom compared to the Hole, moving in a greater sphere, trying to get into position to fire up the pinner and celebrate without anyone seeing me. There are no gun towers at this low-medium–security prison, no guards with binoculars and high-powered rifles watching our every move as they do in Lewisburg, where I started this bid, or Petersburg, where I did most of my time. But there is a hack in a truck circling the compound surveying the double perimeter fence coiled along the top with ribbons of razor wire like a vicious slinky. The cop keeps an eye out for anyone insane or desperate enough to try to climb over the fence and get ground up like hamburger by a million little razor blades.

As soon as the hack in the truck rolls by, I light the joint and suck it up in one long inhale. Bob Dylan's "All Along the Watchtower" plays in my head. Suddenly high and blissfully happy, I rewrite Dylan's lyrics: *All along the razor wire, convicts kept the view / While all the hacks came and went, barefoot snitches too.*

Ah, yes, THC, tetrahydrocannabinol, magic elixir, mysterious chemical compound found in the smoke from this herb that is absorbed by blood in my lungs and carried up to my brain, where it attaches itself to welcoming receptors and miraculously alters my perception of reality. The world around me falls away. My world is a different place. There are no fences, no gates. There is no objective reality, for without some imprisoned consciousness to observe this world, and filter observations through the senses of a locked-up consciousness, who is to say where I am and what is real? A moment ago, I was walking along seeing my world as an enclosed space wrapped with miles of concertina wire and guarded by gun-toting cops. I perceived my fate as an uncertain future to be determined by faceless Bureau of Punishment drones, black-robed judges, and buttoned-down government attorneys. All that has dissolved; it no longer matters. All that has consequence is what is happening inside my head. I'm so high on joy and herb I could float over the fences, disappear in the leaden air.

Now . . . it's princes keeping their view, barefoot servants, too. And, yes, Rojas, a.k.a. Birdman of Ashland. My little friend, round and brown as a nut, crouches beside a shrub. He mutters incantations as he places a cinnamon roll, some packets of jelly, an orange, and a Dixie cup full of sugar carefully in a semicircle at the trunk of the bush.

This is different. I stop and watch.

Rojas has a narrow head covered with sparse tufts of wiry black hair that sprout from his shiny brown skull like moth-eaten upholstery on polished wood. He speaks little English. Someone taught him to say asshole.

"Good morning, asshole!" he greets me cheerfully, though it is late afternoon. He's got a sharp face, foxlike, with a wispy Charlie Chaplin mustache—a naturally comic look. I had noticed odd leavings beneath this bush some time ago, before my vacation in the Hole—bananas, apples, pieces of bread, even mints and hard candies placed on the ground under the bush like the snacks a child might leave under the

Christmas tree for Santa. I was intrigued by this unexplained development in a life of crushing monotony. One day I saw a cigar still wrapped in cellophane alongside the other gifts. Each evening the offerings were there, each morning they disappeared, to be replaced by new oblations.

"Santería," Rojas says. He tells me friendly spirits dwell in the bush and he entreats them to protect his soul from demons sent by Satan to capture him in the night. The bird sounds he makes are his invocation of the winged spirits to ward off the devil. Religion, ceremony, and magic found its way into this godforsaken place. It is as if faith stole in where hope had fled.

"Why this bush?" I ask him.

Rojas explains that, for one thing it is the only bush. And he's right, though I had never noticed it before. There are no other bushes in the denuded recreation yard. One day, Rojas tells me, he saw a tiny bird, "*un pajarito*," fly in and perch on the lower branches. The bird, he claims, looked up at him and then it disappeared. He came to believe that the bush is a portal, "*una puerta*," he says and grins. A door to the spirit world. His eyes shine from his brown face with gleeful excitement that undercuts the solemnity of the occasion. I wonder if Rojas is actually crazy, if he believes his visions. For a moment it all seems unreal.

He can be a clown, this birdman; I never know when he's serious. I watch him at mail call when we are most hopeful and vulnerable. Each time the guard calls a name to deliver a letter, Rojas pops up at the front of the assembled lovelorn and asks, "Rojas? Rojas?" as if he can't understand why his name has not been called. And when it is over, as the Colombians call out, "*Ni chimba!*" Rojas insists on searching the empty mail sack. He turns it upside down and shakes it to make certain no letters drenched with tears and kisses are stuck inside. He speed-walks around the compound with a flexed-knee stride, arms rigid at his sides and swinging like pendulums for extra momentum. When they open the units for the evening meal, Rojas zips along, his gleaming head bobbing like an acorn in the human stream, and he greets his fellow prisoners: "Hello, asshole!"

Axelrod and I worry somebody's going to take it wrong and fuck him up.

The Dixie cup full of sugar persuades me he's on the level. No crack dealer in his right mind would give up crystalline white powder to a shrub unless he really believed it gave him access to magic spirits and a door to another dimension. I tell Rojas to appeal to the sacred bush to grant me a release date.

"You want to go home?" he asks.

"*Si, hombre.* Don't you?"

"Yes, but not yet."

He says he has never eaten so well. "*Cinco niños.*" Five kids back home in Santo Domingo. No prospects for work in Washington Heights. He tells me he can make enough money working in the UNI-COR factory to send some home to his wife and children, and still afford a new pair of sneakers.

"You are my friend," Rojas says and embraces me. "I will speak to the spirits for you also."

THE MAGIC OF the sacred shrub appears to have worked. Spirits taking form as tiny birds nibbling sugar and puffing cigars have saved Rojas from eternal damnation. He's happier than ever, rested and well-fed. More Dominicans have appeared on the compound as if conjured by Rojas. They are his friends; they know him from the streets of New York City and from the villages of the DR. This latest influx of immigrant criminals is a noisy, happy-go-lucky lot. Dressed in baggy army fatigues, they look like shock troops from the Third World. There are so many new prisoners, Bureau of Punishment higher-ups decided to move long trailers onto the compound, park them on the rec yard, and convert them into barracks.

During my forced vacation in the Hole, I had to relinquish my bottom bunk. I lie on the top bunk above the level of the cinderblock walls separating the cubes, and I can see Rojas resting peacefully. No more do his trilling birdcalls shatter the undercurrent of dormitory noise. Light from high-intensity security lamps outside glows in through the windows like pale blue artificial moonlight.

I am wide awake, no embrace of sleep like a lover's arms to fall back into.

Rojas's magic worked for me as well. There is a note stuck to the window of Axelrod's office telling me I have legal mail. But he has been off for two days, and I have not been able to get my hands on what I know must be my notice from the Bureau of Punishment's Central Office in Washington, DC, advising me of my new release date.

I need to know this; I can't sleep thinking about it. I lie awake listening to a symphony of snores and visualize the slack-jawed, dead-looking faces from which the sounds issue. It's like an orchestra or choir, a pond full of croaking bullfrogs. Each sleeping musician plays the unique instrument of his nose.

Even Rojas's name was called at mail call today. More proof of the strength of his magic, or so I thought. But it was only a letter from the Education Department telling him that he had failed his GED exam and would be required to take the test over again.

IN THE MORNING before work call I snag Axelrod to collect my legal mail. Rip open the envelope. Stare at the words on the paper.

What? Three more months! *No way!* These miserable Punishment cocksuckers denied me credit for meritorious good-time I earned working as unit clerk at the MCC while awaiting trial on my second case. They assume the position that because I wasn't sentenced at the time, I was not eligible for the award. This is pure Punishment Bureau jive and bullshit. They have intentionally disregarded the fact that I was already sentenced on the Maine conviction, and serving that sentence even as I awaited trial on the New York case, and therefore I am entitled to the good-time.

I fold the letter and tuck it in my pocket. Show no emotion. Don't let Axelrod see that I am seething inside.

"Not bad," he says. "You got most of your good-time back. Right? So you'll be with us until September."

No, I'm thinking, *I'll appeal.* I must; and I do. A lot can happen in three months. I could get black lung disease or cancer and die. And with the way this joint is filling up, the place could go off. I could get caught up in a riot like what happened at the penitentiary in Atlanta— my greatest fear.

Chapter Sixteen

OF TIME AND SPACE

FCI Ashland, Kentucky, June 30, 1990

TODAY IS MY last day in prison. This time out of time is coming to an end. I could count the hours, the days, the weeks, and months and years that I have been locked up. But it doesn't really matter. I have reached the point where I could spend the rest of my life in here. Because . . . it doesn't really matter. What matters is the new space I occupy inside my head.

I am reminded of the last lines in Byron's poem "The Prisoner of Chillon":

> *My very chains and I grew friends,*
> *So much a long communion tends*
> *To make us what we are:—even I*
> *Regain'd my freedom with a sigh.*

It's a sigh of relief. Yes, of course, I'm relieved. Finally, I can stop fighting. I won, I challenged the Bureau's bean counters and got all my good-time restored. That feels good. To beat the Punishment fuckers out of any time is a victory. As is the knowledge that I held true to at least one fundamental understanding about myself: I am not a rat.

I gave them nothing but time. Eight years. No one else was locked up because of evidence I gave. Actually, make that two fundamental understandings about who I am: I don't snitch, and I do not take it up the ass. Not from the government or anyone else. Still a man. Neither a pitcher nor a catcher in these many years of life in the Big House. I remain virginal. Unrehabilitated. Untamed. Still an outlaw. I continued to smoke, smuggle, and traffic in the magic herb pretty much the entire time I spent in prison, even after I could almost see the end.

Foolish, yes. Hypocritical, no. I am still a soldier in this grotesque war on plants. I may have won my own personal battle, but the war rages on.

And I have more good news. Some time back, I sent the revised manuscript of my novel to Mailer. He liked it enough to send it to a literary agent. The agent sold the book to a publisher who has a check for twenty grand waiting for me after I hit the street. I may have a future in this writing racket after all.

I'M ON THE merry-go-round, going from housing unit to work detail, commissary to law library, education department to hospital, to have the different staff members sign off on my release, stating I have no infectious diseases (the specter of AIDS is upon us); I have no books or outstanding orders or debts that need to be settled before I depart. So I am walking around now knowing that the space I inhabit is about to be greatly, hugely, infinitely enlarged.

Though . . . not quite.

"What do you mean I have to report to my parole officer? I thought this was a non-paroleable sentence. I was *denied* parole," I say to my case manager.

"Yes, that's true," Axelrod says. "But you still owe us the remainder of your sentence on the street. Not parole exactly . . . but parole exactly. You have forty-eight hours to report to the United States Parole Office in the Eastern District, Brooklyn, New York. That's where you'll be living, right?" He smiles. "You do have an alternative. You can refuse to sign the release papers and do the rest of your time here—a little over two years—if that's what you want to do."

"You, white man Axelrod, speak with forked tongue," I say. "Give me the fucking papers. Where do I sign?"

It doesn't really matter. There is nothing more they can do to me. The time I spent in this restricted space went inside; time entered me and changed me. It grew new space in my head. It's like a prison cell I inhabit that I carry around in my consciousness. I'm safe in here. They can't touch me. I am a new person. I live in a dimension that is beyond space and time. Every cell in my body has been renewed. At last I made peace with the lunatic twin, bad Rickie Stratton, that kid who would be Al Capone or Robin Hood or some combination of the two. I left him in the Hole still doing his push-ups, still plotting his release, still running from his fear of mediocrity. The walls have dissolved. The chains and bars and handcuffs have become my nerves and my bones and my flesh. Doing time has become my experience.

But there is still one stop on my personal merry-go-round I know I must make if I am truly a new man. It is not required by anyone but me. As I sit in my cubicle with the minutes and seconds of my internment ticking away, my meager belongings given away, my hand holding the release papers that will allow me to step through the gates and walk away, I know what I have to do, and yet I am fearful. Nervous, afraid, whatever it is—I don't want to do it. I would rather not have to face him, but I know I must. It's the same feeling I used to get before a wrestling match, or before the plane landed and the cargo door flew open. Or before I stood in front of a judge.

The new self takes over. I see myself stand, walk out of the cubicle and pass the TV room, pass Axelrod's office and the guard's station, over to the other side of the barn where the other captives live in their stalls.

Rector stands facing the cinderblock wall in his cube. He's naked from the waist up, his muscular black back to me. He looks like he's preparing a cup of instant soup. I could still wimp out and walk on by.

No one would know but me. What if he spits on me and says, *Fuck you, cracker?* What if he hits me or throws soup and scalding water in my face and we get into it all over again? How fucked up would that be? *Well, your Honor, this fool, inmate Stratton 02070-036, he was on his way out the door to be released. But he got into a fight with another prisoner . . .*

Why can't I just leave well enough alone and let this go, forget about it?

Because—I can't. I must do this or live with the knowledge that I am a coward.

"Rector," I say, and he turns to face me.

Now we are looking at each other. I don't step closer; to enter his cube uninvited would be an act of aggression. I look him in the eye and say, "Respect, man." And the fear disappears.

He puts down whatever it is he's doing and nods, says nothing. I am about to turn and walk away when he steps closer and offers me his hand.

"Yes," he says. "Respect back at you." And we shake hands.

It's over. Now I'm free.

I HAND THE duty officer my fully signed and executed release papers. He looks them over, asks my name and number.

"Stratton, 02070-036," I say for the last time.

He checks my face against my mug shot, hands me back my release papers, and gives me an envelope with an airplane ticket and a hundred bucks.

There is the front door. Just walk down the hallway past the convict with the buffer polishing the linoleum. Show the release papers to the cop on the front gate. See the taxi pull up outside to take me to the airport. Now step out the door into the unrestrained space beyond the fence.

Here it is: the World. I can see the horizon. I look up at the sky, wide, blue and unbounded by fences laced with glinting ribbons of razor wire. Here it is—*freedom*. Here I am. See it. Feel it. Absorb it. Walk and keep walking and know that I am free at last.

Gaze up at the heavens and ask the Creator: *Who am I, God, that you have brought me this far?*

I am nothing. Reborn, I am an empty vessel.